For my grandsons Charlie and Ethan

A M

FO

The b   ›mic
policy   ›een
throug   nder
wheth   natic
events   iews
the his   : last
centur   nsus
of the
    Dr   l for
much   , the
1970s   )80s.
The st   1 the
early 1   )ugh
promis   )7–8
showe   aws,
includi   nd a
revival   ods.
More s   ollar
and the
    Thi   :ater
unders

Christopher Taylor wrote the book while he was a Visiting Fellow at the National Institute of Economic and Social Research, London. He previously worked as an economist at
the Bank of England for 20 years until 1994, including a secondment as UK Alternate Executive Director at the International Monetary Fund, Washington DC, 1981–3. Since 2008 he
has been a lecturer and tutor for the MBA elective course on International Macroeconomics
at the Judge Business School, Cambridge, where he is a Teaching Fellow.

'At last a book that recognises that different policy mixes are appropriate for different circumstances. Christopher Taylor's illuminating book presents macroeconomics as policy choices, rather than a menu of economic models. This gives his analysis a vitality largely lacking in more academic textbooks. No other book explains the complex macroeconomic policy choices faced by governments after the recent financial crisis in such a direct and accessible way'.

Dr. Jan Toporowski, *SOAS, UK.*

'The book provides both a valuable outline of the evolution of macroeconomic policy and a discussion of potential policy options for the future. This is a timely book, given the failure of contemporary economic orthodoxy to anticipate and prevent a financial crisis and global recession. Consequently, it can make a useful contribution to the debate on understanding past mistakes and how economic policy should evolve to meet the needs of the future'.

Prof. Philip Whyman, *University of Central Lancashire, UK.*

A MACROECONOMIC REGIME FOR THE 21ST CENTURY

Towards a new economic order

Christopher Taylor

Routledge
Taylor & Francis Group

LONDON AND NEW YORK

First published 2011
by Routledge
2 Park Square, Milton Park, Abingdon, Oxon, OX14 4RN

Simultaneously published in the USA and Canada
by Routledge
711 Third Avenue, New York, NY 10017

Routledge is an imprint of the Taylor & Francis Group, an informa business

British Library Cataloguing in Publication Data
A catalogue record for this book is available from the British Library

Library of Congress Cataloging in Publication Data
Taylor, C. T. (Christopher Thomas), 1938–
A macroeconomic regime for the 21st century / Christopher Taylor.
p. cm.
1. Macroeconomics. 2. Fiscal policy. 3. Monetary policy. 4. Economic
indicators. 5. Chicago school of economics. 6. Keynesian economics.
I. Title.
HB172.5.T387 2010
339.5–dc22   2010034574

ISBN 978–0–415–59897–2 (hbk)
ISBN 978–0–415–59898–9 (pbk)
ISBN 978–0–203–83063–5 (ebk)

Typeset in Bembo by Swales & Willis Ltd, Exeter, Devon
Printed and bound in the Great Britain by TJ International Ltd, Padstow, Cornwall

CONTENTS

LIST OF FIGURES

LIST OF TABLES

LIST OF BOXES

PREFACE

This book is about macroeconomic policy; that is to say, policy for the economy as a whole. It tries to observe the conventional distinction between macroeconomics, which deals with *aggregate* or collective behaviour in an economy and its broad sectors, and microeconomics, which is concerned with individual agents – households, firms, etc. Thus its main subjects will be the institutions, instruments and modalities of monetary and fiscal policy, which are the chief modes of policy used nowadays in modern market economies. This choice of focus does not of course mean that microeconomics can be ignored: collective behaviour cannot be understood without reference to individual motivations, and discussion of the macroeconomic regime would miss a lot if it ignored them. Indeed the dramatic economic events of the past few years make it essential to look beyond the usual subject matter of macro policy. When leading international banks go down like nine-pins or exchange rates and asset prices gyrate, we have to ask whether macroeconomic measures are not called for. What seems clear is that these events have brought macroeconomic policy back to the centre of attention with a vengeance: any notion that the policy consensus reached towards the end of the last century heralded the end of macroeconomics has been shown to be premature.

The purpose of the book is to devise the best possible macroeconomic regime for liberal democracies – the so-called developed economies – in the 21st century, or at least suggest the kind of regime towards which they should be moving. Although much of the discussion will address policy at the national level, the international dimension will also be prominent. In a world becoming ever more interdependent in economic as in other respects, the external aspects of policy are increasingly dominant: macroeconomic policies and institutions must nowadays be considered in an international context, and the links with developing and emerging-market economies taken into account.

The book was conceived well before the onset of the recent global financial turmoil, at a time when the economic climate seemed set relatively fair, though clouds were visible on the horizon. The breakneck speed of events in the past three years has complicated the author's task by making it impossible to ignore questions of crisis management and short-term recovery. Nevertheless, as the task nears completion (spring 2010), policymakers are naturally still preoccupied with the present troubles, the book aims to look beyond them to address more fundamental questions of policy design. That will naturally mean considering how far the upsets of the past few years can be traced to weaknesses in the existing regime, among other causes.

The author's interest in macroeconomic policy stems from a career of over 40 years as a professional economist, starting with nearly ten years as a Research Officer at the Department of Applied Economics at Cambridge, where he was a founder member of the Cambridge Economic Policy Group; then 20 years as an economic adviser at the Bank of England; then a short spell as a research fellow at the Royal Institute of International Affairs, and since then as a visiting fellow at the National Institute of Economic and Social Research, and latterly at the Judge Business School, Cambridge. He has worked in a variety of fields, including international direct investment, the patent system, macroeconomic forecasting, the operation of monetary and fiscal policy, monetary integration in Europe, and several recent ventures into the teaching of economics. Throughout, macroeconomic policy has been a favourite theme, as this book aims to show in a synoptic and forward-looking way.

In the belief that economic policy is too important to be left to economists, the book is addressed mainly to non-professionals, or those who may have forgotten much of the economics they once learned. For that reason, technical analysis is mostly avoided or segregated in text boxes, annexes or footnotes which may be skipped by those prepared to take the arguments on faith. But professional colleagues may find something to interest them in the policy recommendations later on.

With luck the book will also engage readers in the wider world. It aims to avoid being too UK-centric, and many of its policy recommendations apply to developed economies generally. Indeed it will have missed an important target if the suggestions for a new economic order in later chapters fail to interest those concerned with global issues.

Acknowledgements

The immediate stimulus for the book came from reading Andrew Britton's study, *Monetary Regimes of the Twentieth Century* (Britton 2001). While finding much to agree with there, I felt his message about the failures in policy design in the last century unduly pessimistic. At any rate his conclusions posed a challenge to find a more optimistic answer. The global crisis of the past few years has of course given that challenge extra point, while ensuring that it is indeed a challenge.

Much of the guidance I received in the formative phases of my career came from my mentors at the Department of Applied Economics, Cambridge – its directors Brian Reddaway and Wynne Godley. Later, while engaged on policy analysis at the Bank of England over the next 20 years, I benefited greatly from working to the Bank's chief economists of the time, successively Christopher Dow and John Flemming, both of whom taught me much in their different and inimitable ways. More recently, my association with the National Institute of Economic and Social Research has been a constant source of support and instruction and I am grateful to its director Martin Weale for providing a congenial haven for work on this book among other themes. I have been fortunate in being able to use the National Institute's facilities, including online access to OECD statistics for many of the charts and tables, although of course their presentation and interpretation are entirely my responsibility.

Among others to whom I owe special thanks are my friend and colleague Jochen Runde, Director of the MBA at the Judge Business School, who has been a frequent source of help, including arranging for me to teach courses on international macroeconomics there for the past three years; and my thanks are due to students on these courses for acting as involuntary guinea pigs for some of the book's ideas. Lastly but not least, my heartfelt thanks go to my wife Leslie for putting up with long silences while I have been wrestling with these ideas. Without her encouragement and patience the task would never have been finished.

1

INTRODUCTION

To Utopia and back

An important lesson to emerge from the economic history of the last century is that although a number of different macroeconomic regimes were tried at various times and in various countries, none emerged as superior for all times and countries. This was the main conclusion of Andrew Britton's illuminating historical study some years ago (Britton 2001), which found that different regimes suit different circumstances so that, in a diverse and changing world, no single regime can claim primacy, and no macroeconomic policy can be right for all time. Much depended on the accompanying institutional environment – the political and social institutions, economic structures and behaviour patterns – that confronted policymakers in the 20th century, which also varied greatly through time and across countries, as Britton reminds us (should a reminder be needed).

Change may occur in the institutional environment quite independently of the macroeconomic regime in place. In some cases extraneous institutional change may strengthen the prevailing policy regime, but its effect is more likely to be adverse, creating problems in due course and putting the regime's survival to severe test. This is because macroeconomic regimes tend to be rather specific to their institutional environment, major changes in which are likely to create tensions sooner or later. Thus a regime that succeeds in one era may fail in another. Even if defined rather broadly, no 20th-century regime appears to have lasted more than about 35 years (according to Skidelsky 1998, cited in Britton 2001: 3). On a narrower definition, few regimes have lasted more than 20 years or so, exceptions being the Gold Standard (which however dated from the late 19th century), and the centrally planned regimes of Communist countries.

History also shows that macro regimes tend to *induce* significant changes in their behavioural or institutional environments sooner or later, which therefore cannot be regarded as regime-independent. This property of regimes received famous theoretical recognition in the form of the 'Lucas critique' towards the end of the

Keynesian era (see Lucas 1976 and 1987), which argued that basic macroeconomic behavioural relationships (like the consumption function – the generally stable link between personal consumption and disposable income) are likely to be affected by government policies through their effects on economic agents' expectations. In some cases the induced effects on agents' behaviour may help the regime, as for example when a successful commitment to output stabilisation creates expectations of steady growth which generate high investment and thence become self-fulfilling. But in others they may be unhelpful, as when a commitment to full employment encourages labour-market rigidities (inflexible wage differentials or job-demarcation rules) that make high employment harder to sustain.

This interdependence between regimes and institutional environments might seem to imply that the choice of regime ultimately does not matter, for almost any regime may succeed if it induces supportive environmental change, or fail if it induces disruptive change. It might then be concluded that conscious efforts at 'intelligent design' to create the best policy regime are likely to be fruitless, whereas Darwinian competition between regimes is more likely to throw up the best one for a particular time and place sooner or later. Britton (2001) does not push his argument quite that far, but he does come close to suggesting that all regimes are fatally flawed, in the sense of containing the seeds of their own eventual destruction. Thus his theme is that the 20th century witnessed a grand oscillation between 'laissez-faire' and interventionism – a journey 'to Utopia and back' in policies and theories, which left policymakers at the century's end with no better macroeconomic prescriptions than were available at its start, and economists with no better understanding of how the economy works, apart from some technical improvements in data and analysis. Britton seems to have taken the idea of Utopia from Friedrich von Hayek, who characterised what he held to be the unrealistic goals of socialism as the 'Great Utopia' in *The Road to Serfdom* (Hayek 1944: ch. 2).

Such a pessimistic conclusion, if true, would imply that the mistakes of economic history are bound to be repeated. Although the biggest shocks to the institutional environment during the last century – the two world wars – seem unlikely to recur, at least in the sense of continent-wide conflicts between powerful groups of countries armed to the teeth with conventional weapons, adverse events or tendencies affecting numbers of countries seem bound to happen, and to be very upsetting for those affected. A list of possibilities is painfully self-evident. At the top must come the prospect that systematic climate change, unless mitigated by action to reduce carbon emissions, will bring environmental degradation, with all the implied disastrous consequences: perhaps massive regional impoverishment and conflict. Conflict may also arise from perceived incompatibilities between the main faiths and ideologies, leading to serious political and social disturbances, regional if not global. Given the power of modern technology, the most sophisticated economies seem the most vulnerable to new, organised forms of terrorism, as exemplified by the events of 9/11.

Of more immediate relevance for macroeconomic policy, major political realignments like the formation of the European Union or the collapse of the Soviet empire may occur, calling for the creation (in the former case) or dissolution (in the latter case) of supra-national economic institutions with special regime requirements. Powerful new economic players are now clearly emerging among the developing economies, principally China and India and the thrusting market economies of South East Asia; and others seem bound to emerge in due course among the 'transition' economies of Eastern Europe, principally Russia itself; and these will doubtless create new alignments or new problems for the existing players. The soaring demands for energy, industrial materials and foodstuffs from the emerging giants, whose implications for commodity prices are now becoming painfully apparent, are just one of the more obvious manifestations of such problems. Even the more predictable types of long-run structural change, like the ageing of populations in developed economies, seem likely to add to social tensions and pressure on resources, and clearly have important implications for fiscal-policy objectives and modalities. In the past few years an outbreak of rampant instability in the financial markets has added to these woes. The menu of such possibilities is large and the range of uncertainty about their potential economic implications, unfortunately, very wide.

If macroeconomic policymakers respond to future economic shocks and adverse trends in ways entirely reminiscent of the last century, clinging to regimes tried and then found wanting, or lurching between the extremes of laissez-faire and interventionism in the manner depicted by Britton, they seem condemned to repeat the errors of that century. If this is the prospect, economics will indeed deserve the label of the 'dismal science' it acquired in the time of Malthus and Ricardo.

This book tries to take a more optimistic, if no less speculative, tack. While accepting that no single macroeconomic regime, and no single school of macro theory, has proved universally superior in modern times, it argues that important lessons can be learned from the experience of the main regimes tried in the past century. If these lessons are absorbed and built upon, it should be possible to arrive at a new regime that will be more effective and resilient than any seen previously. In the last decade of the 20th century economists of different persuasions reached a consensus on the key elements of a more durable regime. The denouement was especially prominent in Western Europe, as policymakers striving to achieve monetary union there stumbled upon a new synthesis that held promise for the future. The rapprochement between competing macro-policy doctrines in the 1990s has been called the 'neo-liberal consensus', though that name hardly does it justice. It certainly contains substantial free-market elements, comparable to those that held sway about a century previously; and the associated consensus in macroeconomic theory – which will be reviewed in Chapter 4 – embodies much of the neoclassical thinking of that earlier time. But, as we will argue in more detail later, the 1990s policy settlement also includes elements of the 'new economics' that emerged in the 1930s and gained wide acceptance after the Second World War, including some of the Keynesian apparatus and even the policy activism that Britton dismisses, regretfully but firmly, in his book. In short, the 1990s policy consensus was a genuine compromise between the two main competing macroeconomic philosophies that prevailed at different times and places in the preceding century. That in itself seems an achievement worthy of respect and even some optimism. We may not yet have reached the end of economic ideology, but economists are learning that a mix of ideologies seems to work better.

Nevertheless it is clear from the economic traumas witnessed since 2007 that regimes built on the 1990s synthesis also embody important weaknesses, and further reforms will be necessary if they are to survive and cope well with the threats that seem bound to grow in the present century. One such weakness is the phenomenon of unbridled 'globalisation' – the sweeping removal of barriers to cross-border trade and investment, perhaps the single most powerful and pervasive policy innovation of the second half of the 20th century (though not much mentioned by Britton). Globalisation has brought a near-universal opening-up of economies large and small, developed and undeveloped, to market forces, and with that has come a huge expansion of international trade and investment. Neoclassical economists have hailed it as a triumph of free-market capitalism over interventionist and centrally planned approaches. But several painful episodes have shown that globalisation can bring serious problems if it proceeds indiscriminately and without firm regulation, notably the East Asian financial crisis of the late 1990s and most recently the 'Crash of 2007–8' and the ensuing global credit crunch.

The principal task in what follows will be to identify these key weaknesses and suggest how they might be remedied. This is admittedly a tall order for a rather short book; it calls for more generalisation than the author would like, and considerable selectivity in the range of problems and solutions covered. But if it provokes others to reflect on policy design for the longer term, he will be more than satisfied.

Plan of the book

The first half of the book reviews the policy experience of the later 20th century as a prelude to suggesting what should be done to create a durable regime for the present century. It starts by drawing lessons from the abandonment of Keynesian economic management in the mid-1970s (Chapter 2), and from the experiment in monetarism that largely superseded it in the 1980s (Chapter 3). Chapter 4 describes the '1990s synthesis' – the policy consensus which emerged in the 1990s from the confusion following the successive failure of Keynesian and monetarist approaches; as part of that task it reviews the theoretical model known as the 'New Consensus in Macroeconomics', developed in rationalisation of the 1990s settlement. Chapter 5 explores the weaknesses inherent in the new consensus and the problems it has encountered, with special reference to economic stagnation in Japan and the appearance of China on the world scene. Finally Chapter 6 describes the financial crisis that broke in 2007 and the lessons to be learned from it.

Throughout these chapters detailed consideration will be given to the objectives and methods of monetary policy, reflecting the primacy accorded to it in the 1990s settlement. Attention will also be paid to the diminished role of fiscal policy in post-1990s regimes. Despite its relegation from the mainstream, exchange-rate policy will also receive attention, bearing in mind that it will feature prominently in the recommendations later on. However, the discussion will not venture into policies for promoting productivity and growth, like public support for R&D and industrial development. There may be a role for such policies in modern market economies, and they may have macroeconomic implications, but they generally come under the heading of structural policy and constraints on space argued against their inclusion.

The second half of the book proposes a package of reforms needed in the author's view to convert the 1990s settlement into a durable regime. Chapter 7 recommends the adoption of uniform inflation targets by all major economies and the recognition of output stability alongside price stability as twin primary objectives of monetary policy; it also calls for new instruments to be added to the standard central-banking repertoire, in order to escape from the 'one-club' methodology of monetary policy. Chapter 8 recommends that fiscal policy be given the positive long-term role of achieving a sustainable rate of national saving; it also calls for flexibility to be allowed within that remit for fiscal policy to assist proactively with short-term stabilisation in the event of abnormal cycles or shocks, and for institutional innovations to distance fiscal policy from short-term political interference. Chapter 9 urges that the major economies should proceed cautiously but deliberately towards a stable exchange-rate regime as part of an integrated and cooperative international approach to the use of monetary and fiscal policy. Finally Chapter 10 assesses the package as a whole and speculates that the creation of a fully-fledged exchange-rate system based jointly on the dollar and euro might eventually lead to a merger of these currencies in a North Atlantic Monetary Union around the middle of the century.

A bird's eye view of history

A long sweep of events will be covered in the next few chapters and summary measures of their size and timing may help to lend perspective. In Figure 1.1 four key economic indicators – growth of national output (GDP), the unemployment rate, consumer price inflation and the balance of external payments – are charted for the four major economies that feature most frequently in the story. They span the entire period from 1960 to date. The vertical divisions in the charts mark the three successive policy eras identified later – 'Keynesian Management', 'the Monetarist Experiment' and 'the 1990s synthesis'. Readers may wish to refer to these charts as the argument proceeds.

Some comparable illustration of the evolution of macro policies in our four major economies through time may also be helpful. This is less straightforward, as policies are far from easy to capture by summary statistics. Nevertheless two commonly used indicators of the thrust of monetary and fiscal policy are offered in Box 1.1, and readers may wish to consult them at relevant stages.

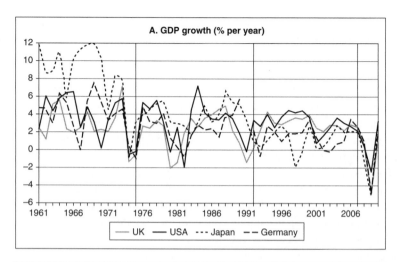

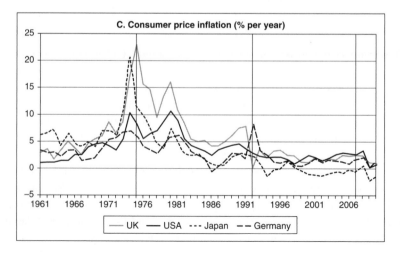

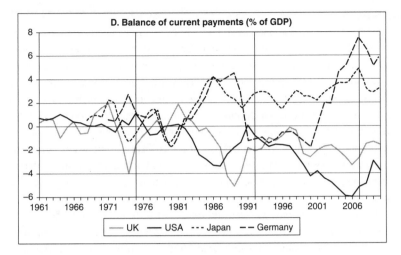

FIGURE 1.1   Key economic indicators, four major economies, 1961–2010 (source: OECD Stat, 'Economic Projections' online database).

Notes: the vertical lines indicate approximate divisions between the three successive policy eras identified in the text: *Keynesian economic management* 1961–75, *the Monetarist experiment* 1976–91 and *the 1990s synthesis* 1992–2007. The divisions are intended only as broad guides to the timing of regime changes, which evolved at different speeds in different countries, as the text explains.

'Germany': West Germany until 1990 and reunified Germany subsequently.

'GDP growth': annual percentage change of national output in real (volume) terms.

'Unemployment': measured on the OECD standardised definition.

'Consumer price inflation': annual percentage change of the expenditure deflator for personal consumption.

'Balance of current payments': balance of external trade in goods and services plus net income from abroad.

Data for 2010 are OECD projections.

BOX 1.1 KEY INDICATORS OF MACROECONOMIC POLICY

The charts below present summary indicators of monetary and fiscal policy in four major developed economies from the 1960s to 2009. They are intended to give a broad impression of the size and timing of changes in the thrust of policy on output in each economy.

Monetary policy

Chart A plots a measure of each economy's real (inflation-adjusted) short-term interest rate. The real interest rate is defined as the nominal interest rate (yield) minus the *expected* rate of inflation over the life of the asset(s) in question. The estimates here are calculated as 12-month averages of a representative three-month rate (expressed as an annual rate) in the relevant economy, *minus* the change in the consumers' expenditure deflator – a measure of the average prices of consumer expenditure on goods and services – in the current year compared with the previous year. They are thus 'backward-looking' estimates (in that inflation expectations reflect inflation in the recent past). Ideally, estimates based on forward-looking inflation expectations (forecasts) would be preferable, but reliable data on them are hard to obtain. Thus these estimates are only approximate measures of the thrust of monetary policy on the assumption that inflation expectations are formed on a backward-looking basis and that policy works through influencing mainly short-term prime lending rates in the economy concerned.

For much of the past half-century real short-term interest rates in our four major economies have varied between about 2 and 6 per cent, except in the early 1960s and again in the early–mid 1970s, when they were heavily negative in the UK and Japan, and unusually low even in the United States and Germany. The apparent slackness of monetary policy at those times was due in large part to the exceptionally high inflation experienced by industrial economies following the massive oil-price hikes of the 1970s. In that highly inflationary period central banks were unable or unwilling to raise nominal interest rates to match the rise in consumer prices. Later, through the 1980s until around 1992, the monetary authorities steeled themselves to raise nominal rates well

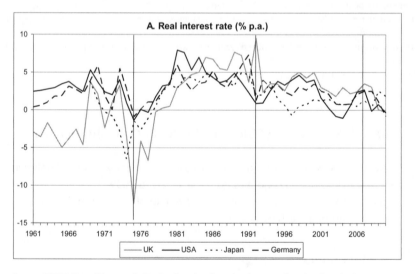

Source: OECD Stat, 'Economic Projections' online database and author's calculations.

Notes: three-month Treasury Bill rate for the United States, three-month interbank rates for the UK and Germany, and three-month CD rate for Japan.

above inflation, in pursuit of the tight monetary stance that was felt necessary to overcome high inflation during the 'monetarist experiment' (see Chapter 3). The high real rates seen in all four majors at times during that era were without post-war precedent and have not been equalled subsequently. Since the mid-1990s, real short-term rates have been near zero until recently in Japan, and have tended to fall to low levels in the United States and UK, reaching near-zero in the recent recession; whereas in Germany (and elsewhere in the Euro Area) they have remained significantly positive through the past decade.

Fiscal policy

Chart B plots the OECD's published measure of the cyclically-adjusted budget balance, expressed as a percentage of potential (full-employment) GDP in our four major economies, for as far back as data are available.

This measure is obtained by separating the budget balance of general government into cyclical and non-cyclical (structural) components, where the cyclical component reflects divergences between actual and potential output (the 'output gap'). The separation is done by estimating the elasticities (proportionate responses) of tax revenues and government expenditure with respect to GDP and applying them to the output gap. The cyclically-adjusted measure therefore abstracts from the effects of changes in capacity utilisation on tax receipts and government spending. Variations in the adjusted measure

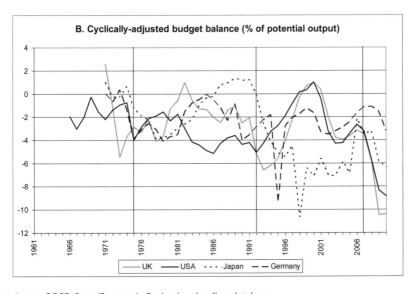

B. Cyclically-adjusted budget balance (% of potential output)

UK ⎯⎯⎯ USA · · · · Japan ⎯ ⎯ Germany

Source: OECD Stat, 'Economic Projections' online database.

are treated as a cause rather than an effect of output fluctuations, and thus provide an impression of the thrust of fiscal policy on output: an increase in the cyclically-adjusted balance represents a policy *tightening*; a decrease represents a policy *relaxation*.

As may be seen, there have been considerable variations in fiscal stance over the short term (1–3 years) in all four economies since this measure has been compiled. Yet until the early 1990s all four governments kept their cyclically-adjusted balances mostly within a range of plus 1 per cent to minus 4 per cent of potential GDP. Japan then became an exception, in that for over ten years after 1992 its cyclically adjusted budget deficit was well over *minus* 4 per cent of potential GDP (reaching minus 10 per cent of potential GDP in 1998). And after the global financial crisis of 2007–8, three of the four majors have run deficits well in excess of minus 6 per cent of potential GDP.

PART I

The new macroeconomic consensus and its problems

2

THE DEMISE OF ECONOMIC MANAGEMENT

A revolution in accepted views about the role and design of macroeconomic policy for developed economies occurred in the last quarter of the 20th century. The essential Keynesian idea that economies should be actively managed to achieve high levels of output and employment was largely abandoned in favour of the different, much less ambitious view that policy should be directed to achieving monetary stability – principally price stability – in the belief that stability will promote growth and prosperity more securely, if less deliberately, than Keynesian intervention.

The idea of economic management

When the author joined the Bank of England as an economic adviser in 1974 he still believed that governments should manage their economies. In this he was probably close to the mainstream of his professional contemporaries in the English-speaking world at the time, at least those brought up in the broadly Keynesian tradition that prevailed in anglophone universities after the Second World War. According to this approach, managing the economy meant using the policy instruments, principally the fiscal ones, actively and fairly frequently to stabilise the level of aggregate demand in the face of cycles and shocks. The approach was well described by economists at the time, notably in Christopher Dow's classic study of British macroeconomic policy in the post-war period (Dow 1964).

This approach had been summed up memorably for the author by his mentor and lead-author of a study of foreign direct investment (FDI), Brian Reddaway, then Director of the Department of Applied Economics, Cambridge. In rebutting trades union criticism of British firms' investment abroad for reducing employment at home, Reddaway wrote: 'We live today in a managed economy and the management tries to take heed of changes in the extraneous factors, so that the combination of these and Government actions may yield, fairly continuously, certain desired results' (Reddaway *et al.* 1967: 27–8). Reddaway's point was that the effects of FDI should be assessed in a situation where governments at home and abroad act to maintain full employment, so although overseas investment may affect international trade and profits it does not affect total employment or investment in either the investing or host economies. This strong expression of faith in economic management was typical of policy thinking in Britain and like-minded countries in the post-war era.

In orthodox Keynesian regimes, the main objective of economic management was to secure and maintain full employment of labour and capital, and if possible to raise economic growth. Most economists brought up in this tradition believed, with Keynes and his disciples, that the self-correcting processes, which in classical theory operated to restore full employment in the face of periodic shocks or cycles, tend to be rather weak in a mature industrial environment. Such disturbances were believed to originate largely on the demand side of the economy, and policy-makers' task was primarily to manage the level of aggregate demand (expenditure on currently produced goods and services, expressed in real terms) to overcome or offset them. This was acknowledged to be a difficult art, bearing in mind the criticisms expressed by such sympathetic observers as Dow (1964) who, while a dedicated protagonist of Keynesian management, was also a stern critic of its short-comings; but it was still thought worthwhile on the whole, if informed by good judgement and the advances in measurement and forecasting techniques that were being made at the time, aided by econometric modelling and computerisation.

BOX 2.1 KEYNESIAN UNEMPLOYMENT AND THE LIQUIDITY TRAP

The precise nature of Keynesian unemployment was a subject of considerable theoretical debate for years after the publication of the *General Theory*. Keynes distinguished two kinds of unemployment – 'voluntary' and 'involuntary' (Keynes 1936: 6, 15). The former reflects activities like job-search and retraining, and depends on the generosity of unemployment benefits. If these factors are given, voluntary unemployment is irreducible in that it exists despite equilibrium in the labour market. Involuntary unemployment is however avoidable in that it represents disequilibrium (excess supply) in the labour market. Keynes saw its causes as essentially twofold: (1) downward rigidity of money wages, reflecting the rise in the collective bargaining power of organised labour in industrial economies after the First World War, and other labour market imperfections; and (2) chronic inadequacy of aggregate demand, principally demand for physical investment, as exemplified by the Great Depression of the 1930s. That was a time of depressed output expectations among businessmen (low 'animal spirits'), in conjunction with the existence of a floor to interest rates – the 'liquidity trap', below which rates could not be driven. The interest-rate floor reflected enhanced 'liquidity preference' (willingness to hold idle money balances) on the part of households and firms when investment intentions are depressed.

In Keynesian market conditions, downward wage rigidity prevents the labour market from clearing in response to a fall in the demand for labour (caused by a fall in aggregate demand). In theory the system should then adjust through a general fall in output prices and thence a rise in the real money supply, which with unchanged real income should induce a reduction in (real) interest rates and thence a rise in investment expenditure. But if the demand for money is extremely elastic at prevailing interest rates, reflecting high liquidity preference among potential investors, the real interest rate will not fall when the real money supply increases and there will be no induced stimulus to demand.

In time, the notion of the liquidity trap was challenged by neoclassical critics, on the ground that it overlooked the operation of the 'real balance effect' originally suggested by the neoclassical economist A.C. Pigou, under which the fall in output prices caused by demand weakness raises the real value of real money balances held by firms and households, and this stimulates increased demand if spending depends partly on agents' real wealth hold-ings (see Pigou 1943). Some economists came to believe that Keynes' liquidity preference arguments were questionable at the theoretical level, though it was still possible to argue as an empirical matter that the adjustment process takes time. In due course Keynesian economists also raised a new empirical point, drawing on evidence produced shortly before and after the Second World War which suggested that goods prices are also rather sticky downwards, if less so than wages. Following these debates, mainstream economists have been content to accept that unemployment characterised as Keynesian may result from inadequate aggregate demand in conditions of downwardly sticky wages and prices, though debate has continued as to how rigid prices really are in the longer term. The onset of deep global recession since 2008 has of course revived concerns about involuntary unemployment and the liquidity trap's role in weakening the ability of monetary policy to address it.

The perceived inability of free-market economies to cope well with big adverse shocks dated from the traumatic experience of the Great Depression in the 1930s, memories of which remained strong in the post-war era. Nowadays macro theorists tend to diagnose those problems rather differently. They attribute them more to the existence of supply-side problems – institutional rigidities and inefficiencies in the labour and product markets of mature industrial economies. Rigidities of this kind had been considerably strengthened by the emergence in post-war Europe of powerful and militant trades unions in highly centralised labour markets, and of nationalised industries, oligopolistic firms and restrictive cartels and practices in wide areas of production and distribution. While recognising these rigidities, traditional Keynesians still emphasised demand-side weaknesses, in particular the myopia and inertia that characterised investment decision-making by private businesses, and the widening institutional gap between physical investment and saving decisions in financially-developed economies, which meant that periodic slumps in investment would not be automatically compensated by booms in consumption.

These different diagnoses grew to dominate policy debate in the 1970s. They continued to be a source of disagreement among theorists and policymakers even after the Thatcher revolution in the UK and comparable phases of market liberalisation in other major economies, some of which preceded the Thatcher government's reforms (as in the United States in the 1970s), or followed them (as in many EU economies in the 1990s). How far the principal sources of market failure and associated 'short-termism' have been largely overcome in modern economies will be considered in later chapters.

The high-employment goal

By the mid-1970s the goals embraced by policymakers in the UK and comparable regimes had shrunk appreciably: the relatively modest aim was to use the macro-policy instruments, which in those days still meant the fiscal rather than the monetary ones, to keep unemployment below 5 per cent of the labour force. This was a much less ambitious target than the unemployment rates of below 2 per cent achieved in Britain and similar economies in the 1950s and 1960s, but after around 1970 it came to be reluctantly accepted that such low rates were unsustainable in the face of seemingly persistent tendencies towards higher inflation and rising balance of payments deficits in many high-employment economies.

As may be seen in Table 2.1, output growth tended to slow markedly in the UK and other major economies during the 1960s and early 1970s, while unemployment tended to rise, suggesting that the slowdown represented a fall in capacity utilisation rather than in the underlying growth of productive capacity. Meanwhile consumer price inflation tended to rise strongly, well before the first oil price shock in 1974–5 (see Figure 1.1C). The rise in inflation during and after the 1960s was a feature common to most Anglo-Saxon economies and reflected a general rise in inflation expectations through this period, for reasons to be discussed later. Policymakers in the UK and elsewhere had hoped that inflation could be kept at bay through voluntary or compulsory wage and price restraints – the prices and incomes policies of the 1960s and early 1970s – but in time it came to be accepted that these were only palliatives which became progressively less effective in the face of rising cost-push forces.

By the early 1970s only a minority of economists on the left of the profession still subscribed to the much more ambitious view, held by socialist theorists of the 1950s and 1960s – among whom Cambridge economist Nicholas Kaldor (an adviser to Labour Chancellors of the Exchequer in the 1960s) was influential – that demand management should aim to *raise* the long-run rate of economic growth, through

TABLE 2.1 Key economic indicators: four major economies in the era of Keynesian management, 1961–75 (five-year averages)

	1961–5	1966–70	1971–5
GDP growth (% p.a.)			
UK	3.3	2.6	2.2
United States	5.0	3.4	2.7
Germany	4.8	4.1	2.3
Japan	9.2	11.1	4.5
Unemployment (% of labour force)			
UK	1.6	2.1	2.8
United States	5.5	3.9	6.1
Germany	0.4	0.7	1.1
Japan	1.3	1.2	1.4
Consumer price inflation (% p.a.)			
UK	3.3	4.5	12.8
United States	1.3	3.7	6.4
Germany	2.9	2.4	6.1
Japan	6.2	5.0	11.3
Balance of current payments (% of GDP)			
UK	0.1	0.4	−1.0
United States	0.8	0.2	0.2
Germany	..	..	1.3
Japan	..	0.7	0.4

Source and Notes: See Figure 1.1.
.. indicates that the data is not available.

persistent demand expansion allied to indicative economic planning. While many orthodox Keynesians still accepted that a sustained high level of demand could raise investment and thence productivity if it were successful in raising expectations of output growth, they recognised that the main efforts made in that direction in the 'mixed' economies of post-war Europe had been mostly unsuccessful.

In the UK, the experiment to raise output growth via the Labour government's 'National Economic Plan' in the mid-1960s, which involved a combination of indicative industry-based planning and sustained demand expansion, was soon perceived to have been a failure. By the mid-1970s little remained, in the UK or elsewhere, of Kaldor's ideas that growth could be raised by force-feeding of investment, sustained by fiscal action – except possibly in France where national economic planning had seemed to contribute to better economic performance. But even left-wing Gallic optimism for planning ran into the buffers in the early 1980s, when the French government under President Mitterand had finally to choose between demand expansion and the disciplines of the European Monetary System – and chose the latter.

Although the most ambitious goals of demand management had been largely abandoned in official circles by the mid-1970s, mainstream economists remained concerned about the tendency of the older industrial economies to stagnate at low levels of activity and slow growth, and many felt that this predicament called for more than mere stabilisation. Continuing dissatisfaction with the relatively weak performance of the UK economy post-war (apparent in Table 2.1) helped to explain the prevalence of this view among British economists of the author's generation. Thus a number of officials at the Bank of England and HM Treasury in the mid-1970s still thought that aggregate demand should be stimulated if necessary to keep unemployment from exceeding 5 per cent; but that belief finally waned with the advent of the first oil price shock in 1974.

Fiscal activism

Until well into the 1970s, economic management in the UK and similar regimes focused mainly on *fiscal* policy. Policymakers continued the routine of quarterly reviews and forecasts of the macro-economy, based on large econometric models built on Keynesian lines, and if necessary they acted on the basis of the results to influence aggregate demand through adjustment of tax rates and public expenditure at least once a year, and sometimes more often. The annual budgeting process followed by most national governments provided the main occasions for such fiscal activism, though actions could take place at other times as well if events seemed to warrant it. The focus on fiscal instruments meant that finance ministries were still very much in charge of the process, with the big government spending departments involved in a subsidiary way, and the central bank consulted but seldom deferred to.

The difficulties of fiscal management had been recognised by its practitioners quite early on. The fiscal instruments were unwieldy for political and administrative reasons, which meant that policy action tended to come too late and thus to be overdone; and such action could be damaging to economic efficiency, by distorting longer-term investment and savings decisions. Thus, in assessing the effects of UK fiscal policy in the immediate post-war period, Dow concluded that in general smaller, more cautious, actions would have been preferable (1964: ch. VII). Unfortunately this advice did not always register with Chancellors of the Exchequer: the 1960s and early 1970s brought a succession of stop-go budgets, culminating in Anthony Barber's dash-for-growth budget in 1972, which created the notorious 'Barber Boom'.

On the other hand, most policymakers in the early 1970s were still highly sceptical about the usefulness of monetary instruments for demand management, a view that had been little challenged officially in the UK since its confirmation as conventional wisdom by the report of the Radcliffe Committee some 13 years earlier (Radcliffe Committee 1959). This report into UK money and banking had concluded that the supply of broad liquidity mattered much more for aggregate demand than money per se, and that, because of the highly regulated nature of the post-war banking system in the UK, interest rates were ineffective in influencing the supply of bank credit and thence the availability of liquidity in the system (see Britton's earlier study, 1991). Moreover the British economy of the post-war era had not been credit-based: rationing and supply shortages had stifled consumer choice and the supply of mortgage and hire-purchase finance (consumer credit) remained subject to strict regulation until the late 1970s.

However, official faith in the power of interest rates received a boost with the adoption in the UK of a liberalised monetary regime known as Competition and Credit Control (CCC) in 1971.[1] This important reform replaced the machinery of quantitative ceilings and other administrative controls on bank lending by a single, uniform, minimum reserve ratio for deposit-taking business across the whole of the banking system. The step was accompanied by simplification of the complex system of special and cash deposit requirements on banks to create a uniform 'special deposit' scheme (a call for all banks to hold reserves as non-interest-bearing deposits at the Bank in proportion to their total deposit liabilities), which could be varied from time to time in accordance with the needs of monetary policy. The aim of these reforms was to enable the Bank to use its own lending rate as the chief tool of monetary policy, while at the same time promoting competition in deposit-taking and lending across the entire banking system. The deregulation of credit creation led to a gradual revival of belief in the usefulness of interest rates for economic management. Policymakers were aware that the Bank's Minimum Lending Rate (MLR) – the interest rate at which it supplied reserves to the banks, thereby setting the floor for the structure of bank lending rates – could be adjusted with much less delay and administrative effort than tax rates. Nevertheless, even in the mid-1970s, the effects of interest rates on aggregate demand were still regarded as weaker and less dependable than those of the fiscal instruments.

Despite the introduction of CCC, UK monetary policy was still substantially hobbled in the 1970s because important parts of the financial system remained highly regulated, so that key lending rates were still relatively unresponsive to money-market rates, or only responded with long delays. Thus mortgage lending, the principal source of finance for house-purchase, and so an important influence on house-building and consumers' expenditure, was still subject to cartel-like arrangements operated by the Building Societies Association (BSA). Under the wing of this association, mortgage lenders combined to 'recommend' a uniform mortgage interest rate, ostensibly in order to create stability for borrowers but in practice also to minimise competition between lenders. This cosy arrangement tended to insulate the mortgage rate from market forces, or at least greatly delay their operation. As a result, the links between MLR and the cost of finance for house purchase were highly variable and subject to long lags. Thus in the years after the introduction of CCC, changes in MLR tended to generate large swings in mortgage lending, and thence house-building and consumer durables' spending: the exact reverse of what stabilisation policy should be achieving. Accordingly changes in MLR were avoided or delayed so far as possible. These arrangements continued until as late as 1983, when the BSA cartel was finally wound up by government action.

The partial liberalisation of the UK financial system in the 1970s created a substantially liberalised banking system alongside a still heavily regulated regime for other credit institutions – mainly building societies and hire-purchase finance companies – and comprised a rather unsatisfactory halfway house. Deregulation unleashed rapid growth in liquidity which fuelled inflation, but the mixed institutional regime made it difficult to use monetary policy to combat the massive inflationary pressures created by the oil shocks of 1974–5, exacerbated as they had been in Britain by the Conservative government's huge fiscal stimulus of 1972 (which generated the Barber Boom); and later, by the ill-conceived sally into wage indexation under Labour's 'Social Contract', an agreement between government and trades unions that attempted to control wage increases by linking them automatically to consumer price increases just after the oil-price hikes.

At the end of 1973 the Bank of England tried to contain the expansion of bank credit by reintroducing emergency credit controls in the form of the Supplementary Special Deposit (SSD) scheme (the 'Corset'), which imposed extra interest penalties on the *growth* of bank deposits beyond a specified rate.[2] In due course this administrative control created serious problems of disintermediation (bypassing of the domestic banking system via other credit channels), which were only removed when the Thatcher government came to power in 1979 and launched a sweeping deregulation of the rest of the financial system. The root and branch liberalisation of the UK financial system in the 1980s led to the rehabilitation of monetary policy in that decade, when official views on the relative efficacy of monetary and fiscal policy as modes of demand management were to be thoroughly reversed, as will be explained in Chapter 3.

Pegged exchange rates

International macroeconomic policy had been revolutionised at the end of the Second World War by the creation of the pegged exchange-rate regime known as the Bretton Woods system. This was a regime change of such far-reaching significance that it is worth recalling in some detail.

The system was designed to overcome the problem of competitive exchange-rate devaluation which had become serious in the inter-war years, when major economies including the UK and United States had sought to mitigate the consequences of global depression by devaluing their currencies, in the hope of obtaining a competitive trade advantage. The competitive leapfrogging had provoked retaliation through trade protectionism which deepened the depression and was seen by some historians as a cause of the Second World War. As the war in Europe neared its end, a scheme to address currency instability was agreed in negotiations between mainly the US and UK governments. Keynes was the chief UK negotiator, and although his ambitious proposals for a new international reserve currency were not adopted, important elements were incorporated later (notably the augmentation of international liquidity by 'Special Drawing Rights' in 1969). The scheme chosen was designed by Harry Dexter White, the official responsible for monetary issues in the US Treasury.[3]

The new scheme was agreed at a conference of the allied economies in July 1944 at Bretton Woods, New Hampshire, under United Nations auspices. The

International Monetary Fund (IMF) and International Bank for Reconstruction and Development (IBRD) – later the World Bank – were set up at the end of 1945 by the 29 countries that ratified the Articles of Agreement. The Fund began operations in March 1947 and by 1981 its membership had grown to 141 countries. Under its rules, participants' rates were pegged within fairly narrow margins (plus or minus 2.5 per cent) to the US dollar, the value of which was fixed to gold at $35 an ounce. Gold was thus the system's nominal anchor via the link with the dollar, which in turn provided the key exchange-rate standard for other currencies. (For this reason most participants saw themselves on a 'dollar standard' rather than a gold standard.) Countries with external payments deficits were allowed to purchase (borrow) reserve currencies from the IMF, unconditionally up to the amount of their 'quota' in the Fund, and they could borrow further amounts up to several times their quota, conditionally on agreeing an adjustment programme with the Fund.

The corrective policies prescribed in such programmes usually centred on a combination of fiscal and monetary tightening, though in time they were broadened to include other measures such as income and price restraints and eventually microeconomic reforms aimed at market liberalisation. In due course adjustment programmes came to include quantitative limits for financial magnitudes, principally the *expansion of domestic credit* via the banking system ('DCE') and public sector borrowing. Observation of these limits was normally a condition of continued Fund assistance, and in time multi-year programmes came to be the general rule. Currency purchases under Fund programmes were repayable over the medium–long term and came to carry a market-related interest rate (which nevertheless reflected the Fund's high credit rating and thus was an attractive bargain for countries with payments difficulties).

Through the system's first two decades the United States was in substantial external payments surplus, which helped US governments to pursue with minimal stress their role as lender of long-term capital on concessionary terms to countries that were either rebuilding their economies after the war or raising their industrial productivity to assist development. The United States also managed to achieve low inflation through much of this era, with the result that the dollar tended to be a hard and sometimes a 'scarce' currency and a number of major industrial economies were obliged to borrow periodically from the Fund to alleviate the dollar shortage.

In principle IMF financing was intended to cope with no more than temporary balance of payments problems, whether reflecting the business cycle, excessive demand expansion, or some other short-term factor. Countries with chronic payments deficits were encouraged to address them by devaluing their currencies, though in an orderly way, avoiding the 'beggar-thy-neighbour' behaviour of the 1930s. Developing and poorer countries in need of long-term capital were eligible to receive it on highly concessionary terms from the IBRD (hence the wisecrack sometimes heard among the staff: 'the Fund is a bank and the Bank is a fund').

The system's architects believed that in order to work satisfactorily it would require effective international consultation under Fund surveillance, hitherto hard to secure among countries experiencing external payments difficulties, and machinery for these activities was set up in the form of regular policy consultations between the Fund and its members.

Although the system was intended to provide an *adjustable peg* for member currencies, when large adjustments of par values (central rates) were needed they were seldom smooth in practice. Major currency devaluations were indeed agreed under the system from time to time, as exemplified by the devaluations of sterling in 1947 and 1967, but they were far from painless and tended to be postponed until crises developed. Governments of countries with payments deficits were generally slow to accept devaluation because it meant loss of prestige, even if postponement meant submitting to sharp demand deflation under IMF conditionality. While domestic political pressures contributed to this attitude, lack of symmetry in the adjustment process was also a problem. Countries in payments surplus usually resisted revaluation of their currencies and the IMF had no power to require them to revalue or to adopt expansionary policies, however warranted such action might seem to impartial observers.

Commentators have nevertheless mainly concluded in retrospect that the system performed well on the whole in helping weaker and slower-growing industrial economies to cope with balance of payments difficulties in the post-war era, while maintaining broad exchange-rate and price stability (see Bordo and Eichengreen 1993 for a review of comparative performance in major economies over the century). However, it became evident towards the end of the 1960s that the conditions essential for stability were being eroded right at its centre, in the US economy itself. The US current balance of payments, having been in substantial surplus since the war, began to deteriorate in the mid-1960s (as Table 2.1 shows), and actually moved into deficit for a time in the early 1970s (see Figure 1.1D). The source of the deterioration was persistent over-expansion of domestic demand, due partly to the burden of the Vietnam War and partly to domestic political pressure. The problem was made worse by a slowdown in US productivity growth, while productivity in the other major economies was catching up, thanks partly to reconstruction financed by the United States. Thus US inflation rose in the late 1960s and early 1970s, both absolutely and relatively to strong exporting economies like West Germany, as may also be seen in Figure 1.1D.

The result was reversal of the post-war global US dollar shortage and strong downward pressure on the dollar, which ceased to provide an effective nominal anchor or an acceptable reserve asset for most participants. A concerted international effort to meet these pressures was made via a general realignment of exchange parities under the Smithsonian agreement (December 1971), which included a devaluation of the dollar against gold, but it did not suffice to overcome them. After further dollar devaluations against other currencies and gold, the exchange parities between major currencies were abandoned with remarkably little fuss during 1972, and generalised floating ensued. The dollar's link with gold was finally severed in early 1973. Apart from the less formal attempts by G7 authorities to stabilise the dollar against other key currencies in the mid/late-1980s, the major currencies have floated virtually freely ever since.

However, although the authorities in charge of key currencies opted for floating when the system collapsed, those in many smaller economies, including most developing and emerging-market countries, chose to retain or consolidate existing links with the dollar or some other major currency; as many still do. In addition several regional currency arrangements were set up to perform the stabilisation role vacated by Bretton Woods, most notably in due course the European Monetary System (EMS), as will be discussed later.

The collapse of the Bretton Woods system was influential in reducing the role of Keynesian management in major economies. Many commentators welcomed it at the time, including some in countries that had been obliged to borrow from the Fund (like the UK): national authorities in slow-growth economies would henceforth be free to pursue expansionary policies without the IMF breathing down their necks. Unfortunately this new policy freedom was acquired just before the oil price shocks of the 1970s, and it allowed national policymakers to respond in very different ways. As a result some oil-importing countries experienced much larger increases in inflation than others, a feature that both contributed to, and fed on, the big increase in exchange-rate volatility under generalised floating.

The switch to exchange-rate floating gave policymakers in open economies much greater scope to use interest rates to influence domestic demand, whereas these had previously been kept mainly for emergency defence of a pegged exchange rate in economies where they could be freely deployed for this purpose. Moreover after 1973 policymakers rediscovered the extra leverage that monetary policy can exert over domestic demand in an open economy if the exchange rate is free to float, reflecting the responsiveness of net exports to real exchange-rate variations. They also discovered the stronger links that operate between monetary policy and inflation in an open economy when the exchange rate floats. But these features made exchange-rate floating a dangerous strategy for countries that chose to expand domestic demand in anticipation of the deflationary effects of the oil price shocks.

In short, the switch from pegged to floating exchange rates in the early 1970s boosted the effectiveness of monetary policy as a tool of demand management in open economies and freed them from the disciplines imposed by fixed exchange rates. Thus the collapse of Bretton Woods hastened the demise of Keynesian economic management and prepared the way for the dash to monetarism at the end of the decade, as will be seen in Chapter 3.

Inflationary bias

The fatal weakness of Keynesian management was its inability to maintain price stability or even, eventually, acceptably low inflation. The technical, administrative and data problems facing policymakers were such that pursuit of high employment was almost bound to create inflationary pressure sooner or later. The high degree of inertia in the economic system, the bluntness and inflexibility of the main policy instruments, and the lateness and unreliability of much output and expenditure data, meant that managing demand in the hope of absorbing 'potential' output more or less exactly, leaving only a narrow margin of spare capacity, was over-ambitious. Over time as firms, trades unions and households increasingly anticipated policy action to stimulate demand in the face of shocks and cyclical downturns, periods of excess demand tended to become more frequent, leading to increasingly serious bouts of inflation, suppressed or otherwise. Boosted also by political pressure for economic expansion associated with the electoral cycle,[4] and perhaps by wishful thinking about the sustainable rate of growth, such periods became dominant, creating a persistent inflationary bias that became harder to correct the longer it lasted. These problems were compounded by the strengthening of downward wage and price rigidity in the UK and some continental economies, as collective bargaining became more centralised in the 1960s and 1970s.

Persistent inflationary bias left the managed economy highly vulnerable to cost-push impulses, whether coming from world commodity markets or from labour markets dominated by powerful and well-organised trades unions. Trades unions found they could press for wage increases at the expense of profits or other incomes (including those of non-organised labour, though the unions were reluctant to admit it), secure in the expectation that governments would expand demand to accommodate higher costs without penalties to output or employment. This problem was amplified in the UK and similar regimes not only by the highly centralised nature of much collective bargaining, especially in the public sector, but also by the emphasis on pay comparability as a criterion for wage setting, which led to leapfrogging in wage bargains (as workers in weaker industries sought to maintain traditional differentials against those in profitable sectors); and also by strong resistance to real wage cuts on equity grounds.

The inflationary dangers inherent in a high-employment economy had been anticipated by the original architects of full employment, principally William Beveridge (1944) as well as Keynes himself and his younger collaborator and critic Dennis Robertson. Keynes' disciples saw the remedy in administrative or political solutions rather than market forces: they hoped that inflation-proneness could be overcome by prices and incomes policies, preferably voluntary restraints based on enlightened cooperation between employers and trades unions, with government acting as referee or chaperon or, failing these, through statutory wage and price controls. It was just about possible to cling on to this hope in the UK for nearly 30 years after the Second World War, during which inflationary pressure, though endemic, never got completely out of control. There was nevertheless mounting unease among policymakers that inflation in Britain and comparable economies seemed on an inexorably rising trend (see Table 2.1 and Figure 1.1C). Fears grew in the early 1970s that these economies were dangerously vulnerable to large price shocks from outside.

These fears were eventually realised: the oil price hikes of 1974–5 and 1979–80 injected large doses of cost inflation across the industrial world, especially in economies that depended heavily on imported energy. In some regimes the shocks were dealt with relatively smoothly, in that sharp and persistent inflationary spirals were avoided, although at the expense of temporary rises in unemployment which were painful in some cases. These were mainly economies where the authorities were willing to forego or suspend high employment goals for the sake of containing inflation (most notably West Germany among the majors). In contrast, most oil-importing economies that strove to preserve high employment by using fiscal policy to counter the demand-deflationary effects of the oil price rises (especially the UK, Italy, France and the Scandinavian countries and even the United States and Japan), suffered prolonged phases of inflation – exacerbated in the UK and Italy by the wage indexation arrangements that had been introduced in the early 1970s as a way of getting trades unions to accept moderate wage rises in conditions of creeping inflation.

The switch to generalised currency floating augmented the inflationary consequences of cost-push pressures in open economies with floating rates. Whereas previously such pressures had tended to emerge as balance of payments deficits, which required correction in association with financing under IMF rules, floating meant that countries with above-average inflation experienced currency depreciation, which added to the inflationary pressure by raising import prices. Thus the removal of the Bretton Woods discipline created a flywheel effect that led not only to accelerating inflation in the industrial economies generally, but also to divergence of inflation rates between countries according to whether they were more or less cautious in their policy responses to cost-plus pressures. Something of this divergence can be seen in Figure 1.1C, which shows inflation rising sharply in the UK, Japan and even the United States, between the first and second oil price shocks, whereas it remained subdued in Germany.

The experience of high and volatile inflation in countries that had adhered faithfully to Keynesian management finally broke the regime and brought a thorough reappraisal of macroeconomic policy. For many observers the crucial policy break in Britain was marked by James Callaghan's 'party's over' speech to the Labour Party conference in 1976, soon after he had replaced Harold Wilson as Prime Minister:

> We used to think that you could spend your way out of a recession and increase employment by cutting taxes and boosting government spending. I tell you in all candour that that option no longer exists, and in so far as it ever did exist, it only worked on each occasion since the war by injecting a bigger dose of inflation into the economy, followed by a higher level of unemployment as the next step.
>
> *(Labour Party 1976: 188)*

According to Denis Healey, then Chancellor of the Exchequer, the speech was drafted by Callaghan's son-in-law Peter Jay, previously a journalist at the London *Times*, who was working at the Treasury and later became UK Ambassador in Washington (Healey 1990: 443). That may be true, but the fact that the new prime minister felt obliged to deliver this message which, according to Healey, 'appeared to reject the concept of demand management, in principle and at all times', is indicative of the despair felt by senior Labour politicians towards the end of the Keynesian era.

Verdict

The Keynesian regimes that operated in a number of major economies for over a quarter of a century after the Second World War, assisted by the exchange-rate stability provided by the Bretton Woods system in its heyday, came to be widely perceived as fatally flawed by the mid-1970s, or at least to have outlived their usefulness. Without the fulcrum provided by relatively stable exchange rates, fiscal policy lost much of its leverage, and without the commitment to high employment, demand management seemed to have lost much of its point. Worse still, the monetary policy freedom permitted by floating exchange rates was misused in weaker-performing economies, with the result that in some of them inflation, having mounted slowly in previous decades, burst through the double-digit barrier and threatened by 1975 to destroy economic stability.

Nevertheless the economies that adopted Keynesian-style regimes after the Second World War enjoyed an uninterrupted period of high growth and activity, unequalled in scale and duration in the 20th century before or since, as a study by Maddison (1995) using long runs of data has shown. The prosperity lasted for nearly a generation after 1945, a period termed the 'golden age' by some commentators, including Britton: 'If the aim of economic policy is to combine stability with growth, then the 1950s and early 1960s must be the high point of success in the twentieth century' (Britton 2001: 121).

Britton cites with approval the statistical study referred to earlier, which concluded that 'The Bretton Woods regime exhibited the best overall performance of any regime' (Bordo and Eichengreen 1993: 27). On this assessment the Bretton Woods system was superior even to the classical Gold Standard which emerged in the late 19th century, and which many economic historians regard as the most successful of pre-Keynesian regimes. Our key-indicator charts (Figure 1.1) show that average GDP growth from 1960 to the early 1970s in the four major economies was substantially higher than during the two subsequent regimes, though output was less stable then and inflation eventually rose higher towards the end of the Keynesian regime than under the latest one (the '1990s synthesis').

How far the record growth achieved in the post-Second World War era was attributable to Keynesian policies has been the subject of much debate. Britton is unsure about the answer, though he thinks too much has been claimed for macro policy in this period. He notes instead the stimulus from rapid growth in the non-developed world, and the helpful background created by years of political consensus and social solidarity in the major economies after the war (except in France). He also notes the absence of adverse shocks, particularly financial panics, which leads him to speculate that 'the golden age may have been prosperous just because it was uneventful' (Britton 2001: 127). Others have argued that the destruction of physical capital in Europe and much of Asia during the war, and the consequent pent-up demand for industrial and housing investment, would have generated high activity for at least a decade afterwards, whatever policy regime had been pursued. Among distinguished economists who took this view in the late 1960s was Robin Matthews, who pointed out that the UK government actually ran large current-account surpluses in the post-war years, and therefore could not have been boosting demand then (Matthews 1968). He found the main proximate cause to have been the high level of *private* investment compared with the inter-war years, which probably reflected post-war reconstruction of the capital stock in industrial economies and 'catch-up' in the developing world; though he accepted that fiscal inducements to investment may also have played a part.

For convinced Keynesians such views may seem unduly sceptical, in that they ignore the supportive roles played by fiscal pump-priming and by the 'balanced budget multiplier', and underestimate the importance of governmental commitments to full employment. At least it can be said that governments guided by Keynesian ideas avoided the policy mistakes that had led to prolonged aggregate demand deficiency in the 1930s. Moreover it is hard to deny that the post-Second World War boom was prolonged by persistent expansionary fiscal policy in a number of major economies, and few have disputed that the mainsprings of growth were on the demand side rather than the supply side, albeit in an unusually favourable low-inflation environment (due to rationing of consumer goods, price controls, credit regulation, etc.) for at least a decade after the war. If so it seems fair to conclude that Keynesian management provided important lessons for policy-makers despite its undoubted inflationary tendencies, and it would be unfortunate if they were forgotten with the regime's demise.

3

THE MONETARIST EXPERIMENT AND ITS LEGACY

While macroeconomic theory was evolving into a fashionable field of academic study with genuine influence on real-world policies after the Second World War, an important ideological rival to Keynesianism emerged in the form of the monetarism of Milton Friedman and his followers in the 'Chicago School'. Monetarism had its roots in classical economic ideas dating from the late 18th century, which evolved in time into the neoclassical economics of the late 19th and early 20th centuries. Classical writers had treated money as a largely passive medium of exchange and store of value, with little recognition that money might play an active policy role in the economy, much less that the quantity of money might be the crucial policy instrument. But they warned that governments could debauch the currency by coining or printing too much of it, and those ideas finally crystallised in the form of the *quantity theory of money* towards the end of the 19th century, which asserted that the price level (and thence inflation) is determined by the size of an economy's money stock. The basic neoclassical assumptions of highly flexible goods prices and competitive and efficient markets were essential elements in this theory, as will be explained shortly.

Monetarism's emergence as an important branch of theory was due in part to the strength of the tradition of free-market liberalism that flourished then (as now) in the universities of the American mid-west. Intense and sometimes bitter disputes between monetarists and Keynesians came to dominate transatlantic academic economic debate during the 1950s and 1960s, with the former, or at least neoclassical theory, tending in due course to find more acceptance in the United States and Keynesian theory mainly preferred elsewhere in the English-speaking world, especially where socialist ideas were an important influence in post-war politics.

However, despite its appeal to neoclassicists, monetarism was generally slow to influence policymaking, even in North America. Only when concerns about inflation came to the fore in the 1970s did monetarists start winning the policy arguments in most market-based economies. Admittedly, regimes with a monetarist lineage had been adopted in a few countries well before 1970, notably West Germany and Switzerland. There, Keynesian ideas had not been widely accepted in either academic or official circles, and post-war policies owed more to the ultra free-market liberalism of the 'Austrian School', a leading modern exponent of which, against the tide of Keynesianism before and after the war, had been Friedrich von Hayek. Hayek's ideas survived the war and were taken up by influential monetarists on the Continent, notably Karl Brunner (who was admired and consulted by Prime Minister Margaret Thatcher and the free-marketeers in her cabinet).[1]

The idea of monetary control

Monetarists of a strict persuasion believe that the essential task of macroeconomic policy, and its only legitimate one, is to stabilise the general price level through *close and continuous control of the money supply*. Pure versions of the approach call for the monetary authority to control the money stock directly through its monopoly of the supply of 'high-powered' money (money issued by the central bank), as will be explained shortly. The key and sole objective of such control is to maintain price stability; strict monetarists firmly reject all ideas of using policy to influence output and activity, for whatever reason.

Monetarism rests on two basic tenets. The first is that the central bank can always control the amount of money in circulation if it sets out to in a determined and systematic way. Control depends on the fact that, in modern economies, money in the hands of the general public (households and firms) comprises mainly deposits held at commercial banks or other credit institutions; by comparison, the amounts of notes and coin in circulation are rather small. Provided commercial banks operate on a 'fractional reserve' basis, so that the volume of bank deposits they create through lending to customers is a constant multiple of their cash reserves held on deposit at the central bank, the latter can determine the total stock of deposit money by controlling the amount of operational deposits it supplies to the banking system. In effect policy is conducted by controlling the size of the 'monetary base', essentially the deposits issued by the central bank and held as cash reserves by commercial banks. (The supposedly constant relationship between proportionate changes in the monetary base and the induced changes in the stock of money in public hands is known as the 'money multiplier'.) Banknotes, which are issued on demand by the central bank via the banking system and mostly held as cash by households and firms, are also included in wider definitions of the 'base', though in developed economies the amounts held are generally too small to affect the total money stock (including deposit money) significantly.

Since in most regimes the central bank is by law the sole supplier of base money in its economy, it should be able to exert close leverage over the money stock, provided commercial banks regularly adjust their lending so as to maintain a broadly stable ratio between their cash reserves held at the central bank and their total deposit liabilities to customers. To reinforce this leverage, monetarist-inspired regimes impose mandatory minimum reserve ratios on commercial banks and other credit institutions in their jurisdictions: banks are required to hold minimum amounts of reserves at the central bank in relation to their total deposit liabilities, and are subject to interest penalties if they fail to do so.

Monetarism's second basic tenet is that a strong and stable relation exists between the money stock (the quantity of notes, coin and bank deposits in the hands of the public) and the general price level, reflecting behavioural and institutional patterns in the economy that tend to change only slowly. This idea, known as the 'quantity theory of money', was formalised in the famous 'Fisher' equation of exchange around the end of the 19th century, by the American economist Irving Fisher (Fisher 1911):

$$MV = PT$$

where M is the stock of money in circulation, assumed to be controlled by the central bank, V is money's 'velocity of circulation', given by institutional and behavioural factors, P is the general price level of goods and services and T is the volume of transactions (or, in some versions, real income or output Y) in the economy concerned. In simple versions of this theory, V and T are both taken to be constant (independent of money and prices), V being determined by factors like the frequency of income payments and the efficiency of the payments system, and T (or Y) by real supply–side conditions (supplies of factors of production, the state of technology, etc.). In consequence, P varies proportionately with the money stock, and price stability is achieved by contriving that money grows at the same rate as the long-term growth of output. More refined versions allow that both V and T (or Y) may vary in the short term, for example because of variations in interest rates and thence relative holdings of money and other assets, and even perhaps in expenditure and thence income. But strict monetarists hold such effects to be weak or transient, so that monetary action by the central bank leaves the link between money and prices unaffected in the medium and longer term. The implication is that inflation is caused by excessive growth of the money stock – growth faster than that of the economy's capacity to supply goods and services over the long run. Hence Friedman's much-quoted dictum that 'inflation is always and everywhere a monetary phenomenon' (Friedman and Schwarz 1963).

Monetarists accordingly believe in the 'neutrality' of money, i.e. that the money stock determines key *nominal* magnitudes over the medium to long term – in particular the general price level of goods and services, and thence the sum of nominal incomes/expenditure – but not 'real' magnitudes. They deny that the money stock can influence physical output, real income, or employment, except in the short term (up to a few years at most), when prices may be sticky or inflexible. This denial rests on the assumption that the prices of currently produced goods and services are highly flexible beyond the short term. If so, in the medium term and beyond, variations in aggregate demand will merely propel the general price level up or down; they will not generate the sustained changes in real wages and incomes needed to move aggregate output and employment permanently.

Monetarists therefore hold that the best way of stabilising output is not to manage demand but to provide *stable monetary conditions*, relying on the supposedly strong self-stabilising properties of the real economy to return employment rather quickly to its sustainable long-run (equilibrium) level in the face of demand or supply disturbances or aberrations. Given that high and volatile inflation rather than unemployment came to be accepted as the main economic problem after the first oil shock in 1974–5 – indeed an acute peril facing some economies – it is hardly surprising that at this juncture monetarism eclipsed Keynesianism with its inflationary tendencies as the basis of policy in much of the developed world.

Nevertheless, the form of monetarism actually adopted in most regimes differed in important respects from the pure version taught until quite recently in most academic textbooks. When policymakers turned to monetarist ideas after the oil shocks they soon decided that tight control of the monetary base would be unsustainable for long in economies with liberalised and diversified financial systems. They got this message from officials in central banks and treasuries whose studies of the new approach, informed by early attempts to apply it in the United States and a few other systems, concluded that it would impose a rigid straightjacket on the banking system and generate damaging interest-rate fluctuations in the event of shocks. We will return to the problems posed by monetary base control later in the chapter.

Accordingly, when monetarist policies were widely applied in major economies in the late 1970s and 1980s, they generally operated by setting official targets for one or more measures of the aggregate money stock and using central banks' ability to influence short-term interest rates as the main control instrument, rather than seeking to ration the money stock per se. The modalities of what came to be known as practical monetarism, with its focus on monetary targets as 'intermediate' policy objectives, will be reviewed shortly.

The dash to monetarism

By the early 1980s, monetarist policies were being pursued in many developed economies, including a number that had practised Keynesian management through much of the post-war era. The Anglo-Saxon economies were prominent among the converts (United States, Canada, New Zealand, Australia and even the UK). This remarkably swift revolution in policy orthodoxy reflected fears that high inflation could become hyperinflation, recalling memories of Germany's experience after the First World War.

In the UK the abandonment of Keynesian economic management by the Callaghan government around 1976 left policy rather rudderless; it was more a gesture of despair at the failure of established policies than a positive acceptance of monetarist ideas. The latter were embraced with much greater conviction by the Conservative government led by Margaret Thatcher which came to power in 1979. Propelled by the new prime minister's drive and her strong attachment to free-market ideas, policymaking in the UK veered sharply towards a monetarist approach, which became for a time the accepted model for macroeconomic policy, under the guidance of uncompromisingly monetarist advisers like Professor Alan Walters, whom the new prime minister summoned from the World Bank in Washington to be her personal economic adviser. Meanwhile fiscal policy was relegated to a subsidiary role, passively supportive of monetary discipline. Almost as soon as the Thatcher government came to power it cut government expenditure in order to reduce public-sector borrowing, with a view to balancing the budget even as the economy was entering recession.

This departure in fiscal thinking attracted fierce criticism from the country's academic economic establishment of the time. It crystallised as a public and uncharacteristically uniform protest in a letter from 364 university economists to *The Times* newspaper after Chancellor of the Exchequer Geoffrey Howe's budget of March 1981. The letter objected to fiscal tightening in the face of the worsening recession and accused the Thatcher government of imposing much too tight an anti-inflationary policy. There has been subsequent debate as to whether so many economists could be right (or wrong). Some commentators believe the letter to have been mistaken, as GDP actually rose quite soon after the 1981 budget. However, one of the signatories, Stephen Nickell, until recently a member of the Bank of England Monetary Policy Committee, has defended it on the ground that GDP growth was below trend for a number of years after the tightening; on his estimate of the Phillips curve at the time, the deepening was more than enough to bring inflation down over a reasonable period (Nickell 2006). The role of the Phillips curve in modern counter-inflation policy will be discussed more fully in Chapter 4.

A detailed account of UK policy in the 1980s can be found in an earlier study by Andrew Britton (1991). However, the modalities of the practical monetarism pursued in the UK and similar regimes merit consideration here because they help to explain why the approach lasted barely a decade. A question that inevitably arose concerned the choice of the monetary aggregate to be targeted. Among the various possibilities, the UK authorities initially chose as their main target a measure of the broad money stock known as Sterling M3 (£M3), which included all bank deposits denominated in sterling – wholesale and retail, interest-bearing and non-interest-bearing – as well as notes and coin in circulation. They also targeted a narrower measure of money, M1, which included just current-account ('sight' or non-interest-bearing) deposits as well as notes and coin. These aggregates were enshrined in a set of financial aggregates termed the 'Medium Term Financial Strategy' (MTFS), which was first published in the Treasury's annual *Financial Statement and Budget Report* (Budget Red Book) in 1980, the publication of which marked the official commencement of the monetarist experiment in the UK. The MTFS contained forecasts for a range of nominal (current-price) indicators over the subsequent four years, including current-price GDP and the Pubic Sector Borrowing Requirement (PSBR) as well as £M3 and narrower monetary aggregates; all built around, and consistent with, the official inflation forecast.

BOX 3.1 NARROW AND BROAD MONEY

One of the vexed questions that confronted policymakers during the monetarist experiment was which version of the money stock they should seek to control. Monetarist theorists taught that the appropriate concept was money in the narrow sense of cash or virtual cash – financial instruments that are instantly acceptable in settlement of economic transactions, large and small. These include coin, banknotes and bank deposits that are transferable without delay or penalty, such as current accounts in the UK and sight deposits in the United States.[1] The rationale harked back to the notion of money's essential function as, among other things, a medium of exchange, with the implication that the amount of cash in circulation in an economy governs the amount of expenditure that can take place within it, in accordance with the quantity theory referred to above.

In contrast the practical monetarists in central banks preferred a broader concept which included less-liquid bank deposits that can be accessed only with some delay or penalty – namely, savings and 'time' deposits in the UK and 'term' deposits in the United States; and also deposits at the expanding category of 'near-banks' that grew in importance with financial liberalization, principally building societies in the UK and savings and loan associations in the United States. Their rationale was that, especially in an era of rapid change in the banking sector, with a growing range of institutions capable of offering money-type assets and rapid improvements in payments technology, broader definitions of liquidity were likely to have a more stable and predictable relation to aggregate expenditure than narrow money. Practical monetarists conceded that broad money might be more difficult to control through conventional central bank operations than narrow money, because the very developments that made it a more relevant target – greater competition between banks and near-banks – boosted its growth outside the controlled sector, and also widened the payment of market-based interest rates on bank deposits (the 'own rate' on money). Thus in innovative regimes the coverage of the money-creating sector was constantly expanding and this reduced the effectiveness of money-market operations for controlling the broad money stock.

In the face of these changes, policymakers found themselves engaged in a continuous search for more meaningful measures of the money stock. In time official statisticians were pressed to compile an increasingly complex repertoire of monetary aggregates. Despite efforts at international standardisation, national definitions varied somewhat with local circumstances, though the same general principles were followed as far as possible. For example in the UK by the late 1980s five main aggregates were regularly published. These were in addition to 'base money' (the monetary base M0, issued by the central bank), which was not money in circulation like the others, although M0 was actually targeted by the UK authorities in the experiment's early years. By 1990 the UK published the following six aggregates, in increasing breadth of coverage:[2]

M0: notes and coin in circulation outside the Bank of England *plus* banker's balances held with the Bank of England.

Non-interest-bearing (Nib) M1: notes and coin in circulation with the public *plus* non-interest-bearing sterling sight deposits held by the private sector.

M2: Nib M1 plus private-sector interest-bearing retail sterling deposits (deposits of less than £100,000 and with less than one month to maturity) at banks and building societies, and national savings bank ordinary deposits.

M4: M2 plus private-sector sterling holdings of time deposits and *certificates of deposit* (CDs, a type of time deposit of fixed maturity) at banks; and of shares, deposits and CDs at building societies.

M4C: M4 plus private-sector *foreign-currency* bank and building society deposits.

M5: M4 plus private-sector holdings of money-market instruments (bank bills, Treasury bills, local authority deposits, certificates of tax deposit and national savings instruments (excluding long-term).

At the time M1 and M4 were the Bank's preferred measures of narrow and broad money respectively. Initially the Bank had included interest-bearing deposits in its measure of M1 but the Nib version was preferred after the early 1980s, when it was found that the original aggregate was increasingly swollen by rapid growth of interest-bearing deposits, reflecting the introduction of market-related interest rates on sight deposits. The Bank had also previously published M3 and sterling M3 (excluding foreign-currency deposits), both including M1 *plus* essentially all private-sector sight and time deposits at banks (but not building societies). But these intermediate measures were progressively downgraded, and their publication was eventually discontinued in 1989, as a consequence of the breaks in the series caused by the conversion of the Abbey National Building Society into a corporate bank. Publication of M1 was also discontinued then.

Other central banks, notably the US Federal Reserve, continued through the 1980s to focus mainly on the narrow and intermediate measures of money, M1, M2 and M3, which they had embraced at the commencement of monetary targeting (see Meek 1982: Part 2); so too did the Bundesbank in Germany. However, the Bank of Japan preferred to focus on a variant of M2 including CDs, and a wider measure known as 'broadly-defined liquidity', which resembled a cross between M4 and M5; and it continues to publish and monitor them. (A comprehensive account of its policy strategy and operating procedures can be found in Bank of Japan 2009a: ch. 6; its monetary aggregates are also described there in ch. 7, Box 1). Nowadays most of the main central banks continue to publish and monitor a variety of narrow and broad aggregates. However, the ECB is alone in using a monetary aggregate (growth of M3) as the *reference value* for one of the two 'pillars' of its monetary policy strategy, the other pillar being the conditional inflation forecasts derived from its mac-roeconomic projections. (A full account of its policy framework and operating procedures is available in ECB 2001: ch. 3.)

As may be seen later in Figures 3.1 and 3.2, the behaviour of narrow and broad money in the 1980s and early 1990s tended to bear out policymakers' concerns. Figure 3.1 shows that broad money (M3 in the United States, M4 in the UK) was much less stable than narrow money M1 (Nib M1 in the UK) in relation to the monetary base, and in that respect was harder to control. On the other hand Figure 3.2 suggests that narrow money was much less stable than broad money in relation to aggregate expenditure (GDP) in these two economies, and in that respect was a less reliable indicator of the thrust of monetary policy. But Figure 3.2 also suggests that broad money also turned out to be a rather unsatisfactory indicator of the thrust of policy in both econo-mies, with velocities of circulation that were far from stable through the 1980s and early 1990s.

Notes

1 This concept should not be confused with that of 'legal tender' – the types of coins or notes that are legally acceptable in settlement of transactions up to a certain size, unless the parties agree otherwise beforehand. The purpose of legal tender is to avoid foreign currency, or inconveniently large amounts of domestic coin, being offered in routine domestic transactions without prior consent.
2 The following definitions are based on those in UK Central Statistical Office (1990, Section 11, especially p. 106). See also Bank of England (1987).

In Britton's judgement the official UK emphasis on broad money was a mis-take, which he attributes to blinkered views in both the Bank of England and the Treasury (Britton 1991: 105–7). He says that the Bank favoured a broad measure of money because it closely matched the stock of domestic bank credit, an aggre-gate which the Bank was used to controlling (though previously by administrative controls rather than interest-rate action) and with which he thinks the Bank was obsessed, but which had no explicit role in monetarist theory. The Treasury also favoured the wide, bank-credit-related, measure because it gave a rationale for controlling the PSBR and financing it outside the banking system. These were both longstanding Treasury obsessions, which also played no clear role in monetar-ist theory.

Britton is probably right that it would have been easier for the British authori-ties to control a narrower measure of money like M1, especially the version from which (after 1981) interest-bearing deposits had been excluded, and which was thus more responsive to changes in short-term interest rates as the control instrument than the previous version.[2] Some corroboration of this is offered in Figure 3.1, which presents money multipliers for narrow and broad money in the UK and United States – the supposedly stable relation between the money stock and the underlying 'wide' monetary base (including notes in circulation), which depends on the public's note-holding habits and the relevant reserve ratio(s) in the banking system. It can be seen that even during the 1980s, when there were large changes in real short-term interest rates, these ratios tended to be much more stable for narrow than for broad money.

However, aside from controllability, it is hard to see what other factor would support a preference for narrow over broad money. In an economy with a financial sector undergoing far-reaching institutional and technical changes driven by deregulation, as in Thatcher's Britain, the transactions demand for narrow money was more variable and less predictable than the demand for broad liquidity, which should

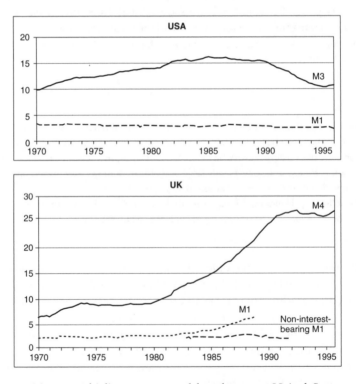

FIGURE 3.1 Money multipliers, narrow and broad money, United States and UK, quarterly 1970–96 (sources: for United States, Federal Reserve Bank of New York online database; for UK, Central Statistical Office/Office of National Statistics, *Financial Statistics*, HMSO, London, various issues back to 1975).

Notes: money multipliers here are ratios of narrow money (M1) and broad money (M3 for United States, M4 for UK) to Monetary Base (M0). Annual averages of amounts outstanding at end-quarters. See also the text for explanations.

reflect credit conditions more generally. Thus any link with the general price level should be much more tenuous in the case of narrow money than broad money.

In fact the evidence from this period suggests that neither narrow nor broad money had a stable enough link with nominal GDP, or the price level, to provide an effective inflation control mechanism. This continued to be so in the UK despite the broadening of the main broad money target in due course (May 1987) to include the sterling deposits of building societies as well as banks, in a new aggregate known as M4.[3] As may be seen in Figure 3.2, the velocity of circulation of M4

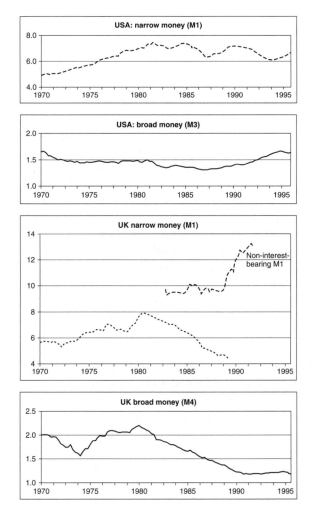

FIGURE 3.2   Velocity of circulation, narrow and broad money, United States and UK, quarterly 1970–96 (source: for money stocks see Figure 3.1. Current-price GDP from OECD online database).

Notes: velocity here is the ratio of GDP at current market prices (quarterly at annual rates) to money stock outstanding at end-quarters (M1 and M3 for United States; M1 and M4 for UK).

fell rather sharply in the UK throughout the 1980s, from about 2.2 in 1980 to about 1.2 in 1990. (The vertical scales of the charts are drawn so that, over the relevant magnitudes, equi-proportionate changes in velocity are represented by approximately similar distances.) The strong competition that gripped the UK banking system during this decade boosted M4 lending to such an extent that it became impossible to use it as a reliable measure of the thrust of monetary policy. In short, it is doubtful that any feasible approach to monetary targeting, whether narrowly or broadly based, would have succeeded in an era when the financial systems of the UK and other major economies were undergoing such radical liberalisation.

The retreat from monetarism

Despite the enthusiasm for monetary discipline displayed by many of the newer converts to monetarism in the late 1970s (who were, however, more likely to be senior politicians than officials or central bankers), even the pragmatic versions of the monetarist approach that focused on monetary targeting were generally not pursued seriously for long into the 1980s. This was so even in economies where Keynesian ideas had never taken firm root and where monetarist regimes had been adopted at an earlier stage. Thus the authorities in the small number of countries that continued to voice strong support for monetarist ideas through the 1980s, notably West Germany, quietly watered them down in practice over time, as will be seen in a moment. In less ideologically committed countries, enthusiasm for the monetarist discipline tended to wane almost as quickly as it had arisen.

To recap: in the UK and other economies with relatively sophisticated and diversified financial markets, the monetary aggregates turned out to be unreliable and even deceptive guides to the thrust of policy; and such monetary discipline as was achieved had disappointing effects on inflation, bearing in mind that unemployment remained worryingly high. Thus monetary targeting failed to achieve the high degree of credibility among agents and markets needed to puncture inflation expectations.

Although the MTFS continued to feature in the presentation of policy until it was finally abandoned by the incoming Labour government in 1997, serious monetary targeting in the UK was progressively overtaken after a few years by interest in an exchange-rate target as a counter-inflation device. As early as 1987, in an extraordinary volte-face by Chancellor of the Exchequer Nigel Lawson, the UK authorities began informally shadowing the Deutsche mark, and this led eventually to formal pegging of sterling against other European currencies when the UK joined the Exchange Rate Mechanism (ERM) in 1990.

When that long-anticipated but short-lived venture came to grief with sterling's abrupt departure from the ERM through the traumatic events of 'Black Wednesday' (16 September 1992), it seemed to some weary officials in the Treasury and Bank of England that all feasible methods of overcoming inflation in the UK had been exhausted. Nevertheless, surprisingly soon after the ERM debacle, Chancellor of the Exchequer Norman Lamont announced a novel and little-tried approach to the problem. The approach focused directly on inflation itself as the policy target and assigned both monetary and fiscal policies to bringing it steadily but securely down towards price stability. Within a few months of leaving the ERM, the UK authorities were firmly attached to the new approach, which was soon seen to be delivering a clear reduction of inflation.

The strategy that became known as 'inflation targeting' was pioneered in New Zealand, a country which had also been struggling to overcome acute and deep-rooted inflationary problems.[4] Introduced in 1990, the new approach achieved notable early success there and in due course was copied in a number of other Commonwealth countries as well as the UK, and in South America and elsewhere. Against the initial expectations of many sceptics, inflation targeting maintained its early success in the UK, overcoming claims that the inflation slowdown was due simply to the sharp monetary tightening applied to keep sterling in the ERM. In general the new approach met with marked success in the growing number of inflation-prone economies that embraced it, and it has remained the central focus of macro policy in these economies, at least until the recent financial crisis. The key point here is that it did not rely on control of the money supply, and cannot therefore be regarded as a form of monetarism in the strict sense.

In other countries that chose to pursue monetarist policies more or less seriously during the 1980s, the results were at best mixed and often almost as discouraging as those in the UK. By the mid-1980s such policies could claim a degree of success in countries where inflation had peaked alarmingly in the 1970s, but relatively little elsewhere, despite still historically high rates of unemployment. Inflation picked up again alarmingly in developed economies as the 1980s came to a close, and sizeable inflation divergences re-emerged between the majors, as may be seen in Figure 1.1C. This divergence was particularly apparent in the European Community, despite the progressive hardening of the ERM around its anchor currency the Deutsche mark in the late 1980s.

Meanwhile the costs in terms of unemployment and lost output in many economies that tried monetarism were substantial. As shown in Table 3.1, average GDP growth in the UK and United States in the late 1980s was below that of the preceding ten years of 'stagflation', and unemployment in all four majors was markedly higher through the 1980s than before 1980.

Even where monetarist policies were regarded as relatively successful in controlling inflation, most obviously in West Germany, monetary targets did not appear instrumental, notwithstanding the authorities' lip service to them. Indeed the monetary targets themselves were often missed by significant margins even in Germany, where the Bundesbank had pursued an annual target for growth of 'central bank money' since 1974, a narrow aggregate akin to the monetary base. In Germany's case, this narrow aggregate was heavily affected by changes in the official foreign exchange reserves, which fluctuated widely as a result of Germany's membership of the ERM, despite the Bundesbank's attempts to sterilise them (i.e. to offset their effects on domestic money; see the account of German experience in OECD 1985: 51–7). In the 1980s, public belief in the efficacy of German monetary policy

TABLE 3.1 Key economic indicators: four major economies during the monetarist experiment, 1976–92 (six-year averages)

	1976–80*	1981–6	1987–92
GDP growth (% p.a.)			
UK	1.8	2.3	1.9
United States	3.7	3.3	2.7
Germany	3.3	1.4	3.4
Japan	4.4	3.1	4.2
Unemployment (% of labour force)			
UK	5.1	10.9	8.1
United States	6.8	8.1	6.2
Germany	2.0	5.5	5.4
Japan	2.1	2.6	2.3
Consumer price inflation (% p.a.)			
UK	13.9	6.5	5.2
United States	7.7	4.7	3.8
Germany	4.0	3.0	2.9
Japan	6.6	2.6	1.9
Balance of current payments (% of GDP)			
UK	−0.0	0.3	−3.2
United States	−0.2	−1.6	−1.6
Germany	0.1	1.5	2.2
Japan	0.1	2.0	2.5

Source and Notes: see Figure 1.1.

* five-year average.

came to depend less on meeting the monetary target than on the Bundesbank's enviable (and much envied) record of success in controlling inflation, thanks to its demonstrated willingness (backed up by the German government) to accept the short-term costs of doing so.[5]

In general among economies that were successful in containing and then reducing the inflationary pressures of the 1970s, success seemed to owe at least as much to factors other than tight monetary control: stagnation of activity due to weak external demand, high rates of private saving induced by the 'real balance' effects of previous high inflation, and, above all, a reassertion of fiscal restraint.[6] In most developed economies by the late 1980s, monetary targeting had been superseded by other approaches, in many cases exchange-rate targets, which were widely favoured by small open economies, as shown by the number that were, or became, members of the ERM; or among larger, less open, economies, by eclectic versions of what had started out as rather pure monetarist approaches (notably in Germany and the United States).

Nevertheless monetarist theories and policies left a considerable mark, especially in economies that became ever more dedicated to financial market liberalisation from 1980 onwards. The rest of this chapter will focus on monetarism's weaknesses and the lessons to be drawn.

Monetarism's weaknesses

On the face of it, it may seem surprising that the monetarist policies adopted to overcome the inflationary crisis of the mid-1970s seldom survived for long, even in countries where Keynesian ideas had taken relatively shallow root, for example in Western Europe's least anglophone countries. In general the monetarist experiment lost support because its results were on the whole disappointing, in that it either failed to overcome inflation quickly enough to satisfy the governments that adopted it, or did so at excessive cost to output and employment. It is worth reflecting on why it failed to live up to its protagonists' hopes.

Difficulties in controlling base money

When addressing the practical task of controlling the money stock, central banks operating in liberalising financial environments found that they could not exert close enough control over base or high-powered money – essentially the stock of commercial-bank reserves at the central bank – to meet broader monetary targets without risking serious disruption to their financial systems. The few that moved quickly to introduce strict forms of monetary base control, notably the Federal Reserve in the United States, soon ran into difficult problems, principally high interest-rate volatility in the money markets when they intervened in order to influence the stock of commercial banks' cash reserves; and they were obliged to adopt more flexible arrangements.

Those in more cautious regimes like the UK quickly drew back when they contemplated the likely consequences of controlling base money. Thus when the Bank of England considered adopting monetary base control in 1979, its experts concluded that a strict regime (i.e. one in which the monetary base was predetermined by the central bank's operations, and banks were required to achieve their reserve requirements exactly on a daily basis) would put enormous potential pressure on financial markets (Foot *et al.* 1979: 149–59. See also Goodhart 1989 for a longer-ranging evaluation). The reasoning was that if the central bank preset the monetary base at below the level existing in the system, banks collectively would not be able to replenish their shortages by bidding reserves from each other, and could only meet their required ratios by cutting back lending or selling marketable assets by a *multiple* of the initial shortage; or by attracting notes and coin from the public. Either course would be fraught with difficulty: attracting currency from the public would probably mean offering a variable interest premium, which would break convertibility between currency and deposits; and the system collectively could not increase its reserves by asset sales unless the Bank stepped into the market to buy the assets, thereby creating more reserves and exceeding its target. The conclusion was that 'strict control of the base . . . would continually threaten frequent and potentially massive movements in interest rates, if not complete instability' (Foot *et al.* 1979: 153). It was conceded that a looser form of the control might be technically viable, for example by allowing reserve requirements to be met on average, and only approximately, over a period of months, or by attenuating or even eliminating the interest penalty (thereby effectively weakening the reserve requirement and converting the base into merely a leading indicator of broader money). However, such steps would weaken the thrust of the policy, and would also bring about large structural changes in the financial system, which would make targets difficult to interpret for years to come. In the event these arguments won the day.[7]

As explained earlier, similar though less serious problems arose where central banks tried to control 'narrow money' – notes and coin in circulation plus sight deposits. It was soon recognised that close control over this type of money would also lead to serious interest-rate volatility in short-term financial markets.

As a result of these experiments, the onus for achieving monetary restraint in liberalised regimes came to rest on influencing money-market interest rates rather than rationing monetary base or narrow money; central banks came to accept that control meant operating on the *price* rather than the quantity of high-powered money, though still generally with a view to achieving a target path for the money stock on some measure. In most jurisdictions the preferred measure came to be 'broad' money on some definition – generally notes and coin in circulation plus 'retail' deposits held in the domestic banking system, as explained earlier. However, a different sort of problem was then encountered, in that the market-based links through which central banks could influence the broad money stock, whether through monetary base control or management of money-market interest rates, proved to be much less stable than academic monetarists assumed. This problem was due mainly to the big institutional changes that occurred in banking systems following financial liberalisation.

A key change in this respect was the general decline that took place during the 1970s in commercial banks' reliance on central-bank reserves as their main source of liquidity. Whereas previously commercial banks had tended to maintain fairly stable *voluntary* cash ratios of 'central bank money' (commercial bank deposits at the central bank or notes issued by it) of 10–15 per cent of deposit liabilities, such ratios became smaller and more variable in the 1970s. As a result of the diversification and specialisation that occurred in deregulated banking systems, banks which ran short of liquidity found they could normally replenish it by bidding for deposits in the liquid and efficient interbank markets that developed then, through which they were able to trade near-money assets dependably and on narrow margins. The greater variability of reserve ratios in the banking system weakened the links between the monetary base and banks' deposit liabilities, so making the impact of open market operations by central banks on the money stock weaker and less predictable.

Another kind of institutional change was the introduction after the late 1970s of market-based interest rates on *money* itself, not just on savings or time deposits but also on many current or sight deposits; a development stimulated by rising competition between banks and near-banks after de-cartelisation. Thus, central-bank action to control the money stock by changing interest rates increasingly generated counteractive responses via the 'own' rate on money. For example, open market operations to reduce the monetary base by raising its cost also tended to raise the public's demand for money at precisely the time when its supply was being reduced, with unpredictable consequences for lending rates and yields on non-monetary assets. These factors combined to make the control of both narrow and broad money more difficult than before deregulation.

Instability of demand for money

A second source of weakness in approaches that sought to overcome inflation by controlling money was the variable influence of the *demand* for money in deter-mining the size and behaviour of the money stock, a feature that strict monetar-ists, with their emphasis on money-supply arguments, had tended to ignore or minimise. Doubts had existed about the stability of money demand since Keynes' time and experience in the 1970s and 1980s confirmed that it is generally much less stable than implied by the crude quantity theory. The improvements in pay-ments technology and the development of substitutes for traditional bank money (credit cards and other sources of consumer credit, overdrafts, etc.) and alternative savings vehicles (like building society accounts in the UK) in the last quarter of the century meant that established relationships between deposit money and income or transactions flows were increasingly breaking down. Deregulation of banks and near-banks, starting with reforms like CCC in the UK, contributed to the break-down; so also did the new competitive dimension added by financial globalisation, which greatly augmented the alternatives to domestic sources and uses of liquid-ity in developed economies, especially for multinational firms with sophisticated treasury operations. As a result, not only did control of the money supply become harder but also the demand for traditional forms of money became less predictable and less responsive to market mechanisms.

Accordingly, even in regimes – generally less liberalised ones – where monetary control proved relatively effective, relations between the money stock and aggre-gate income/expenditure tended to vary, thereby weakening the supposed link between money and prices. And where attempts were made to tighten control by imposing mandatory cash reserve ratios on commercial banks and varying them in response to changing monetary conditions, these distortions were magnified by 'disintermediation' – diversion of credit flows away from controlled to uncon-trolled areas of the financial system, whether via domestic near-banks or offshore intermediaries. (This problem resembled the difficulties encountered earlier by the Bank of England when it introduced the 'Corset' in the mid-1970s, as seen in Chapter 2.) Distortions of this kind inspired the dictum known as 'Goodhart's law', which remains familiar in the policy sphere.[8] Thus even in regimes where mon-etary restraint was relatively effective, it was found that money's velocity tended to change unpredictably when efforts were made to control the money stock. Such distortions greatly complicated the policy task and were liable to defeat their objective if great weight was placed on the control mechanism.

For these reasons the practical objections raised by Keynesians, in debates before the dash to monetarism, turned out to be mostly well-founded. Although a number of countries that practised monetary restraint managed to achieve sustained falls in inflation after the inflationary shocks of the 1970s, little of the credit could be claimed by monetary control per se. An impression of the confusing signals visible in the major economies can be obtained from Table 3.2. For example in the UK it proved possible to achieve a deceleration of nominal aggregate demand and consumer prices through the 1980s while failing to meet the announced monetary targets closely, and often considerably exceeding them; growth of the broad money stock tended to exceed that of nominal GDP by a large margin, thanks in part to the exceptionally high real yields on bank deposits engineered by the Bank of England after 1980. Qualitatively similar if less extreme pictures are evident in Germany and Japan during the same period. Elsewhere, a relatively high degree of success

TABLE 3.2 Real interest rates, growth of money stock and nominal GDP, and consumer price inflation, four major economies, 1971–95 (five-year averages, per cent per year)

	1971–5	1976–80	1981–6	1987–92
United States				
Real ST interest rate	1.6	1.6	6.2	3.2
Growth of money stock	10.2	9.5	9.3	3.9
Growth of nominal GDP	9.5	11.3	8.1	6.0
Consumer price inflation	6.8	8.9	4.9	4.2
UK				
Real ST interest rate	−2.8	−2.1	5.0	6.5
Growth of money stock	16.9	14.5	14.6	12.5
Growth of nominal GDP	15.6	16.9	8.8	8.2
Consumer price inflation	13.2	14.4	6.6	5.4
GERMANY				
Real ST interest rate	1.8	1.7	4.1	4.2
Growth of money stock	10.9	8.5	5.5	8.7
Growth of nominal GDP	8.8	7.4	4.7	8.2
Consumer price inflation	6.1	4.0	3.2	2.7
JAPAN				
Real ST interest rate	−2.4	0.5	4.0	3.7
Growth of money stock	18.8	11.1	8.5	7.2
Growth of nominal GDP	15.2	10.1	5.8	5.9
Consumer price inflation	11.6	6.6	2.4	1.9

Source: OECD *Statistical Compendium 2003–1*, CD-ROM.

Notes: 'Money stock' is M3 for United States and Germany; M2 for UK and Japan.
'Nominal GDP' at current market prices.
'Consumer price inflation' measured by the consumer price index.
'Germany' relates to West Germany until 1990 and reunified Germany subsequently.

in meeting monetary targets failed to deliver price stability or even a satisfactory degree of inflation slowdown. Canada's short-lived experience of monetary targeting in the late 1970s exemplified this failure. In this period the Bank of Canada more than achieved the targets for declining growth of narrow money adopted in 1975, only to find that Canadian inflation markedly exceeded that of the United States, largely because of sharp depreciation of the Canadian dollar against the US dollar (see OECD 1985: 83–9). This illustrated the particular difficulties of using monetarist policies to control inflation in an economy so open to trade and capital flows with a large neighbour. By the late 1980s, monetary targets had been effectively abandoned there, as well as in the UK and most other Western European economies, or had been much downgraded in practical significance (as in Germany and the United States).

Alternative transmission mechanisms

The difficulties encountered by monetary targeting in the 1980s heightened debate among economists about the 'transmission mechanism' of monetary policy – the chain of links from the monetary instruments to inflation. The links from short-term interest rates to the money stock proved unreliable because of the instability of money demand referred to above. After a decade of experimentation, the idea of monetary policy operating via control of the money supply foundered against the myriad of practical difficulties encountered in liberalised monetary regimes, as Goodhart's law predicted.

However, it proved possible to retain more faith in an alternative transmission mechanism working from short-term interest rates to bank lending rates and hence the *cost and supply of credit*, and thence to aggregate demand, output and finally inflation. Because of the balance-sheet identities through which the stock of domestic bank credit is approximately matched by the domestic stock of bank deposits (ignoring banks' long-term liabilities and external effects arising through transactions in foreign currencies and/or with non-residents), manipulation of interest rates provided an indirect means of influencing nominal demand and hence inflation. This mechanism was helpfully augmented by wealth effects, given that short-term interest rates affect long-term rates and thence financial securities' prices; and by external effects, since international interest differentials are a major determinant of exchange rates and thence the import prices in domestic currency.

The switch to exchange-rate floating after the collapse of Bretton Woods strengthened this transmission mechanism in open economies because monetary policy gained leverage by inducing exchange-rate variations. Extra channels then operated for transmitting monetary action to demand and inflation: not only import-price effects on domestic prices but also competitiveness effects on exports and import substitution. Under free floating, monetary policy worked in ways that monetarist theorists had not anticipated. A drawback was that reliance on the demand-side route was subject to the information delays, variable response lags and unpredictable effects that had dogged Keynesian demand management.

The view that monetary policy works by influencing the supply and cost of bank credit rather than the money stock raises a basic issue that will be returned to in Chapter 4: whether slow and steady money-stock growth over the medium and longer term is the crucial (necessary and sufficient) condition for maintaining low inflation, or merely the by-product of an approach that works through the *control of aggregate demand*. If the latter is really the case it can be argued that, despite appearances, monetarist regimes are obliged to rely on the procedures of Keynesian demand management, albeit with a different objective – price stability rather than full employment. In the late 1980s Keynesians (Dow and Saville 1990) put forward the latter view, whereas monetarists (especially Laidler 1989 in response to their 1988 edition) argued that monetary control was the key.[9] Subsequent experience seems to have settled the issue in Dow's favour, in that demand management aimed at price stability has succeeded in overcoming inflation in many countries despite often failing to deliver stable monetary growth, a result that appears to show that the latter is not a necessary condition for price stability; whereas in other cases, stable monetary growth has not delivered price stability, a result showing that it is not a sufficient condition either.

Other counter-inflation targets

In due course the impracticality of pure monetarism and the perceived failure of practical monetarism in inflation-prone economies like the UK and other open economies of Western Europe and the older Commonwealth, brought disenchantment with the monetarist experiment. As stagflation persisted into the 1980s, policymakers in these economies, still committed to controlling inflation and to avoiding the discretionary excesses of Keynesian demand management, felt obliged to seek other approaches. For many small and medium-sized open economies that were willing to sacrifice monetary independence, the logical alternative was to adopt an external anchor in the form of a hard-currency exchange rate, and many EC economies chose this approach via the ERM after the mid-1980s. By that time the obvious anchor currency was the Deutsche mark. West Germany continued to achieve relatively low inflation through the 1980s, thanks to the Bundesbank's skill and single-mindedness in maintaining a good inflation record through firm monetary restraint supported in principal by monetary targets, though without close adherence to them. This performance was so well sustained that the D-mark remained a globally strong currency through the traumas of German reunification in 1990 and the subsequent turbulence in the EMS's Exchange Rate Mechanism. The D-mark's credentials as a nominal anchor for Germany's neighbours were therefore hard to resist.

However, among economies that remained strongly attached to monetary independence, disappointment with monetarism led to interest in inflation targeting, as noted earlier. Their authorities were still keen to find a reliable touchstone for monetary restraint but were unwilling to accept the thrust of policy provided by the Bundesbank or some other foreign central bank with a good inflation record.

In the UK, umbrage and desperation at being forced out of the ERM in 1992 drove this novel policy choice. Policymakers there and in other open economies were encouraged to try inflation targeting by the hope that a floating exchange rate would provide powerful leverage for monetary policy, if only a credible policy focus could be found. The new free-market enthusiasm associated with globalisation also influenced their thinking: in the environment of liberalised trade and capital markets, little support could be found in developed economies for fixed exchange-rate regimes, whether driven by the political imperatives of European unification or not.

One advantage claimed for currency floating was that it would banish the balance of payments worries that had dogged weaker-performing economies through the era of Keynesian management. Instead the conventional big-economy view became, and largely remains, that under liberalised capital markets it should always be possible for an economy with a floating exchange rate to finance an external payments deficit without difficulty, provided it avoids inflation and has a good reputation for debt repayment. Whether this is indeed so will be among the issues discussed in later chapters.

Verdict: the lessons from monetarism

Most economies that turned to monetarist policies after the demise of Keynesian management found them, within ten years or so, to be an unsatisfactory remedy for the high inflation inherited from the previous regime. In most cases it either proved difficult to control the money stock closely enough to meet official targets; or where monetary targets were more or less achieved, overcoming inflation within acceptable time horizons proved either impossible, or possible only through demand deflation that raised unemployment to unacceptable levels, or kept it there. The difficulty of meeting monetary targets was a special disappointment. The few central banks that set out initially to control the monetary base, or some other narrow aggregate, found tight control impracticable or ineffective; and the majority that chose to target some broader version of money found such targets difficult to meet, especially in economies undergoing widespread financial liberalisation and structural change. An equally important source of weakness was the instability that developed in the demand for money, on any consistent definition, in economies where the main onus for controlling inflation was placed on monetary control.

Yet the experience undoubtedly left its mark. Most policymakers who lived through it would probably agree that things could never be quite the same again. No return to Keynesianism appeared thinkable after the searing inflation experience of the 1970s. Henceforth, maintenance of stable monetary conditions would be the main objective of macroeconomic policy, with price stability the prize for those who succeeded.

In summary, the key elements of monetarist thinking that survived to influence policymaking in the last decade of the century were:

1. An emphasis on *rules rather than discretion* for the conduct of policy.
2. The abandonment of commitments to full or high employment, or any targets for output or activity, or at least their relegation to a subsidiary status.
3. A focus on a *nominal* target or targets of some kind; if not a monetary or nominal income target, at least an exchange-rate or inflation target.
4. A large measure of restored faith in the *self-stabilising powers of the real economy*, implying empirical judgements about behaviour of goods and labour markets, namely, that in general goods and services markets have flexible prices that enable them to clear fairly quickly and continuously at efficient levels (that maximise buyers' and sellers' utility).
5. Considerable emphasis on the role of *rational expectations*, or at least forward-looking expectations of some kind, especially in relation to the formation of general and relative prices and interest rates.

These are all features not just of monetarism but also of neoclassical economic theory generally, reflecting that monetarism has drawn its analytical foundations from neoclassical theory, and indeed may be said to be a special branch of neoclassical thinking.

The end of fiscal activism?

One seemingly robust legacy of monetarism was its rejection of the fiscal activism that had been a central feature of Keynesian management. In order to mount this attack, monetarists drew on the rational expectations arguments which were developed largely by neoclassical theorists in the 1970s. (The rational expectations ideas and their important contribution to the 1990s synthesis will be discussed in Chapter 4.) Serious doubts had arisen in the 1970s not only about the usefulness of Keynesian demand management but also the effectiveness of fiscal instruments for that or any other policy purpose, and this scepticism became dominant as monetarists gained real-world influence. Both theoretical and empirical reasoning contributed to the downgrading of fiscal policy. At the theoretical level, the Lucas critique and the doctrine of 'Ricardian equivalence',[10] both incorporating rational expectations in consumer behaviour, were deployed to show that on standard assumptions a fiscal stimulus can only have transient effects on aggregate demand; and at a more practical level it was argued that fiscal stimuli must sooner or later result in 'crowding out' private investment if monetary policy is non-accommodating.[11] By the start of the 1990s fiscal activism had been thoroughly discredited. In a radical role-reversal, the 1990s settlement assigned chief responsibility for price stability (via demand management) to monetary policy, while fiscal policy was given the subsidiary role of supporting monetary policy, with little recognition of other objectives. This subsidiary role was taken to require the maintenance of broad government budget balance over the medium and long term. In modest qualification of this non-accommodating fiscal stance, it was generally accepted that the automatic fiscal stabilisers should be allowed to operate, which perhaps suggests some residual acceptance of a stabilisation role for fiscal policy, though only within a rules-based framework.

In retrospect, and in view of the widespread resort to fiscal stimulus in response to the recent recession, it is fair to ask whether the downgrading of fiscal policy in the past 30 years has not been overdone. Little firm empirical evidence has ever been presented to show that fiscal instruments are ineffective for demand management. Empirically, Ricardian equivalence is hard to detect except when fiscal deficits and government debt accumulate to such high levels in relation to GDP that long-term real interest rates are boosted to historically high levels. Crowding-out arguments certainly come into play when monetary policy is non-accommodating, but not when it accommodates fiscal action (by maintaining constant real interest rates in the face of fiscal expansion or contraction), unless government debt grows so large in relation to GDP that it threatens to become unserviceable.

Some critics of fiscal activism emphasise different arguments, namely that there is little genuine need for demand management because the economy is believed to be sufficiently self-stabilising to make policy intervention unnecessary; or that fiscal activism is usually misapplied and therefore does more harm than good. At the empirical level the first argument is hard to accept, given the manifest persistence of large fluctuations in economic activity among developed economies, large and small. By no means all of these fluctuations can be ascribed to supply-side events, or dismissed as unavoidable technical corrections, as some free-market adherents tend to argue. The second argument (fiscal policy misapplication) is harder to contest, given the manifest policy errors of the 1960s and 1970s, but it leaves room for hoping that a degree of fiscal activism might be useful if applied with caution and skill, and subject to appropriate longer-term objectives and constraints. These themes will be resumed in Chapter 8.

4

THE 1990s SYNTHESIS

As foreshadowed in earlier chapters, policymakers in the market economies reached a radical compromise in the design of macroeconomic policy in the early 1990s which, despite initial doubts, has appeared to offer genuine promise for the future. An important precursor was the inflation targeting pioneered in New Zealand. Much of the new thinking crystallised slightly later in the blueprint for European Monetary Union (EMU) laid out in the Maastricht Treaty (1992) and the changes that flowed from it. The new consensus represented a reconciliation of the two conflicting ideologies that had been embraced in turn in market-based economies during the previous 50 years, and eventually found wanting. Out of the failure of Keynesian demand management in the 1970s and the monetarist experiment of the 1980s emerged a hybrid approach which combined successful features from both approaches. Despite early scepticism, the 1990s settlement turned out to be effective for around 15 years in maintaining price stability and steady economic growth with (eventually) falling unemployment in economies where it was put into practice, as may be seen in the right-hand segments of Figure 1.1. But it has recently run into such severe turbulence that its very survival is now in question, and few would deny that some rethinking is necessary.

The key focus of the 1990s consensus was monetary stability but this did not equate with monetarism. Given that the 1980s experiment with monetarism showed, for most of the countries which ventured on it, that controlling the money stock was not after all the solution to overcoming inflation, the new consensus can hardly be viewed as a monetarist victory, despite some resemblance to such an outcome. There are perhaps stronger grounds for regarding it as a vindication – how secure will be considered shortly – of the neoclassical philosophy from which monetarism sprang, as Britton (2001) implies. But while the neoclassical features are arguably dominant, close inspection shows that some Keynesian elements are important too, and in that case it seems more appropriate to regard the settlement as a mixture of the two ideologies; hence our preference for the '1990s synthesis' rather than the 'neo-liberal consensus' in more common usage. The latter term seems more appropriate for the free-market package which had been identified rather earlier and in a different context.[1] This chapter will discuss the main elements of the 1990s settlement and argue that they represent a genuine compromise between the two dominant but conflicting economic doctrines of the later 20th century.

Principles of the 1990s synthesis

The main principles of the 1990s synthesis are summarised below. Not all of them have been universally embraced by the main national or trans-national regimes now in existence, but most developed-economy regimes subscribe to most of them, and some to all. The following list is intended to be broadly representative, starting with the key objectives and modes of policy and then moving on to the institutional framework.

1. The primary objective of macroeconomic policy is overall price stability, and this should be formally recognised by law, treaty, pact or code. Price stability should be given definition and transparency by adopting one or more explicit targets, among which a target for inflation itself is increasingly the preferred option. The inflation target should be set by government or the central bank, and should preferably have legal backing. It should be expressed in low single figures, which for most major economies means an annual rate of about 2 per cent for the consumer price index, either as a point target or the centre of a range, or simply a narrow range (of say 0–2 per cent per annum). The target should cover a run of years (the medium term) and be publicly announced. It may be supplemented by other intermediate targets, such as the European Central Bank's 'reference indicator' for broad-money growth.[2]
2. Price stability should be achieved through the exercise of monetary policy, for which it should be the primary objective, though not necessarily the only one. It should be pursued through the active use of market-based monetary instruments, principally official short-term interest rates, to influence monetary conditions, which should be tightened or loosened according to whether CPI inflation is above or below target.
3. Responsibility for monetary policy, and thus for securing price stability, should lie exclusively with the central bank. To this end the bank must be free from political interference in the pursuit of its objectives, as preferably defined by statute; or at least it must have full autonomy in the conduct of monetary policy. This implies a clear separation of responsibility for monetary policy from that for fiscal policy (for which national finance ministries generally retain responsibility).
4. The task of fiscal policy is to support monetary policy in achieving price stability. To that end the fiscal instruments should be set so to keep the government in broad financial (budget) balance over the medium and longer term. These

instruments should be passive (not actively managed) in the face of cycles and shocks. The automatic fiscal stabilisers should be allowed to work, but otherwise the thrust of fiscal policy should be constant and demand-neutral. For most major economies this is held to imply an annual government net borrowing requirement averaging not more than around 2 per cent of GDP over the business cycle. Such objectives should preferably be embodied in a formal statute, treaty, pact or code. For EU economies these budgetary objectives are enshrined in the Maastricht Treaty (now part of the EU Treaty), and are supplemented by mandatory limits of 60 per cent on government debt/GDP ratios, though some elasticity is permitted in observing these.

5. A large public sector in relation to GDP is undesirable on both efficiency and counter-inflation grounds. In many developed economies the size of the public sector in GDP has been reduced from the excessive levels reached in the 1970s, and any reversal of that movement should be resisted. Where the overall public sector is larger than in the best-performing low-inflation market economies – generally not much more than 40 per cent of GDP – governments should privatise public-sector enterprises, cut subsidies and social security benefits, and reduce overall tax burdens.

6. In normal circumstances developed economies, other than small open economies and those that have joined a monetary union or aspire to do so, should allow their exchange rates to float freely, apart from minor smoothing.

7. In contrast, developing and emerging-market economies should generally link their currencies to an external currency, either formally via a pegged-rate system with the help of the IMF or a regional development bank, or bilaterally and less formally with a major trading partner. Those concerned to control inflation should link to a strong currency (traditionally the US dollar, though dollar weakness in recent years has made the euro a genuine contender); those seeking stable external trading conditions should stabilise their real (inflation-adjusted) exchange rates against their main trading partner(s).

8. Banking and financial systems should be liberalised so far as possible, subject to effective regulation on prudential and anti-cartel grounds. Liberalisation requires complete removal of administrative controls and mandatory reserve requirements on banks and other credit institutions, and of demarcations between commercial banks and other credit institutions on activities like deposit taking, mortgage lending and investment banking. Corresponding liberalisation should extend to create a level playing field across all financial institutions, short term and long term.

9. International trade and investment should be liberalised so far as possible, subject only to protection for infant industries in developing economies and for industries that are essential to national defence or security. The protection and subsidisation still widely accorded to domestic agriculture in developed economies should be removed in return for free access to markets for manufacturers and services throughout the developed and developing world.

10. There should be periodic multilateral policy consultation between the largest

developed economies via the G7/G8 group of finance ministers and central bank governors, and regular policy surveillance should be exercised over all market economies by the International Monetary Fund through Article IV consultations. However, surveillance carries no obligation for policy action unless a country seeks Fund assistance. Beyond these activities, there is no economic case for macroeconomic policy cooperation, much less coordination, between major economies.

Acceptance of this set of principles did not of course happen overnight; many of them gained recognition at different speeds through the ebb and flow of events over preceding decades. Nor were they announced by a single body or in a single document, with the important exception of the Maastricht Treaty, as pointed out above. Outside the European Union they mostly emerged piecemeal as uncoordinated responses to persistent economic pressures.[3] Yet inflation targeting spread widely across both industrial and developing economies between 1990 and 1998, as may be seen in Table 4.1.

The movement to embrace monetary stability and fiscal balance as central features of macroeconomic policy also spread quickly through the developed world, and in those respects most of the major market-based economies may be said to have joined the 1990s synthesis, as Box 4.1 explains. By the end of the century most OECD countries had adopted inflation targets, though often with support from other monetary-policy targets (usually a broad monetary aggregate, as in the case of EMU participants after 1998). As also noted in Box 4.1, all member countries of the European Union accepted the fiscal limits introduced in the Maastricht Treaty (1992).

The main bystanders from these movements are the United States and Japan, as Box 4.1 points out. Neither has adopted explicit inflation objectives or mandatory fiscal limits, and in those respects neither can be regarded as card-carrying members of the 1990s synthesis in the sense that EU countries can. Yet in both the United

TABLE 4.1 International spread of inflation targets, 1990–8

	1990	1998
Number of countries with:		
Inflation targets	8	54
(Of which, inflation targets only)	(1)	(13)
Targets not including inflation	38*	33
No target for monetary policy	37*	4
Total countries responding	83*	91

Source: Sterne (1999: 275); and author's calculations.

Notes: these results are from a Bank of England survey of 91 industrial, developing and transitional countries undertaken in late 1998 (EMU countries were surveyed pre-entry). Countries were asked to report whether they had explicit targets for monetary policy and, if so, whether the target related to inflation or some other objective.

* Approximate (estimated from Chart 2 of the source article).

BOX 4.1 WHICH COUNTRIES HAVE EMBRACED THE 1990s POLICY SYNTHESIS?

If commitment to price stability via an inflation target is the essential feature of the 1990s synthesis, the pathfinder was New Zealand in 1990. Other countries followed soon afterwards, including the UK (in 1992), Canada, Chile, Finland, Sweden, Australia, Israel, Switzerland, Mexico and Brazil, in all of which the central bank was required to observe an explicit inflation target. In addition, from the beginning of its operations in January 1999 the European Central Bank has pursued an inflation target supplemented by a broad-money target, on behalf of the member states (then 11) of the newly-formed Euro Area. Thus by the end of the 1990s over 20 of the 30 member economies of the OECD pursued inflation targets. (That number has since risen to 24.) The important exceptions were, and continue to be, the United States and Japan, neither of which has adopted an explicit inflation target. But both the US Federal Reserve and the Bank of Japan are required by law to pursue price stability, along with high employment and moderate interest rates in the Fed's case.[1]

With inflation targets came another key feature of the 1990s synthesis – independence for central banks in the pursuit of monetary policy. In virtually all regimes that have adopted inflation targets, the central bank has exclusive responsibility for conducting monetary policy in pursuit of its objectives, free from political interference. This also applies in the United States and Japan.

During the 1990s a number of the countries that had adopted inflation targets also moved to adopt broad government budgetary balance, or something close to it, as an explicit target for fiscal policy. A decisive step in this direction was taken by EU governments through the introduction of mandatory fiscal rules via the Maastricht Treaty (1992), which limited annual financial deficits of 'general government' to a maximum of 3 per cent of GDP. This was followed for EMU participants by the Stability and Growth Pact (1996), which strengthened the Treaty's excessive deficit procedure by imposing financial penalties of up to 0.5 per cent of GDP on governments that persistently infringe the fiscal rules. The UK government adopted a comparable commitment in the form of the 'golden rule' (zero balance on current account) under its 'Code for Fiscal Stability', introduced when the new Labour government passed responsibility for monetary policy to a newly independent Bank of England in 1997 (but now abandoned).

However, neither the US nor Japanese governments have yet made explicit commitments to fiscal targets or limits. The US Constitution does not require the Federal government to balance the budget, unlike the position in most US states. Several attempts have been made in the Congress to introduce a 'Balanced Budget Amendment', starting as far back as 1982, but none has gained enough support to be passed into law. In these respects neither the US nor Japanese authorities have yet accepted the entire 1990s settlement, though both generally subscribe to broad budget balance as a long-term objective.

Note

1 The US Federal Reserve Act (1913) requires the Fed to 'promote effectively the goals of maximum employment, stable prices and moderate long-term interest rates' (see US Federal Reserve 2005). The Bank of Japan Act (1997) states that 'currency and monetary control by the Bank of Japan shall be aimed at achieving price stability, thereby contributing to the sound development of the national economy' (see Bank of Japan 2009b).

States and Japan price stability is high among the goals set for their central banks, and the authorities in both clearly subscribe to the free-market elements in the synthesis, notably the emphasis on market-based monetary policy to achieve price stability; the attachment to fiscal discipline, floating exchange rates, free international trade and capital mobility and ultra-liberal financial markets; and, especially in the case of the United States, aversion to international macro-policy cooperation beyond G7 consultation and IMF surveillance.

The urgency of macroeconomic reform in the 1990s was due partly to the hasty retreat from the monetarist experiment in the late 1980s and the need to put something convincing in its place, and partly to a remarkable feat of politico–economic diplomacy at the start of the 1990s: the agreement on EMU in the Maastricht Treaty (signed in February 1992).[4] This negotiating tour de force between Europe's governments and central banks, orchestrated by the European Commission and conducted largely behind closed doors and under great pressure of political events, gave form and precision to much of the new policy synthesis at a vital moment. Yet the driving force behind EMU was political rather than economic: the imperative of anchoring reunified Germany in Western Europe, at a time when Europe's centre of gravity was shifting eastward after the disintegration of the Soviet empire.

Inevitably, given the variety of national interests at stake and of institutions involved in the reform process, some of the principles outlined above have received more acceptance than others, and some have undergone criticism and revision as time has passed. One of the earliest to attract criticism was the blanket extension of free international trade and investment – globalisation – to the developing world. Some influential Washington economists like John Williamson and Joseph Stiglitz (2002) were highly critical of the indiscriminate application of ultra free-market remedies to the problems of emerging-market economies in the late 1990s, when some half a dozen East Asian 'tiger' economies underwent a serious financial crisis from which they have only recently recovered; and also to 'transition' economies of Eastern Europe, seeking to convert previous centrally planned systems to market regimes after the collapse of the Soviet empire around 1990. The problems created by premature liberalisation, especially in the Far East, are nowadays seen as forerunners of the recent global crisis.

Other features of the 1990s synthesis have also been subject to criticism. One that has come under increasing attack in the past few years is the downgrading of *output* stabilisation as a policy objective. Not surprisingly, the global recession of 2008–9 has greatly boosted this concern. Another is the attachment to floating exchange rates for major currencies, given the problems that a depreciating US dollar has created for America's main trading partners in the past decade. Last but certainly not least, the freedom accorded to banks and other financial institutions in liberalised financial centres of the developed world to undertake risky long-term lending financed increasingly by short-term borrowing in the wholesale markets, has attracted scathing condemnation as the denouement from the US sub-prime mortgage crisis has unfolded. These and other concerns will be revisited after considering the foundations of the 1990s synthesis in more detail.

The revival of free-market economics

Among the neoclassical principles underlying the 1990s synthesis was a revival of belief in the self-righting properties of market economies, which grew to displace traditional Keynesian market pessimism from the late 1970s onwards. For markets to be efficient in an economic sense, prices have to be able to adjust flexibly to changes in supply and demand. Price flexibility requires not just that prices are free from controls, whether legal or institutional, but also that no individual buyer or seller can influence them through their own actions, so that markets habitually clear sooner rather than later in response to shocks. In such conditions, all participants will be content with the prices and quantities established through free trade when markets settle into equilibrium following a disturbance. This property of efficient markets requires in turn that large numbers of individual buyers and sellers are well-informed about the commercial and technological possibilities available in their economy and are free to enter (or 'contest') markets or leave them, if they see advantage in doing so. If these conditions hold in near-perfect form, general under- or over-utilisation of resources cannot persist for long. Thus, if a shock occurs to reduce aggregate demand for labour, other things being equal, unemployment may emerge in the short term, but in the longer term real wages should fall (i.e. nominal wage rates should fall more, or rise less, than prices), until the excess supply of labour is eliminated; and the converse should apply if there is a positive shock to labour demand.

The crucial role played by freely competitive markets in securing economic efficiency is one of the basic tenets of neoclassical economics, and belief in the existence of such conditions as an empirical generalisation is an indispensable assumption of neoclassical theory. Price flexibility, above all flexibility in the key relative prices that drive economic activity – real wage rates, real interest rates and the real exchange rate – is held to provide the essential mechanism by which the macro-economy adjusts to periodic shocks and adverse trends. It had been the erosion of price flexibility by market imperfections associated with industrial con-centration and state ownership of key industries in the early and middle years of the 20th century that had given rise to Keynesianism. The neoclassical revival held that the eradication of these imperfections through root-and-branch deregulation and privatisation of public-sector industries from the late 1970s onwards would deliver large improvements in efficiency and productivity in the stagnating heartland of the developed world.

The onward march of globalisation

The revival of faith in free-market competition during the final quarter of the 20th century gave new impetus to the long-running campaign for international market liberalisation that had been launched at the end of the Second World War. During the 1970s the focus of that campaign moved beyond removing tariffs and quotas on manufacturing trade towards liberalisation of trade in services and international capital flows, and at the same time it spread to embrace increasing numbers of emerging-market and developing economies. The drive for liberalisation of finan-cial markets in the late 1970s had been led by the United States, where in any case few markets had reached the degree of imperfection, regulation and state owner-ship found in the 'social market' economies of Europe, which had been much more heavily affected by wartime controls, nationalisation and restrictive measures favoured by socialist or left-leaning governments.

The re-launching of the liberalisation process was taken up by other Anglo-Saxon economies in the late 1970s, notably older members of the Commonwealth such as Australia and New Zealand, and famously in the UK under Prime Minister Margaret Thatcher after 1979. The spread of deregulation across the wider UK financial services industry in the late 1980s was so rapid that it became known as 'Big Bang' in the City of London.[5] The process was driven by a wish to stem the loss of London's global financial market share to more competitive centres, princi-pally New York; it precipitated a revival that led to London regaining parity with New York in many markets and eventually surpassing it as an international invest-ment and foreign exchange market in the 1990s.

The economies of Continental Europe were generally slower to follow this trend but eventually became committed to it as the Common Market evolved into the European Community in the 1970s and then into the 'Single Market' via the Single European Act (SEA), signed in 1986, which called for the completion of a genuinely unified pan-European market in goods and services by 1992. The movement towards harmonisation of standards and removal of barriers to cross-border trade in services initiated by the SEA spread in due course to Community economies' financial sectors. It received a big boost from the Maastricht Treaty in 1992, which created the European Union and launched the drive towards mon-etary union. EMU was finally formed in 1999 and was seen by its architects as crowning the long process of European economic integration begun under the Rome Treaty (1957).

A succession of negotiating rounds under the GATT and eventually the WTO (formed in 1995) in the last three decades of the century removed the remaining restrictions on manufacturing trade between the major economies, and went on to dismantle the still-extensive systems of controls on international capital flows between them. It also extended the liberalising process to many of the emerging-market economies of East Asia and South America and in doing so, launched the pervasive phenomenon known as globalisation. Thus globalisation grew out of the post-war elimination of barriers to international trade and investment to which the main industrial economies had resorted in the 1930s. In due course it spread to embrace more of the developing world, including numbers of poorer economies which had a legitimate stake in protection from the more extreme pressures to which the international capital markets are prone. Unfortunately, international capital flows were liberalised too fast and too indiscriminately in a number of emerging economies and for that reason globalisation came to be viewed with suspicion as an instrument of US foreign policy.

The progress of globalisation in the last quarter of the 20th century drew strength from the rebirth of faith in free-market economics and also contributed to it. Indeed globalisation may be said to have been an essential precondition for the 1990s synthesis and a powerful catalyst for it, by boosting output growth through cross-border trade and investment, and indeed spreading the view that the capitalist system was succeeding the world over. Had such a change of perception not occurred, it is hard to imagine that the synthesis would have been possible, or that the neoclassical elements would have been as dominant in it.

The influence of rational expectations

The revival of belief in competitive markets drew on institutional reforms in the 1970s and 1980s and also on radical new academic thinking in the neoclassical tradition: the development of rational expectations. Ever since Milton Friedman had mounted his criticism of Keynesian economics in the 1960s, critics of Keynes' theories had argued that they depended excessively on myopia on the part of economic agents – a failure to foresee the indirect or longer-term consequences of economic events, even when they are fairly predictable, for example the effects of tax cuts, the longer-term implications of which for expenditure, incomes and government finances are observable and relatively well-documented.

The kind of myopia in Keynesian economics that Friedman and his followers felt particularly unrealistic was the assumed prevalence of 'money illusion' in wage bargaining: failure of wage bargainers to foresee that if money wage rates are raised faster than output per head, while the government continually raises aggregate demand to prevent higher unit wage costs from generating unemployment, inflation will result and will erode the real value of the wage increase. Critics argued that experience teaches employees sooner or later to foresee the inflationary results of above-productivity wage increases and learn to anticipate future inflation when forming wage demands.

Early Keynesians had not ignored such dangers but they had hoped that the inflationary consequences of full-employment policies could be contained by income restraints on wage bargainers (statutory if not voluntary), supported if necessary by price restraints on oligopolistic businesses. As explained in Chapter 2, the failure of these hopes after more than a decade of unsuccessful prices and incomes policies in the UK and similar regimes made Keynesian management hard to sustain. But the latter's demise was hastened and magnified by a further shift in perceptions of labour market behaviour, induced by the severity of the inflationary shocks in the 1970s; namely a shift in the way in which wage bargainers' inflation expectations were supposed to be formed. The intellectual explanation for this shift was provided by the development of a powerful new body of theory focusing on 'rational expectations'.

The notion that expectations influence economic decisions had of course featured much earlier in the work of Pigou, Keynes and others, but rational expectations theorists formalised this thinking and gave it a new thrust. They started from the neoclassical proposition that in competitive markets characterised by large numbers of well-informed and highly rational buyers and sellers of homogeneous goods, prices adjust relatively quickly towards the levels implied by long-run equilibrium, and therefore provide the best possible indicator of the true or underlying price. Individual agents may make errors but in competitive situations these are randomly distributed so, on average, prices reflect the fundamentals implied by the 'true model'. Markets can sometimes get prices wrong, but this can only be because unpredictable events occur and change the fundamentals. The new approach was originally formulated in a paper on modelling price expectations by John F. Muth (1961) and went on to be applied to the behaviour of stock market prices, in a theory that became known as the 'efficient markets hypothesis'. According to this theory, a daily index of share prices follows a 'random walk', meaning that the spot (current) price gives the best possible prediction of the future price. This conclusion came to be generalised to other markets characterised by free competition and price flexibility.

The approach was taken up in the 1970s by Robert Lucas, who used it to develop the 'Lucas Critique' of government policy (Lucas 1976), as mentioned earlier. His main conclusion, termed the 'policy ineffectiveness proposition', was that if market participants are well-informed and rational, government attempts to influence activity by measures that induce false expectations will be ineffective. Thus, fiscal action to stimulate aggregate demand by, for example, cutting taxation will be ineffective because consumers will foresee that future taxes will have to rise in due course to service the debt created by extra government borrowing.

In the 1970s and subsequently, rational expectations theory was also applied to labour market behaviour, notably by Sargent and Wallace, among others.[6] The thinking behind this development will be explored more fully later when we address the Phillips curve. The essential point is that, whereas the pre-1970s assumption had been that wage bargainers base their inflation expectations on price behaviour in the recent past (backward-looking or 'adaptive' expectations), the sharp acceleration of inflation in the 1970s caused them to switch attention to expected *future* price behaviour (forward-looking expectations). Such expectations might involve simple extrapolation of past trends, but logically they should derive from knowledge of the 'true model' supposed to underlie economic behaviour. If purely rational expectations of this kind are applied to wage bargaining they tend to short-circuit the process by which changes in inflation are fed into wage demands, greatly speeding up inflation rates in buoyant labour markets, so that almost any significant departure from price stability soon tends to become unstable and thus unsustainable.

It was not necessary for policymakers to accept as fully realistic the more extreme projections of accelerating inflation produced by the rational-expectations models that became fashionable during the 1970s and 1980s.[7] The big surges in inflation seen in the 1970s in economies with strong trades unions and centralised wage bargaining, especially where wage indexation had been widely adopted as in the UK and Italy, were sufficiently alarming to convince governments of the urgent need to puncture inflation expectations. In an environment conditioned by rational expectations this meant making commitments to avoid inflation altogether, even if it meant abandoning other important aims like output stabilisation.

The searing inflation experienced in economies where policymakers had given priority to maintaining high employment through the 1970s oil shocks, and the stagflation into which these economies lapsed in the 1980s, were strong motivators behind the 1990s synthesis. In that these painful experiences appeared to bear out the implications of rational expectations only too well in practice, this new branch of neoclassical theory may be said to have been a key influence determining the counter-inflationary character of the 1990s policy package. Moreover, because rational expectations also provided a persuasive rationale for promoting free competition in labour, goods and financial markets, it may also be said to have been a key influence behind the liberalisation that characterised the 1990s synthesis.

A reprieve for demand management

Nevertheless, although many of the intellectual foundations of the 1990s synthesis were neoclassical, the new approach also included important Keynesian elements. A central Keynesian feature of the 1990s package, despite appearances to the contrary, was the retention of demand management as the main mode of policy implementation, together with much of the accompanying apparatus of measurement and forecasting – albeit subject to new rules and with a crucially different objective, and relying on monetary rather than fiscal instruments for its execution. From a Keynesian perspective, the switch from fiscal to monetary techniques for managing demand was anyway warranted, and indeed required, by the widespread liberalisation of financial systems in the 1980s and 1990s; arguably the substitution of price stability for output stability as the primary objective merely gave the policy a different motivation.

Accordingly the shift to reliance on monetary rather than fiscal instruments did not imply a rejection of demand management per se; indeed it can be said that demand management got a new lease of life under the 1990s synthesis. Furthermore, demand management in consensus regimes involves the regular exercise of *discretion* by monetary policymakers, and in that respect the view that the 1990s approach represents a victory for rules over discretion merits significant qualification. As is clear from official reports, minutes, debriefings, etc. from bodies like the US Federal Open Market Committee (the committee that determines the Federal Reserve's monetary policy), the ECB Council in the Euro Area and the Bank of England's Monetary Policy Committee in the UK, a considerable degree of judgement is routinely exercised in the conduct of policy by the central bankers and expert advisers who have been appointed to them. Admittedly the fact that this discretion is subject in most regimes to explicit targets for inflation, supplemented by intermediate targets or reference indicators in some cases, represents a key departure from orthodox Keynesianism. Whether the preferred monetary policy instrument – manipulation of short-term interest rates – is an efficient tool for controlling inflation, in the sense of having strong and predictable effects via the transmission mechanism, is more open to debate. Those questions will be revisited in later chapters.

Output stabilisation as a subsidiary objective

Although price stability is generally accepted as the primary objective of macroeconomic policy in the 1990s synthesis, with output stability a subsidiary objective, this does not mean that output and employment have been ignored in practice. Despite the priority given to avoiding inflation in the Euro Area and the UK for over a decade, policymakers in these regimes have at times seemed almost as concerned to avoid downturns in activity – even before the recent deep recession. The same is true a fortiori in the United States, where high employment still features among the formal statutory objectives assigned to the Federal Reserve, almost on a par with the avoidance of inflation, as seen earlier (Box 4.1). Thus despite the rhetoric of 1990s regimes, the Keynesian notion that macroeconomic policy should be concerned with the level of activity has not been entirely abandoned.

On the face of it, the survival of concerns about output stability might appear to conflict rather sharply with the commitment to price stability. Macroeconomic theory has long taught that the number of policy objectives should not exceed the number of instruments available for achieving them. In that case, and if monetary policy in the sense of managing short-term interest rates is the only instrument capable of securing price stability, it would appear mistaken or at least ambivalent to use this instrument to pursue output stability as well. Such ambivalence might not arise if fiscal policy were still available for pursuing output stability, but that is not so in 1990s regimes as we have explained.

However, the apparent conflict implied by simultaneous pursuit of price and output stability can be resolved if it is accepted that these two objectives are not independent. It can indeed be argued that the latter proposition holds. There are good theoretical grounds for believing that price and output stability are highly congruent, mutually compatible objectives in modern market economies, at least if external inflationary influences (commodity price hikes or import-price increases due to currency depreciation) are left out of account. This conclusion arises from the widely-accepted body of theory built around the concept of the Phillips curve and its successors, as will be seen next.

The Phillips curve and the NAIRU

The resort to discretionary demand management, rather than non-discretionary control of the money stock, as the preferred technique for controlling inflation under the 1990s synthesis can be seen as an answer to one of the profound macroeconomic debates of the late 20th century: what causes inflation and how does the process actually work in modern market economies? If excessive growth of the money stock is not after all inflation's basic cause as monetarists claim, what is? In the 1970s many economists came to a different view, that inflation in industrial economies is due to excessive demand pressure in labour and goods markets, an idea that had received support from the discovery of the functional relationship known as the Phillips curve. Some Keynesians still clung to the more traditional Keynesian view, that wage and price inflation are due to cost-push forces, independent of demand pressure,[8] but they steadily lost the argument as repeated attempts at prices and incomes restraint proved ineffective in economies that experienced excess demand through much of the post-war era.

The Phillips curve did not originate with Keynes or his immediate followers: it arose from empirical research done in the 1950s by an economist trained initially as an engineer, A.W. Phillips, though his work was taken up and extended by economists of a mainly Keynesian persuasion. The original Phillips curve described a negative statistical relationship between aggregate unemployment and wage inflation in the UK over nearly 100 years, such that lower unemployment (higher employment or activity) generates higher inflation (Phillips 1958). Follow-up research claimed to identify a stable causal link in a number of industrial economies, running from the pressure of aggregate demand as measured by the unemployment rate (or alternatively, the gap between actual and potential output) to the rate of wage inflation, other factors being given, including external price influences. If labour productivity growth is broadly constant in the long run, this translates into a negative link between unemployment and general (consumer-price) inflation.

Among its key properties, the Phillips curve implied that there is a specific, unique, level of domestic activity at which inflation is zero (the overall price level is stable). If aggregate demand is managed so as to stabilise output at this level, price stability can be maintained indefinitely, aside from external disturbances with which policy must deal separately. In due course the Phillips-curve construct was taken up by Keynesian policy advisers, for whom it provided the rationale for a supposed 'trade-off' between output and inflation: the view that an economy could be run permanently at a relatively low rate of unemployment if policymakers are prepared to accept a relatively high rate of inflation, other things being given. As explained in Chapter 2, this idea entered the conventional wisdom of policymaking in the UK and similar regimes in the early 1960s and survived until the mid-1970s.

However, there continued to be much debate about the nature and stability of the supposed trade-off. It was found that the original Phillips curve broke down in many economies from the mid-1960s onwards, suggesting that the original relation was a casualty of the behavioural and institutional changes experienced then. As observed earlier, neoclassical theorists attributed the breakdown to the growing influence of systematic inflation expectations in wage bargaining. Friedman himself was influential in challenging the theory underlying the original curve, pointing out that, in an inflationary environment, employees involved in regular wage bargaining learn to anticipate inflation by adding an estimate for expected inflation over the life of the wage contract to their usual wage target framed in real terms (Friedman 1968). The outcome in due course was a revised version known as the 'inflation-augmented' Phillips curve, which converted the original unemployment–inflation link into a link between the unemployment rate and the *rate of change* of wage inflation. Independently Edmund Phelps (1967) formalised the revised curve and used it to develop the notion of the 'natural rate of unemployment' – the rate of unemployment which, if maintained, would be consistent with a stable rate of inflation (equivalent to the 'NAIRU', see pp. 63–4).[9]

Research on the Phillips curve for periods after 1970 found that the inflation-augmented version of the curve, with inflation expectations on an 'adaptive' (backward-looking) basis, captured experience in the major economies relatively well. On this evidence mainstream economists came to accept that the systematic incorporation of inflation expectations into wage bargaining was behind the breakdown of the original Phillips curve. The outcome is sometimes called the 'accelerationist' theory of inflation.

The replacement of the original Phillips curve by the inflation–augmented version in mainstream theory had far-reaching implications for policymaking. After this jolt to the conventional wisdom, policymakers could no longer hope to exploit a stable trade-off between unemployment and inflation, except in the short run. Henceforth the best they could aim at was to keep activity or unemployment at or near the rate found to be consistent with price stability, in the face of periodic disturbances. This required policymakers' attention to focus on the unique rate of unemployment at which inflation tends to be stable. This rate was named inelegantly the 'NAIRU' in the literature – the *non-accelerating-inflation rate of unemployment*. A summary of the main analysis is offered in the Annex 4.1.

The NAIRU is the unique rate of unemployment at which inflation is stable, and above which it tends to accelerate.[10] Thus where wage increases are systematically augmented by adaptive inflation expectations, the NAIRU is also the unique unemployment rate at which the overall price level may be stable (i.e. the inflation rate is stable at zero).

These conclusions apply a fortiori if wage expectations evolve from being systematically adaptive (backward-looking) into being systematically forward-looking in some way. If fully rational expectations are assumed, even the possibility of a short-run trade-off between unemployment and inflation disappears, as Annex 4.1 explains. In these extreme conditions the iterative, step-by-step, wage-price responses envisaged under adaptive expectations are short-circuited, with the result that any sustained shortfall in unemployment below the NAIRU immediately results in rapidly accelerating inflation. Although this argument is in the nature of a limiting case adopted for theoretical exposition, it does illustrate the inflationary dangers of allowing the economy to operate appreciably below the NAIRU, and the difficulty of controlling inflation once forward-looking expectations have taken hold.

The inflation-augmented Phillips curve and the NAIRU provide the underlying rationale for managing the level of aggregate demand in order to achieve price stability in the 1990s synthesis: demand must be managed so as to maintain unemployment at or near the critical level implied by the NAIRU. Moreover given the relative stability of the largely technical links between output, employment and unemployment, over the short–medium term (the context of stabilisation policy),[11] the strategy effectively entails *stabilising output as well as the rate of inflation*. As argued above, this congruence of policy objectives has been of great help to counter-inflation policy in 1990s regimes, because it means that action to stabilise prices should also tend to stabilise output, at least in the absence of external inflationary shocks.

Nevertheless the inflation-augmented Phillips curve, and thus the NAIRU, can at times be rather unstable. The curve may be disrupted over the short–medium term by external price shocks, and over the longer term by institutional changes that affect competition in labour and goods markets, such as the removal of restrictive practices, monopolies and other sources of market rigidity. Thus cost-push or institutional shocks of various kinds may influence the level of the NAIRU temporarily or permanently. For this reason inflation targeting based (implicitly if not always explicitly) on the NAIRU cannot be a mechanical exercise. It often has to operate through trial and error, an approach that is likely to require small and frequent policy adjustments. In that respect it superficially resembles Keynesian fine-tuning, though the parallel is not close, since the objective is nowadays a medium-term target, not a short-term target as under orthodox Keynesianism, and the new regime involves a strong political commitment to price stability. Yet a large element of judgement is usually needed to identify where the economy stands at any given time in relation to the price-stability target (which in effect means in relation to the NAIRU), and what action should be taken to keep it operating close to that position, or return it there. Fortunately for 1990s regimes, in practice the NAIRU spans quite a wide range of unemployment rates (possibly as much as 2 percentage points) rather than a single point, because in strongly unionised labour markets wages and prices still tend to be rather rigid downwards in nominal as well as real terms. Thus precision is not necessary for inflation targeting to work effectively, provided the markets remain convinced that the authorities will not shrink from raising interest rates if they judge such action necessary to maintain price stability over the longer term.

During the 15 or so years through which 1990s regimes have been in operation, until the big external price shocks of 2007–8, the central banks of the United States, the Euro Area and the UK have for the most part been remarkably successful in maintaining that conviction. As Table 4.2 shows, consumer price inflation in our four major economies has been kept in low single figures on average throughout this period, while a comparison with Table 3.1 shows that unemployment has fallen below 1980s rates in the two Anglo-Saxon economies (though not in Germany or Japan).

To sum up: the inflation–augmented Phillips curve is a central concept underlying the 1990s policy approach, and one that represents a combination of Keynesian and neoclassical ideas. The inflation–augmented curve is compatible both with the neoclassical critique, which held that the un-augmented Phillips curve is vertical in the long run (though it may be downward-sloping in the short run), and with the Keynesian belief that real factors like the level of activity and output can indeed influence the price level and the inflation rate, over the long as well as the short term. Monetarists may question whether the NAIRU adequately explains what determines the price level in the first place, but given the central role played

TABLE 4.2 Key economic indicators: four major economies under the 1990s synthesis, 1993–2007 (five-year averages)

	1993–7	1998–2002	2003–7
GDP change (% p.a.)			
UK	3.1	3.1	2.6
United States	3.5	2.9	2.8
Germany	1.4	1.7	1.5
Japan	1.5	0.2	2.1
Unemployment (% of labour force)			
UK	8.7	5.6	5.1
United States	5.8	4.6	5.2
Germany	8.3	8.1	9.5
Japan	3.1	4.8	4.5
Consumer price inflation (% p.a.)			
UK	3.0	1.6	2.2
United States	2.1	1.7	2.6
Germany	1.9	0.9	1.4
Japan	0.1	–0.8	–0.6
Balance of current payments (% of GDP)			
UK	–1.0	–1.8	–2.5
United States	–1.6	–3.6	–5.4
Germany	–0.9	–0.4	5.1
Japan	2.3	2.7	3.9

Source and Notes: see Figure 1.1.

by the Phillips curve and the NAIRU in the pursuit of inflation targets, it can be regarded as an essential element in the 1990s synthesis, though not always officially acknowledged as such.

The attachment to exchange-rate floating

On the face of it, the coexistence under the 1990s synthesis of free floating by the major currencies – including the euro, the single currency for much of the EU since 1999 – and EMU in Europe, which irrevocably fixed exchange rates between participants, might seem to suggest a degree of ambivalence about the merits of exchange-rate stability. In locking their exchange rates permanently together, many of Europe's open trading economies would appear to have rejected currency floating, but such an impression would go too far: although EMU participants have adopted a fixed exchange-rate regime for intra-area trade and investment, they retain a floating regime for trade and investment with the rest of the world, which are important and growing for most of them. Thus the 1990s synthesis respects the notion of the 'inconsistent quartet' that arose from the policy debates of the preceding 20 years – the proposition that in an environment of free international trade and capital flows, open economies cannot enjoy both monetary independence and fixed exchange rates.[12] EMU participants have opted for the benefits of a single currency in their trade and investment with each other, and to that extent they have sacrificed scope to pursue *independent* monetary policies. Instead they must accept, and adapt to, the single monetary policy set for the Euro Area as a whole by the European Central Bank. Yet these economies retain a degree of monetary power through their ability to influence the ECB's monetary policy, so long as the euro floats freely.

Most other countries which have embraced the 1990s synthesis have preferred to retain full monetary independence and accept that this means forgoing all notions of fixing or managing their currencies, even if that means periodic exchange-rate instability. For the largest, relatively closed, economies like the United States and Japan, this was a straightforward choice and policymakers there have shown little interest in currency stabilisation since the late 1980s. For other economies, more open to trade and investment but large enough to want, and feel capable of pursuing, an independent monetary policy, the choice has been less straightforward. For the UK in particular, with its strong tradition of monetary sovereignty but with an important and growing stake in EU markets, the decision not to join the euro has been a difficult one, and EMU membership remains a latent policy issue.

For a number of years after the 1990s synthesis emerged, instability between the major currencies was not regarded as a serious problem, except briefly in autumn 2000, when rapid euro depreciation against other major currencies threatened such strong cost-push inflation in the Euro Area that the European Central Bank (ECB) was moved to orchestrate intervention in support of the euro, an exercise that proved effective in arresting its depreciation. However, key-currency instability has become a more serious concern subsequently. The sharp and persistent depreciation of the US dollar against most other floating currencies that started around 2003 has led the United States' main trading partners to worry increasingly about their loss of competitiveness in world markets, and some in Europe (notably the French government) have questioned the unalloyed commitment to free floating.

The 'New Macroeconomic Consensus' model

The principles of the 1990s policy synthesis outlined above are inevitably broad-brush in character, given the settlement's wide scope. However, in the past ten years academic economists have sought to capture the core of the new approach rigorously in a small analytical system which has become known as the 'New Consensus in Macroeconomics' (NCM) model. This has been principally the work of New Keynesians and so has a strong neo-Keynesian flavour. Yet its behavioural foundations are very much those of the neoclassical economics discussed above – freely functioning competitive markets displaying high price and wage flexibility in the medium and longer term and motivated by forward-looking expectations based on rational expectations principles applied by large numbers of well-informed and far-sighted market participants. In that respect as in others, the NCM model is fully compatible with the 1990s synthesis as described above, and indeed is encompassed by it. In view of the model's importance as a rationale for the new regime, a résumé is offered below.

In essence the NCM model comprises, for a closed economy, just three basic functional relationships: an Aggregate Demand (AD) function; an Aggregate Supply (AS) function which might alternatively be called an Inflation function; and a Monetary Policy (MP) rule.[13] The AD function depicts aggregate demand for output as linked negatively to the real interest rate among other arguments. Other things being equal, real expenditure on goods and services rises as the real interest rate falls, and conversely if the interest rate rises. The AD function thus resembles the 'IS curve' originally proposed by J.R. Hicks in his seminal article synthesizing Keynesian and neoclassical theory (Hicks 1937: 147–59), familiar to generations of economics students. However the function in the standard NCM model is more forward-looking, as will be explained shortly.

The AS function relates the rate of change of the general price level positively to aggregate output, other things being equal, including crucially the *level of trend or potential output*. It therefore resembles the inflation-augmented Phillips curve also familiar to macroeconomists, as outlined earlier in this chapter and the annex; except that, like the AD curve, it is more forward-looking. In the NCM model the usual inflation-augmented Phillips curve is modified to incorporate forward-looking inflation expectations, and the output measure is replaced by the 'output gap' (difference between actual and trend or potential output). Other things being equal, the inflation rate rises as the output gap rises and conversely if the gap falls; and inflation is constant when output is at its potential or 'natural' level (the level that matches the NAIRU, where the output gap is zero).

The third key relationship in the model, the MP rule, is a policy reaction function which depicts how the central bank adjusts the short-term interest rate in response to deviations in inflation from the official inflation target, and deviations of output from its natural (trend or equilibrium) rate. The official interest rate in the MP rule also depends on the 'equilibrium' real interest rate – the rate consistent with output at its 'natural' level, and thus with constant inflation – which is treated as exogenous to the model. A policy reaction function of this kind is often referred to as a 'Taylor rule' after the American economist John Taylor, who was among the first to propose it (Taylor 1993: 195–214).

The NCM model for a closed economy works as follows. Starting from a position of equilibrium with low and constant inflation on target and output at its natural rate, suppose there is a positive demand shock to the economy; for example a jump in expenditure due to an improvement in confidence about long-term growth prospects. The increase in aggregate demand raises output above the natural rate and this raises inflation in accordance with the AS function (Phillips curve). If no policy action is taken, the higher inflation rate will raise inflationary expectations and in due course inflation will accelerate as these are built into successive wage rounds. The central bank must act quickly to head off the inflationary pressure by tightening monetary policy in accordance with the MP rule. The resulting increase in the *real* interest rate (provided underlying inflation expectations are unchanged) reduces output via the AD function and this works to reverse the initial rise in inflation via the Phillips curve. The tighter stance of monetary policy will be maintained until inflation settles back in due course towards its target rate, the initial interest-rate hikes being unwound when equilibrium is re-established.

The open-economy model

In the past few years the closed-economy NCM model has been extended by the Cambridge economist Philip Arestis and others to cover an open economy by adding just three more equations to the three above (making six simultaneous equations in all), together with three new dependent variables – real and nominal exchange rates and the current balance of external payments. The real exchange rate is made to depend positively on the difference between the domestic and foreign real interest rates and on the current account balance, among other factors, and the nominal exchange rate is determined by the real exchange rate and the difference between domestic and world prices. In this way the AD and AS functions are augmented to include exchange-rate effects. In the open-economy AD function output depends negatively on the real exchange rate as well as on the previous arguments; and in the Phillips curve, inflation is made to depend positively on expected changes in world prices and negatively on the nominal exchange rate, as well as on the previous arguments. Details of the equations comprising the standard open-economy NCM model can be found in Box 4.2.

In the open-economy model the effects of a given change in the central-bank interest rate are augmented by exchange-rate movements in an economy with a

BOX 4.2 THE 'NEW CONSENSUS IN MACROECONOMICS' MODEL FOR AN OPEN ECONOMY

In recent years the NCM model has been extended to cover an open economy by adding an exchange rate and current account balance, together with world output and inflation, to the arguments of the closed-economy model. The equations below summarise the version proposed by Philip Arestis (2007), which he developed from the closed-economy analyses by McCallum (2001) and Meyer (2001), and the detailed exposition by Woodford (2003).

The extended model comprises just five functional relationships and one definition. For brevity the summary here gives just the general forms of the relevant functions; and it omits lagged independent variables which provide for smoothing or partial adjustment of dependent variables, and the error terms representing stochastic (randomly distributed) shocks in Arestis' equations:

$$Y_t = f_1[K_1, E_t Y_{t+1}, (R_t - E_t p_{t+1}), rer_t] \tag{1}$$

$$p_t = f_2[(Y_t - Y^*_t), E_t p_{t+1}, (E_t p_{wt+1} - E_t \Delta er_t)] \tag{2}$$

$$R_t = f_3[RR^*, E_t p_{t+1}, (Y_{t-1} - Y^*_{t-1}), (p_{t-1} - p^T)] \tag{3}$$

$$rer_t = f_4[K_4, (R_t - E_t p_{t+1}), (R_{wt} - E_t p_{wt+1}), CA_t, E_t rer_{t+1}] \tag{4}$$

$$CA_t = f_5[K_5, rer_t, (Y_t - Y^*_t), (Y_{wt} - Y^*_{wt})] \tag{5}$$

$$er_t = rer_t + P_{wt} - P_t \tag{6}$$

The symbols here should be interpreted as follows. The terms K_i (i = 1,4,5) in equations 1, 4 and 5 respectively represent groups of underlying influences which are treated as exogenous to the model: K_1 could reflect the economy's fiscal stance among other factors; K_4 could reflect the economy's underlying productivity compared with the rest of the world, among other arguments; and K_5 could reflect its underlying import propensity, etc. Y is actual domestic output (GDP) and Y^* is trend, potential, or 'equilibrium' output; thus $(Y-Y^*)$ is the domestic 'output gap' (which featured in our discussion of the Phillips curve earlier). Analogously, Y_w is actual world output, Y^*_w is trend world output and $(Y_w-Y^*_w)$ is the world output gap. All 'Y' terms are expressed in logarithms. The terms 'rer' and 'er' stand for the real and nominal exchange rate respectively, both expressed as units of foreign currency per unit of domestic currency. R and R_w are respectively the domestic and world nominal interest rates while p and p_w are respectively domestic and world inflation rates and p^T is the domestic inflation target. RR* is the equilibrium *real* rate of interest, i.e. the real interest rate consistent with a zero output gap, which implies, via equations (2) and (6), a constant rate of domestic inflation. CA is the current account of the balance of payments. P and Pw are domestic and world price levels respectively, both in logarithms. E is the expectations operator (E_t refers to expectations held at time t). The change in the nominal exchange rate, which appears in equation (2), can be derived from equation (6) as $\Delta er_t = \Delta rer_t + p_{wt} - p_t$.

Equation (1) is the aggregate demand function or 'IS' curve, in which real expenditure on output depends positively on expected future output and negatively on the real interest rate and here also on the real exchange rate, the latter working though the effects of changes in competitiveness on net trade; and on exogenous factors including the fiscal policy stance. Equation (2) is the Phillips curve, in which inflation depends positively on the output gap, and on expected inflation at home and now also in the rest of the world, the latter offset by any expected exchange-rate change (a rise in the nominal exchange rate reduces import prices in domestic currency). Equation (3) is the 'Monetary Policy Rule' (unchanged from a closed economy), in which the official interest rate depends positively on the 'equilibrium' real rate of interest (consistent with a zero output gap and thus a constant rate of inflation), the output gap, and the gap between actual and target inflation. Equation (4) determines the real exchange rate as a function of the differential between domestic and foreign real interest rates, the balance on current account and exchange-rate expectations (influenced by such factors as risk premiums and the credibility of the inflation target), and exogenous factors including underlying trade competitiveness. In equation (5) the economy's balance on external current account is a function of the real exchange rate, the domestic and world output gaps, and underlying factors like domestic and foreign import propensities. Equation (6) defines the nominal exchange rate in terms of the real exchange rate and relative world and domestic price levels.

There are six equations and six unknowns (Y, R, p, rer, CA and er), so the model is determinate and can be solved to give values for all the dependent variables if all the relevant parameters and the constants and exogenous variables are known. Particularly important among the latter are trend or equilibrium output Y^* and inflation expectations Ep_{t+1} in the domestic economy, and their counterparts in the rest-of-world economy. Y^* is assumed to be determined by long-run supply-side factors (labour force, capital stock, technology, employee preferences for work and leisure, etc.) which are not affected by aggregate demand; inflation expectations Ep_{t+1} are regarded as being set by the credibility of the central bank in achieving its inflation target over time in the face of inflationary shocks.

In the open-economy model, as in its closed-economy predecessor, control of inflation works through the consistent and predictable manipulation of the economy's representative interest rate by the central bank, responding to periodic disturbances that drive the economy away from its equilibrium path. The ability of the central bank to influence expectations, especially inflation expectations, is crucial to the policy's effectiveness, as Arestis explains (2007: 25–8ff.). The exchange rate per se plays no direct role in the setting of interest rates but in an open economy it is an important channel through which their effects may operate, owing to exchange-rate dependence on the interest differential in equation (4). One such route is relatively direct, through the prices of finished goods and services imports on domestic consumer prices (and perhaps on wages in response to the effects of exchange-rate changes on consumer price expectations); another, less direct, is via the prices of imported materials and intermediate products on domestic production costs.

Other key features of the model and problem areas for further research are extensively debated by Arestis and the other contributors to his collection (Arestis 2007), which also provides full bibliographies.

floating exchange rate. Thus in the event of a positive demand shock, the exchange rate will appreciate in response to the rise in the interest differential implied by the policy tightening, and this will reduce import prices, other things being equal, and thence reduce inflationary pressure. In that way monetary policy gains leverage from a floating exchange rate, as we pointed out earlier in this chapter. Of course, inclusion of world output and prices in the model also creates the possibility that an open economy will be subject to external shocks, and in that respect the tasks facing monetary policy may be made more difficult.

Criticisms of the NCM model

Among the distinctive features of the standard NCM model several merit special attention. Principal among them are: the absence of money from the model and, allied to that, the absence of any role for banking or credit; the inclusion of only one interest rate, which implies an implausibly direct and stable transmission mechanism from monetary policy to inflation; the independence of natural (potential) output from demand-side influences; and the absence of any role for fiscal policy. These and other features have attracted criticism of various kinds in the subsequent, and continuing, academic debate.

The complete absence of money from the NCM model has brought predictable criticism from a monetarist perspective: since inflation is a monetary phenomenon, how can a theory that seeks to explain inflation and its control omit all mention of money? Above all, where is the nominal anchor that the theory surely needs? The model's defenders argue that the anchor is provided by the MP rule: the modern central-bank commitment to price stability provides the necessary nominal anchor, *provided the policy is credible and expected to remain so.* This is a crucial proviso, but the remarkable worldwide success of disinflationary policies in the era since major central banks became independent in the 1990s, and the contribution of policy action resembling the Taylor rule to securing that success, have convinced markets that the anchor is credible (see Woodford 2009: 12–13).

A major reason given for preferring an inflation target to monetary targets is that the former signals the central bank's commitment to price stability much more clearly and less ambiguously than the latter. Links between the monetary aggregates and inflation are tenuous and uncertain, given the variability observed in money's velocity during the era of monetary targeting. The difficulty of controlling the monetary stock in liberalised financial systems, and the instability of the demand for money when policy focuses on monetary targets (explained in Chapter 3) – have persuaded many economists of the superiority of inflation targets. However, some leading apologists for the moneyless construction of the NCM model go further than this. Some, like the American neo-Keynesian Michael Woodford, argue that, quite apart from problems of controlling the money stock and the variability of money demand, targeting monetary aggregates can achieve little or nothing that the more structural approach in the NCM model cannot achieve equally well (Woodford 2006: Sec. 3.2). He denies that the absence of money in the standard model makes it incomplete (provided the model is correctly specified), even with respect to maintaining price stability over the long run (2006: 6–9).

Other critics, including some non-monetarists, feel that a moneyless approach omits elements that should be included in a model that purports to show how central banks target inflation. In particular they believe the NCM model relies too heavily on the Phillips curve, which is unstable because it is much affected by institutional changes and market disturbances like cost-push shocks (see Goodhart 2007: 62–3). Moreover, empirical estimation suggests that inflation expectations in labour and goods markets are mainly backward-looking rather than forward-looking, because of the uncertainties involved and the unreliability of inflation forecasts (Wren-Lewis 2007: 50–2).[14] In addition there are known to be difficulties in measuring actual output and, more especially, natural (or potential) output. Apologists for the model like Woodford concede these difficulties but argue that they are inherent in any inflation targeting approach of a structural kind, and that the inclusion of monetary aggregates as additional arguments in the AS curve would not overcome them. In mitigation Woodford suggests that the inflationary excesses, which threaten if policymakers persistently overestimate potential output as happened in major economies through the 1960s and 1970s, can be avoided by making inflation targets look *backward* as well as forward. Thus if central banks begin to exceed their inflation targets they should claw back past excesses when setting current and future targets. This could be done by targeting the price level rather than the inflation rate, or by setting inflation targets as averages calculated over past as well as future periods.

The rudimentary nature of the monetary transmission process based on a single interest rate has also come under strong attack from non-monetarists, notably Charles Goodhart (2007: 61–81). As early as 2005 he pointed out that short-term interest rates are not the only possible channel of monetary policy and that monetary expansion via open market operations may offer a solution to the liquidity trap. More basically Goodhart thinks the implicit assumption of perfectly-clearing banking markets and absence of credit rationing in the NCM model is unrealistic and prevents the model from addressing changes in the structure of interest rates associated with credit risk and liquidity shortages. In his view monetary policy in liberalized banking systems should be concerned with asset-price fluctuations as much as goods-price inflation. Yet he does not support the broadening of inflation targets to include asset prices (other than the inclusion of mortgage servicing costs in CPI targets) as this would muddy the signals and detract from the price stability commitments that have played such an important part in post-1990s regimes. Neither does he favour adopting separate targets for asset prices, owing to uncertainties about their equilibrium or sustainable values, particularly for financial assets. Instead he recommends actions by central banks and regulators to target aggregate bank lending as a percentage of GDP, for example through counter-cyclical variation of capital-adequacy requirements.

From an orthodox Keynesian perspective an important weakness of the NCM model is its assumption that potential output is independent of aggregate demand. This feature arises from the form chosen for the AD function, which differs from the traditional IS function in several key respects. Arestis (2007: 25) describes the model function as 'a forward-looking expectational relationship which implies that the marginal rate of substitution between current and future consumption, ignoring uncertainty and adjusted for the subjective rate of time discount, is equal to the gross real rate of interest'. Thus in the standard model all debts are ultimately paid in full, thereby removing all credit risk and default, so it cannot address situations in which expenditure is credit constrained, as in the recent credit crunch. Moreover, changes in the cost of capital have no effect on firms' investment decisions, other than those that operate via household saving decisions. A related feature of the AD function is that investment has no effect on the future path of the capital stock and thus potential output. This means that variations in aggregate demand have no effects on productive capacity or equilibrium production costs through time.

Verdict on the NCM model

The exclusive dependence of potential (i.e. natural) output on supply-side arguments and its independence of demand-side arguments is a standard property of neoclassical models and it is bound to worry most Keynesians. While the model may offer an acceptable approximation of real-world developments when economic conditions remain smooth and disturbances are minor, it is unlikely to do so in the event of major shocks that drive output a long way from normal levels, even if only for a few years. Such shocks may affect the path of potential output for long periods afterwards and may have lasting effects on output and inflation unless policy can somehow contain them. Other less prominent features of the NCM model raise allied concerns. The log-linearity usually assumed for the key functional relationships means that a given type of shock has the same proportionate effect on inflation and output regardless of its size. This may be an acceptable approximation for small shocks but it is unlikely to be for big ones. Similarly, the time–invariance of key functional links in the model means that shocks have constant effects on inflation or output whether they are short or long-lasting, whereas the effects of such shocks may evolve through time.

These real-world problems are likely to complicate the conduct of monetary policy in ways not captured in the standard NCM model. Ideally central banks should be able to identify the nature and size of shocks accurately enough to gauge quickly how far interest rates must be adjusted in order to counter the effects on inflation. But in many real-world situations these factors will be unclear when they happen and central banks are obliged to make difficult judgements about the size and timing of their actions. Such uncertainties, and the fact that sharp movements (spikes) in interest rates are particularly damaging for financial businesses that borrow short and lend long, mean that official interest-rate adjustments in post-1990s regimes tend to be made in series of small steps, allowing the policymakers to assess effects through trial and error as they go along. Nevertheless it is essential to the effectiveness of the policy that central banks should be credible 'managers of expectations'. As Arestis points out:

> . . . by acting directly on lowering expectations of inflation, a manager of expectations may allow the temporary gap of output (now below the natural rate of output) to be less than would otherwise be needed for the same reduction in inflation.
>
> *(Arestis and Ross 2007: 4)*

It follows from the above that the most severe tests for the NCM model, as indeed for the regimes it represents, are posed by economic disturbances which are so large and persistent that they surpass the capacity of monetary policy to deal with them. This may be because there is a practical floor below which official short-term rates cannot be driven – even real interest rates, when inflation expectations are very subdued – or because the shock induces distortions in the transmission mechanism, for example when spreads between official rates and bank lending rates diverge from normal levels, owing to pressures on banks to replenish lost capital and avoid risky lending, as happened in the recent banking crisis. Such shocks have thankfully been rather rare, although they may become less so in future. Less rare have been sustained periods of very slow growth, low inflation, and near-zero short-term interest rates, as experienced in Japan since 1990. It is perhaps understandable that a model built to reflect the favourable circumstances enjoyed by Western economies for 20 years before the 2008 crash should fail to address such problems. But experience since then must surely lead to some reappraisal of the passive role accorded to fiscal policy in the NCM model.

Some apologists for the NCM model (and indeed for the 1990s synthesis more generally) have sought to rationalise the downgrading of fiscal policy by reference to the assumption that inflation is a monetary phenomenon and should therefore be addressed by monetary means, using interest rates as the monetary instrument.[15] However, this reasoning seems highly debatable. Monetary policy is the preferred policy mode because it has proved more efficient in achieving price stability under normal conditions. But it has done so by influencing the *balance of demand and supply in labour and product markets*, and thence the general price of goods and services in terms of money, not by exploiting a supposed direct causal link from money to the price level. In abnormal conditions fiscal policy may be a more effective, if less flexible, tool for stabilising aggregate demand, and it may also have an important long-term role to play in relation to aggregate saving, as will be argued in later chapters.

The NCM model cannot claim to have been the inspiration or the blueprint for the revolution in policy under the 1990s synthesis; governments and central banks resorted to inflation targeting for largely political and practical reasons, and they have adhered to it because of its remarkable success in maintaining broad price stability over nearly two decades. Success in this area has depended, not on the particular policy rules that central banks have chosen to follow, or the mechanisms believed to underpin them, but on the consistency and determination they have shown in controlling inflation whenever it has appeared. The NCM model offers an elegant rationale for the new regime and it has proved useful for teaching purposes and as a test bed for ongoing research. Yet, well before the recent global crisis, academic critics were pointing to its shortcomings. The events of the past few years have shown beyond doubt that new thinking is needed if the model is to survive the difficult environment of the present century. Chapter 5 will develop this theme in relation to the broader 1990s synthesis, and suggestions for reform will follow.

ANNEX 4.1

Mechanics of the Phillips curve

The original Phillips curve was a statistical relationship between wage inflation and unemployment in the UK economy, estimated over the period 1861 to 1957. The curve had a downward slope and was convex to the origin, as shown in Figure 4.1, which uses the parameters of the original curve. Subsequent research identified similar curves for other industrial economies.

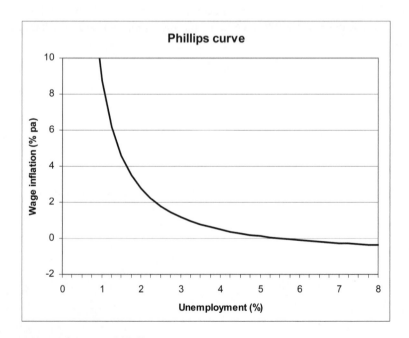

FIGURE 4.1   The original Phillips curve

The negative slope implies that the annual rate of wage inflation (on the vertical axis) tends to fall as the rate of unemployment of the labour force (on the horizontal axis) rises, other things being equal. This reflects that employees engaged in collective bargaining tend to be less aggressive about bidding for wage increases at higher unemployment rates, because competition for jobs becomes more intense as the number of jobless rises. An alternative though compatible explanation is that as aggregate demand rises and firms employ more labour, they have to raise wage rates because the supply of labour of any given quality is limited. The convexity of the curve is then due to the increasing difficulty of recruiting an extra unit of labour as unemployment falls, because labour of a given quality becomes increasingly scarce as full employment is approached.

As can be seen in the figure, wage inflation is 2 per cent per annum when unemployment is just over 2 per cent (strictly 2.3 per cent according to the parameters of the original curve), rises to about 4 per cent per annum when unemployment is down at about 1.5 per cent, and falls to zero when unemployment is just over 5 per cent (strictly 5.5 per cent in the figure). If trend productivity growth is about 2 per cent per annum, prices should therefore be stable at an unemployment rate of 2.3 per cent. In these circumstances, if the authorities wish to reduce unemployment to, say, 1.5 per cent (by boosting aggregate demand), they must be prepared to accept inflation of around 2 per cent per annum (i.e. wage inflation of 4 per cent per annum minus productivity growth of 2 per cent per annum). This represents a segment of the policy trade-off offered by the traditional Phillips curve.

The Phillips curve implies that there is some critical unemployment rate at which general or consumer price inflation is zero. In this example the critical unemployment rate needed for price stability is 2.3 per cent if productivity growth is 2 per cent per annum and 5.5 per cent if productivity growth is zero. In principle the relationship should be symmetrical for unemployment rates above the critical rate: for example, if productivity growth is zero, inflation should be negative and constant through time at all unemployment rates above 5.5 per cent. However, in practice, downward real wage rigidity is likely to prevent negative inflation emerging unless unemployment reaches very high rates. If real wages are perfectly rigid downwards the Phillips curve will be flat in the range where U exceeds 5.5 per cent.

Crucial to the traditional Phillips curve was the assumption that although workers are concerned with real wage rates, they repeatedly fail to foresee the effects of consumer price inflation in frustrating their attempts to bid up real wage rates when unemployment falls. In other words they suffer from myopia about future inflation – a form of 'money illusion'. An alternative situation is next envisaged in which employees overcome this myopia, anticipating that higher wage settlements will raise output costs and prices.

More specifically, suppose now that at the start of a new wage contract employees expect inflation over the contract period to be the same as it was in the previous contract period, and they add this percentage to the annual real wage increase (which varies inversely with the unemployment rate, as before) in their new wage bid. Employees adopt this simple form of 'adaptive' or backward-looking inflation expectations systematically through succeeding wage contracts. The effect of incorporating inflation expectations of this kind into the Phillips curve is shown in Figure 4.2.

To keep the picture simple, zero growth of labour productivity is assumed, so that wage inflation on the vertical axis is identical with consumer price inflation, and the rate of unemployment needed for both wage and price stability is just over 5 per cent. Imagine that at the start of year one the economy has for some time been in equilibrium at position A in the figure, with unemployment at 5.5 per cent, and both inflation and inflationary expectations zero. Suppose that at that stage a policy-induced increase in aggregate demand reduces unemployment to 2.3 per cent and holds it at that level. In year one there is a movement leftward along the Phillips curve to position B, indicating that employees respond to the rise in activity by bidding their wages up by 2 per cent, which results in inflation in year one of 2 per cent. Anticipating that inflation will remain at this rate, at the start of year two employees bargain in real terms by adding 2 per cent for expected inflation to their previous wage demand of 2 per cent, giving a nominal wage increase of 4 per cent. In that case, the year-two Phillips curve shifts up the chart by a uniform 2 per cent at all rates of unemployment. With aggregate demand held at its new level in real

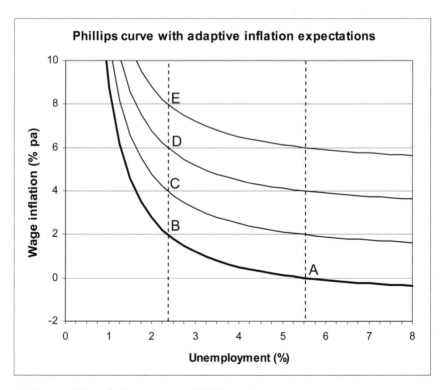

FIGURE 4.2   The inflation-augmented Phillips curve

terms (requiring a rise in current-price terms to allow for inflation), the equilibrium position moves up to C in the chart.

If unemployment remains at 2.3 per cent in year three and employees continue to anticipate inflation of 2 per cent per annum, average nominal wage rates rise by 6 per cent in that year, the year-three Phillips curve shifts uniformly upward by a further 2 per cent, and the equilibrium position moves up to D. This pattern will recur so long as unemployment remains at 2.3 per cent, with equilibrium shifting annually up the vertical line C-D-E . . . through a family of Phillips curves consistent with U = 2.3 per cent. In other words, with unemployment held constant at that rate, inflation accelerates through time at a constant 2 per cent per annum.

In general, corresponding families of curves would emerge at other rates of unemployment, though distances between successive curves in any family would be larger at lower unemployment rates. The only exception to this general pattern occurs if unemployment remains at the critical value of U = 5.5 per cent, in which case inflation and inflation expectations remain at zero and the curve is unchanged through time. This critical unemployment rate came to be termed the NAIRU (non-accelerating-inflation rate of unemployment) in the literature. A strict interpretation of the adaptive expectations hypothesis implied that the Phillips curve is vertical (at the NAIRU) in the long run, although it may be downward-sloping in the short run.

In this way, the introduction of systematic inflation expectations into wage bargaining implies a progressive upward shift of the Phillips curve (or a downward shift, if inflation is negative), at a speed that depends on how far unemployment deviates from its critical zero-inflation rate.

This example has assumed that wage bargainers form inflation expectations in an 'adaptive' (backward-looking) way, focusing simply on last period's inflation. If that simple adaptive approach is accepted, the traditional Phillips curve in Figure 4.1 translates into an 'inflation-augmented' curve, where the vertical axis represents the *rate of change* of inflation, not its level. The adaptive expectations theory had revolutionary implications for demand management in that it suggested that although the unemployment-inflation trade-off may hold in the short run (namely, the shift from A to B in year one), it does not do so in the long run, since attempts to reduce unemployment below the critical zero-inflation rate will result in permanently accelerating inflation that become unsustainable beyond the short run.

More sophisticated approaches to expectations formation can of course be envisaged and may be more plausible in some conditions. (This applies even to adaptive expectations. For a discussion of alternative methods of backward-looking expectations formation and their practical implications, see Flemming (1976: ch. 7).) Thus expectations may be formed on a forward-looking basis, for example by extrapolating the past trend of inflation into the future, or by forecasting inflation in some way, perhaps using the 'true model' of the economy, as recommended by rational expectations theorists. Forward-looking expectations tend to boost the inflationary consequences associated with any deviation of unemployment from the NAIRU. Indeed the logical implication of strict rational expectations is that any significant deviation of unemployment below the NAIRU will generate such rapidly rising inflation expectations (or increasingly negative inflation expectations, if unemployment exceeds the NAIRU), that even the *short-run* Phillips curve is effectively a vertical straight line, cutting the horizontal axis at the NAIRU. In other words, under strict rational expectations there is no possibility of a trade-off between unemployment and inflation even in the short run. Nevertheless this extreme version of the curve still implies the existence of a unique non-inflation level of unemployment and output.

5

PROBLEMS UNDER THE 1990s SYNTHESIS

At first the 1990s policy settlement did not seem very auspicious. Sceptical observers saw it as a last-ditch attempt to restore credibility after the inflation traumas and policy confusion of the preceding 20 years. It nevertheless made a remarkably good beginning. Through the remainder of the decade and into the new century, inflation stayed well under control in the major economies, fiscal retrenchment proceeded satisfactorily, and activity stabilised and eventually picked up – even in Germany and Japan (as shown in Figure 1.1A). Indeed performance in North America and Western Europe through the new regime's first ten years seemed so promising that optimism spread to other regions, especially among the EU's neighbours in Eastern Europe and emerging economies in the Far East and the Americas. In due course hopes were raised that the new synthesis would not merely guide policymakers through a particularly challenging transition but also become the pattern for developed and emerging economies for much of the new century.

Nevertheless, despite impressive early progress, a number of warning signs were evident from the start. Notable among these was the continuation through the 1990s of economic stagnation in Japan, the high-performance economy which had led the post-Second World War revival in Asia and inspired economic miracles among East Asia's tiger economies. Japan's inability to shake off the debilitating effects of the banking collapse which had struck it in the late 1980s and the subsequent 'debt deflation', despite very low interest rates under the 'zero interest rate policy' and recurrent efforts at fiscal stimulus, meant that it could not regain its rapid growth of earlier decades or reverse the steady rise in unemployment dating from then (Figure 1.1B). Japan's economic doldrums, and the financial tsunami that struck some half-dozen small East Asian economies towards the end of the decade, were massive setbacks to confidence in the region, and serious warnings that the policy package might not transfer well to the emerging world. With hindsight these events can be seen as harbingers of the financial crisis that afflicted the developed world ten years later.

This chapter considers in more detail the faults detectable in, and threats to, the 1990s synthesis, some of which have been mentioned already. First it will address the *endogenous weaknesses* – defects that are inherent in the new regime, and in some cases peculiar to it. Then it will turn to the *exogenous threats* – shocks or adverse trends that are likely to originate or recur outside the regime and might damage it sooner or later. Some of the latter are fairly familiar from previous experience but others are novel, and their incidence and severity are especially hard to predict, as shown by the events of the past few years. Most of these phenomena are complex and prone to interact, so any categorisation has to be somewhat arbitrary. This was especially evident in the severe crisis that hit the global economy in 2007–8, as will be seen in Chapter 6.

The 'one-club' methodology

Virtually everywhere in 1990s regimes, control of inflation relies heavily on manipulating short-term interest rates. This choice of methodology followed from the primacy accorded to monetary policy in the new synthesis and its preference for flexible, market-based tools. Unfortunately dependence on a single policy instrument may pose problems. One is that the links between the official interest rates set by central banks and the main lending rates charged by commercial banks to their customers are not always stable and may vary markedly when financial markets are under stress. This problem became troublesome after the onset of the global credit crunch in 2007–8, which led to sharp increases in the margins customarily observed between central-bank lending rates and interbank rates (the rates charged by commercial banks for provision of liquidity to one another, which provide a fulcrum for the structure of lending rates) in a number of the main centres. As may be seen in Figure 5.1, a large gap opened up between official and interbank lending rates in London between 2006 and 2008 and made it difficult for monetary policymakers to maintain a stable and predictable thrust of policy in the face of the sub-prime mortgage crisis and the ensuing credit crunch. Similar gaps emerged in other centres, though the problem was less serious in some than others, depending on the severity of the liquidity shortages in domestic banking systems and the steps that central banks took to relieve them.

A further problem arising from the one-club methodology is that the lending rates charged by commercial banks and other credit institutions tend to bear unevenly on different sectors. In most market economies some sectors rely much more heavily on bank finance than others, much of it charged at variable rates. This is the case in the United States and UK, where a high proportion of household borrowing takes the form of variable-rate mortgages; other economies (notably Italy, Ireland) exhibit similar though less acute dependencies. Moreover, in the Anglo-Saxon economies small businesses generally, and the construction industry in particular, rely heavily on short-term borrowing, much of it from banks. Problems are liable to arise in these sectors when stability in the property market requires different lending rates from those needed by the rest of the economy. Such problems have

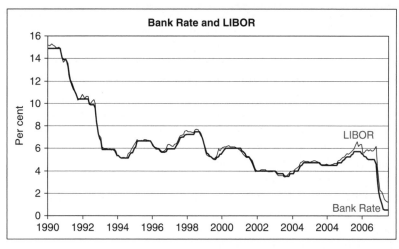

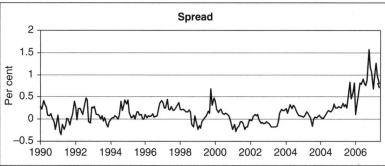

FIGURE 5.1 UK Bank Rate and three-month interbank rate, January 1990 to June 2009 (source: Bank of England online database).

Notes: 'Bank Rate' is the official interest rate at which the Bank of England supplies reserves to the banking system; termed Minimum Lending Rate earlier. LIBOR is the three-month interest rate at which banks lend to each other in the sterling interbank market. Both are monthly averages of daily rates. The spread here is calculated as LIBOR *minus* Bank Rate.

been experienced periodically in the UK since the de-cartelisation of the mortgage market in the 1970s, and have been blamed for the long-term instability in house prices seen since then. Somewhat similar problems developed in the United States in the early 2000s, when low real interest rates resulting from an expansionary monetary policy fuelled an unsustainable house price boom and created the preconditions for the US sub-prime mortgage crisis in mid-2007, as will be explained later.

The problems arising from the one-club methodology may become acute in situations where the central bank is expected to fulfil more than one role, as may happen if a systemic bank liquidity shortage develops quite independently of the overall level of economic activity, especially if the shortage spreads across national boundaries via globalised markets. In such circumstances, the central bank may face a difficult dilemma between its traditional responsibility as lender of last resort to commercial banks seeking to restore liquidity and its post-1990s commitment to overall price stability, for the maintenance of banking liquidity in the face of a systemic threat will create pressure for interest-rate cuts while price stability may call for a non-accommodating monetary stance. These were the circumstances witnessed during the recent global credit crunch, as will be seen in Chapter 6.

Unevenness in interest-rate dependency may also arise from differences in exchange-rate exposure between different economic sectors. In open economies with flexible exchange rates, manufacturing industry tends to be especially vulnerable to interest-rate variations, owing to the strong links between international interest differentials and floating exchange rates. In most industrial economies, shares of (gross) output exported and imported are considerably higher in manufacturing than in other sectors, so changes in short-term lending rates tend to impinge much more on manufacturing than on other industries, or most services. We will return to this problem in the context of exchange-rate instability below.

The uneven impact of changes in short-term lending rates across different sectors is an important drawback for the one-club policy because, when faced with shocks and disturbances, the single-minded pursuit of a non-accommodating monetary policy tends to generate instability and inefficient resource allocation between sectors. The big fluctuations in property prices, house-building and mortgage lending, and the marked cycles in non-residential construction and manufacturing production in the UK and the United States in the past 10–15 years are manifestations of these unintended but damaging effects. Inevitably they lead to criticism of the monetary policymakers from those affected – industry or trade associations, lobbyists for small businesses, homeowners, etc. Although most central banks are more protected from such pressures in post-1990s regimes than previously, it would be surprising if they remained entirely unaffected by them at times of abnormal stress, and this must raise questions about the durability of the new regimes when put to serious test.

Asset-price instability and financial-market fragility

Large and persistent swings in asset prices have occurred in all the major economies since the mid-1990s. (In Japan they emerged ten years earlier.) Since 2007 these have reached proportions that exceed those in earlier regimes, at least since the Wall Street crash of 1929. Fluctuations have been evident in the prices of both financial and physical assets (property and land). The sustained boom in US and UK house prices after around 1995 is illustrated in Figure 5.2, which shows that by 2007 real (earnings-adjusted) house prices were well above their long-term trends in both economies. And as mentioned earlier, there was a violent boom and bust in commercial property prices in Japan and the East Asian emerging economies from the mid-1980s onwards.

Large movements have also occurred in equity prices in the major markets since the mid-1990s (earlier in Japan). As may be seen in Figure 5.3, they have

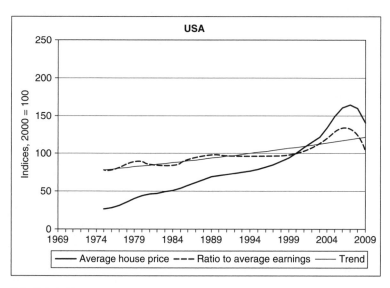

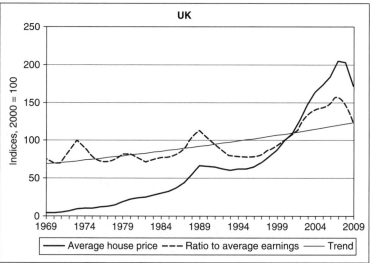

FIGURE 5.2 House price indices, nominal and real, United States and UK, 1969/75–
2009 (sources: US house price index from US Office of Federal Housing Enterprise Oversight online database; UK house price index from
UK Department of Communities and Local Government database; average earnings indices calculated from OECD Stat online database. All are
rebased to 2000=100).

Notes: nominal prices are indices of mix-adjusted averages of house prices, base year 2000=100;
annual averages of monthly data. The broken line is an index of the ratio of average house prices
to average hourly earnings in the private sector (or 'all activities' in the UK), rebased to 2000=100.
Log-linear trends in this ratio were estimated for 1975–2008 in the United States and 1969–2008
in the UK.

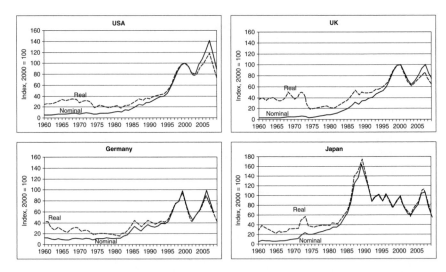

FIGURE 5.3 Share price indices, nominal and real, four major economies, 1960–2009 (source: OECD Stat online database and author's calculations).

Note: real share prices calculated by deflating indices of nominal prices by the consumers' expenditure deflator, both indices having base year 2000=100. Monthly averages of daily data.

proportionately exceeded those going back to the early 1970s, even in real terms and allowing for the rising trend in real equity prices over the past 50 years.

Capitalist economies have of course long been prone to large and persistent swings in share prices, often characterised as 'bubbles' which burst sooner or later and are followed by sharp downward corrections. The unusually long and powerful stock-market boom that began around 1980 and lasted through the 1990s meant that, by around 2000, equity prices on the US stock market and other major markets had become substantially overvalued according to standard market criteria (dividend yields and price-earning ratios).[1] This overvaluation was checked by the 'dot com' crisis in 2000–2, which burst the bubble in Internet stocks. But subsequently equity prices surged ahead again until their progress was punctured by the financial crash of 2007–8.

The increase evident in stock-market instability during the 1990s can be attributed largely to the rapid process of deregulation which the financial markets of many developed economies were then undergoing. This process was exacerbated by increasing use of devices like electronic trading systems with built-in trading points, which are triggered automatically regardless of traders' judgements about the fundamental causes of market shocks. These sources of systemic fragility were compounded by deficiencies in securities firms' financial reporting and control systems, as exemplified by the collapse of Barings Bank, a UK merchant bank, in 1995 and of Long-Term Capital Management, a US hedge fund which developed exceptionally high-risk trading strategies, in 1998. They were made

worse by weaknesses in corporate governance and auditing standards and procedures in a number of high-profile cases, principally in the United States, as exemplified by the major frauds (over-reporting of profits) found at Enron in 2001 and
WorldCom in June 2002. These uncomfortable events signalled quite early on that
corporate managements were taking advantage of the freer market conditions to cut
corners, and were being driven to take bigger risks by incentive payment schemes
that linked traders' and managers' remuneration directly to share performance.

The spread of financial deregulation under the 1990s synthesis and the associated increase in asset-price volatility was almost bound to create systemic problems
sooner or later. In time systemic fragility percolated not only across the financial sectors of deregulated economies but also among the non-financial firms and
households which became heavily reliant on bank credit for financing investment,
inventory holding and other commercial operations. Moreover, through globalisation, the instability originating in liberalised centres spread to others where risk-
taking and financial engineering had been less aggressive or more conservatively
regulated; and eventually developing countries with rudimentary banking systems
but heavy reliance on exports to liberalised economies.

As will be apparent when we come to review of the crash of 2007–8 and its
aftermath, there is now widespread agreement among independent commentators, practitioners and officials that there have been important failures of regulation
and prudential supervision in liberalised financial centres, and that remedies are
urgently needed. How far the traumas in the financial sector can also be blamed
on macroeconomic policy and institutions is less clear. Before the recent upsets,
few would have challenged the view in the 1990s consensus that remedies for
asset-price instability and imprudent bank lending lie mainly with financial regulation, and so fall outside the ambit of macro policy. Moreover, as will be seen later,
some free-market economists still argue that capitalist economies cannot function
effectively without a high degree of risk-taking and periodic asset-price volatility.
However, the events of the past few years have clearly made it much harder to
exonerate macro-policy regimes from blame in these respects.

Exchange-rate instability

One of the more confident hopes after the 1990s settlement was that overcoming
inflation in developed economies would promote exchange-rate stability, given
that differences in national inflation rates had been regarded as an important cause
of the much increased volatility seen in key currencies after the collapse of Bretton
Woods. But this hope has been largely disappointed: it is now evident that floating
exchange rates are still prone to large fluctuations, if not quite on the scale experienced in the post-Bretton Woods era. As may be seen in Figure 5.4, since 1990
there have continued to be swings of the order of 30 or more percentage points in
both the nominal and real exchange rates (adjusted for movements in relative costs)
of the Deutsche mark (and its successor the euro) and yen against the US dollar,
lasting 5–10 years or more. The long-run instability of the sterling/dollar rate since

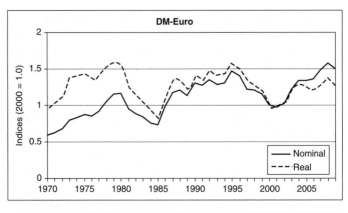

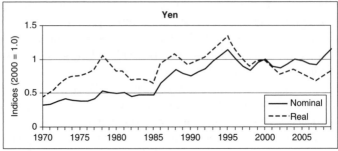

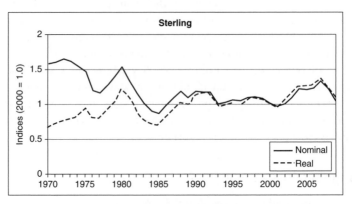

FIGURE 5.4   Nominal and real exchange rates against US dollar: Deutsche mark-euro, yen and sterling, 1970–2009 (source: OECD Stat online database and author's calculations).

Notes: index numbers of nominal rates calculated from annual averages of daily market rates; amounts of US dollars per unit of home currency. 'DM-Euro' relates to the Deutsche mark before EMU (January 1999), converted into euro equivalents (1.95583 D-mark = 1 euro); and to the euro subsequently. Real exchange rates were calculated by dividing relative total-economy unit labour costs in domestic currencies by market exchange rates. A rise here represents a deterioration in home-economy competitiveness against the United States.

1990 has been somewhat less marked but still substantial; for example a real sterling appreciation of around 30 per cent occurred between 2000 and 2007. It is reasonable to think that swings of this magnitude in real exchange rates are damaging to industry in open economies because they represent changes in competitiveness which are hard to predict and hedge against.

In an era of inflation convergence like that of the past 20 years, large and persistent exchange-rate fluctuations ('low-frequency' instability) imply phases of substantial currency over- or undervaluation, a problem termed misalignment under the original Bretton Woods system. Thus for example the large depreciation of the US dollar against most other major currencies between 2002 and 2008 has led to considerable dollar undervaluation – in excess of 20 percentage points in 'effective' (average trade-weighted) terms. Advocates of free floating believe that dollar undervaluation on this scale is warranted by the mushrooming US external trade deficit in recent years. Thus Martin Feldstein, former Chairman of the US Council of Economic Advisers under President Reagan, insisted in March 2008 that 'the dollar is falling at the right time': 'Investors and policy officials should recognise that the dollar's current decline is part of a natural process for reducing the US trade deficit' (Feldstein 2008).

While others are less convinced of the merits of dollar depreciation, most agree that the weak dollar gives US manufacturers a substantial competitive advantage in world markets. However, opinions differ considerably among economists as to how damaging such instability really is. Many in the mainstream as well as towards the free-market end of the spectrum favour exchange-rate floating for major currencies because they trust the ability of markets to identify the 'correct' level for an exchange rate more than that of governments and central banks; and/or because they doubt the authorities' ability to control rates for long; or because much empirical research suggests that exchange-rate volatility has little effect on productivity or growth in developed economies. This sceptical view has been pungently expressed in an op-ed column by one of its leading protagonists Kenneth Rogoff, a former research director of the IMF and leading researcher in this and other fields: 'When taming volatile currencies, policymakers are trying to rein in forces they can't control – much less understand' (Rogoff 2005: 74–5).

Other economists, some mainstream as well as those of a more interventionist inclination, find it hard to accept the free-market philosophy in this context because they are impressed by the weight of historical opposition to exchange-rate instability, as manifest by repeated efforts to overcome it; and they doubt that exchange rates can be 'correct' if they settle for long periods at values which are manifestly unsustainable in the long term.

Critics of floating rates believe that large and persistent (long-period) exchange-rate swings are very harmful to industry and trade in open economies. Their concerns are principally relevant to small and medium-sized economies which trade heavily in world markets, but they also apply to the tradable-goods sectors of less open economies. Thus the big US dollar undervaluation of recent years is regarded as harmful not only to activity and employment among the United States' main trading competitors but also in the long run to industry in the United States itself, because it gives misleading signals which eventually lead to resource misallocation. On the other hand there is general agreement that short-term currency fluctuations ('high frequency' volatility) are a much less serious problem for most kinds of business, except very small firms. The monthly and quarterly exchange-rate fluctuations that characterise floating currencies, which are also undiminished under the 1990s synthesis, can generally be overcome by hedging in the forward markets, at least by larger firms with the necessary expertise and creditworthiness. But the forward markets are much less useful for covering the risks created by low-frequency instability, because forward cover beyond a year ahead is generally either not available or prohibitively expensive for all but the largest firms.

Unambiguous evidence on the effects of currency instability on international trade is hard to obtain because the industrial adjustment processes tend to be complex and long drawn out. Many of the econometric studies that are inconclusive or negative in this respect focus on short-period volatility rather than misalignment.[2] Other studies find that changes in real (inflation-adjusted) exchange rates do have fairly strong and systematic effects on trade flows between developed economies, when they persist beyond the short run (1–2 years). Manufacturing exports in particular are generally found to be negatively related to relative unit labour costs, a standard measure of competitiveness. For major economies the effects in estimated equations are generally stable, with well-identified and plausible coefficients, though the lags tend to be long (two years or more on average), and the coefficients may change over time for structural reasons.[3] Variations in competitiveness also have appreciable impacts on manufacturing output and employment in open economies in due course, and also on profitability and investment, though the latter effects are harder to identify. Non-manufacturing industries are generally less heavily affected, though internationally traded services like travel and tourism respond significantly when their relative costs change.

Some new evidence on the effects of low-frequency exchange-rate instability on manufacturing output in open economies is offered in Box 5.1. As explained there, a significant negative relationship is detectable between relative unit labour costs (a measure of competitiveness) and manufacturing output in both the UK and Germany since 1970; the large variations in trade competitiveness which have continued into the present century appear to have led to marked output instability in manufacturing in those countries. It is reasonable to conclude that such instability damages long-term growth of productivity and international trade in the affected industries.

Low-frequency exchange-rate instability tends to be damaging not only because it gives misleading price signals that distort long-term investment and lead to resource misallocation in the tradable sectors of open economies but also because it creates uncertainty which discourages investment in the countries affected. One of the main benefits expected from monetary union in Europe was elimination of the interest penalties borne by weak-performing currencies as a result of exchange-rate uncertainty. As may be seen in Figure 5.5, during the 15 or so years before

BOX 5.1 COMPETITIVENESS AND MANUFACTURING OUTPUT IN THE UK AND GERMANY SINCE 1970

This box examines what has happened to competitiveness and output in the manufacturing industries of the UK and German since 1970, a period covering the entire era of key-currency floating since the end of Bretton Woods (though the Deutsche mark participated in the Exchange Rate Mechanism of the European Monetary System from 1979 until 1999, when it was merged with nine other EU currencies to become the euro). These two countries were chosen as exemplifying medium-sized open economies with well-established manufacturing industries.

In each of the charts below, the dark line shows an index of real manufacturing output with base year 2000=100, and the broken line is an exponential (log-linear) time trend fitted to output over the period 1970–2008. The light-coloured line is an index of relative *manufacturing unit labour costs* (MULCs), also with same base year. The MULCs index is a measure of the real exchange rate often used to indicate trade competitiveness in manufacturing: each economy's home costs per unit of output are divided by a weighted average of trading partners' costs expressed in a common currency, the weights reflecting partners' shares in the relevant countries' manufacturing trade. A fall in the MULC line indicates an improvement in competitiveness.

As may be seen, manufacturing output has tended to rise considerably faster in Germany than the UK, a feature that may be partly explained by the fact that German manufacturing competitiveness has deteriorated much less than that of the UK overall since 1970. Statistical tests confirm that both countries' real exchange rates have been slightly more unstable since 1990 than in the preceding two decades (the standard deviation of MULC for the UK rose from 11.7 in 1970–90 to 14.3 in 1991–2007; and from 4.9 to 5.8 in Germany's case).

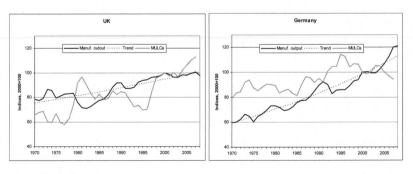

Source: OECD online database and author's calculations.

Inspection of the charts suggests there is a marked negative relationship in both countries between manufacturing output and relative unit labour costs: increases in MULC appear to be associated with falls in output relative to trend. This link was confirmed by OLS regression analysis, in which each country's manufacturing output was regressed on its MULCs and a time trend, using annual data from 1970 to 2007. For both countries the estimated coefficients of output on MULC were found to be well identified (significant at the 95 per cent confidence level) and had the expected negative sign. Introduction of a one-year lag in the operation of MULC gave the best-defined effects for both countries. The results suggest that a change of 10 percentage points in MULC causes manufacturing output to deviate from trend in the reverse direction by about 3 percentage points on average in the UK after one year, and about 3.5 percentage points in Germany, other things being equal.

Similar tests of the link between MULCs and manufacturing output were carried out for the United States and Japan but the estimated effects were found to be statistically insignificant at the 95 per cent level. These latter results may reflect that both economies are much less open to external trade than their European competitors, so domestic influences tend to dominate the effects from competitiveness on manufacturing output.

the formation of EMU the EU's highest-inflation economies – Spain, Italy and the UK – suffered periodic real interest differentials well over two percentage points (annual rate) against the lowest-inflation currency (the Deutsche mark); and at times even Germany's low-inflation neighbours – France and the Netherlands – experienced adverse differentials up to two percentage points. (The rates in the chart apply to short-term low-risk assets – three-month treasury bills or interbank rates; so the differentials must have reflected exchange risk rather then credit-risk premia.) As would be expected, most differentials fell sharply in the late 1990s when it became clear that monetary union would actually happen and even the high-inflation economies would be included; though not the UK, which had opted out of EMU by then.

The continuation of long-period instability among the main floating currencies is arguably one of the biggest disappointments to come out of the 1990s policy synthesis. Moreover there is little reason to hope that such instability will recede in due course, unless action is taken to reduce it. Membership of the Euro Area will probably continue to grow as more CEE and Mediterranean countries are permitted to join the single currency; and other regional currency unions or exchange-rate systems may emerge in time if other groups of countries seek to emulate EMU. Participants may be able to shelter from the worst effects of currency instability, but the creation of a small number of expanding but inward-looking regional currency zones would threaten to increase instability among surviving floating currencies in the long run.

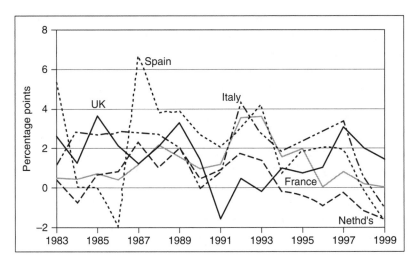

FIGURE 5.5   Real short-term interest differentials against D-mark, five EU currencies before EMU, 1983–99 (source: OECD *Statistical Compendium* 2003–1, CD-ROM, and author's calculations).

Notes: differences in percentage points (at annual rates) between representative three-month interest rates on selected EU currencies and the Deutsche mark. Real interest rates were calculated as annual averages of monthly rates minus the percentage change in the national consumer price index on the previous year.

Inflexible fiscal targets

For many economists and policymakers the firm commitment to fiscal discipline in the 1990s synthesis was a crucial break with the past, given the blame attached to lax fiscal policy for the inflationary tendencies of earlier regimes. Yet some doubters feared that rigid fiscal targets in developed economies would create problems sooner or later, and these fears have grown with the passage of time. One concern was that the new fiscal orthodoxy would turn out to be destabilising in the event of major cycles and shocks. The automatic stabilisers built into developed fiscal systems might be adequate to cope with moderate cycles and shocks but not with the swings in aggregate demand due to the oil-price shocks of the 1970s; or a fortiori the scale of the 1930s depression. Moreover, if interpreted strictly, the 1990s orthodoxy seemed to require fiscal authorities to adopt pro-cyclical measures to keep deficits near target, for example expenditure cuts during recessions. Hard battles had been fought by Keynes and his followers to free fiscal policy from the 'Treasury view' which had prolonged the chronic shortage of demand in the 1930s. A related concern was that too much would be asked of monetary policy in reformed regimes, as argued in relation to the 'one-club' methodology above. On this view, fiscal policy needs to be proactive at times of unusual stress if it is to give adequate support to monetary policy.

The pros and cons of mandatory limits on government deficits and debt stocks were vigorously debated during the run-up to EMU. Those in favour of such limits felt they were necessary to deter governments with suspect fiscal records from free-loading on the reputations of Germany and other fiscally responsible states, thereby inflating long-term interest rates for all participants. Others questioned this view: City advisers argued that market forces should be sufficient to discipline govern-ments after EMU, provided it would be made clear that they would not be rescued by others; hence the strong 'no-bailout' clause in the Maastricht Treaty. Some economists were critical of what they saw as undue uniformity and rigidity in the treaty rules; notably Willem Buiter (Buiter et al.1993). A number of critics pointed to the difficulties that the treaty constraints would create for less-adaptable partici-pants in adjusting to adverse shocks if monetary policy is set for the Euro Area as a whole and exchange rates cannot contribute to individual-economy adjustment.[4] For us this is a vital concern and more will be said on it below.

Lack of a central fiscal authority for EMU

In the academic debate that preceded EMU, a chief concern had been that absence of a central government with substantial tax and expenditure functions, or at least a strong central fiscal authority with powers to influence national fiscal policies, would be an important weakness in the prospective monetary union. The literature on optimal currency unions had warned that unless labour and capital can move freely across national borders, countries should not join together in a union that removes all capability of exchange-rate adjustment as a way of accommodating 'asymmetric' shocks – exogenous events that affect individual economies differ-ently – or persistent differences in rates of national productivity growth. One semi-nal contribution concluded that even in the most propitious case, where countries with highly diversified industrial structures join to form a monetary union, 'a wide array of budgetary policies to deal with stubborn "pockets of unemployment"' would be needed (Kenen 1969: 54). Subsequent empirical research investigated the stabilization role played by central fiscal systems in successful existing monetary unions. One much-quoted study found that the automatic fiscal stabilizers operat-ing at the federal level in the United States compensated for some 35–44 per cent of the effects of region-specific shocks to personal incomes (Sachs and Sala-i-Martin 1989); and earlier studies had found broadly comparable results for other industrial countries (MacDougall Report 1977). In contrast it was estimated that no more than about 1 per cent of shocks to income in EC member states were compensated by variations in EC taxes (Eichengreen 1990).

The European Commission and their advisers were well aware of these results, to which attention had been drawn in one of the many official studies of prospects for EMU (European Commission 1993). The Commission were under no misap-prehension that a greater onus would fall on fiscal policy for preserving internal balance in EMU. On the one hand they hoped that national fiscal policy would exert greater leverage in EMU's fixed exchange rate regime than under floating exchange rates, for if rates are flexible the effects of fiscal policy actions tend to leak overseas through currency adjustments driven by interest differentials; but on the other hand they were aware that the scope for fiscal action in EMU would be limited by market discipline based on the 'no bailout' rule, and by the mandatory fiscal limits also being written into the rules. For these reasons, although the Commission hoped national fiscal policies would be effective in addressing temporary shocks under EMU, they did not see fiscal policy as a solution to permanent shocks in the new regime. Their main hope for addressing them was that the new regime would boost wage and price flexibility enough to overcome longer run problems like different national productivity trends.

Some economists felt the Commission was too optimistic on these issues. They feared that national fiscal policies would be less effective in an integrating area with growing cross-border trade and investment 'spillovers'; and increasing factor mobility would make it difficult for national authorities to pursue differential tax policies. They also pointed to the absence of effective obligations or incentives for national governments to coordinate fiscal stances (see Goodhart 1993). Several proposals were put forward for Community stabilisation schemes which would operate through the central budget (Italianer and Vanheukelen 1993; Goodhart and Smith 1993). The essential features of such schemes were that they would be automatic and rapid, and cover only temporary asymmetric disturbances. They should therefore work on the insurance principle and not involve cumulative net income transfers between member states. Critics argued that the benefits from such schemes would be small but the risks of moral hazard, through encouraging governments to adopt irresponsible policies, would be large. But in any case, political considerations at the time made them totally unacceptable to EU governments and the Commission was obliged to kick them into the long grass on that account. (For a fuller discussion and bibliography see Taylor 1995: ch. 6.)

For nearly a decade after EMU came substantially into effect (in 1998, when participants' exchange rates were locked and the single monetary policy began to operate) worries about the lack of a central fiscal authority remained in abeyance; some member states exceeded their fiscal limits but the excesses were mild and did not trouble the financial markets unduly. But worries about them eventually came to the fore with the onset of the global credit crunch in 2008. Many governments responded to that crisis by applying fiscal and monetary stimuli, as well as shoring up banks caught in the US sub-prime crisis. Although the escalation of fiscal deficits in the United States and UK initially attracted the headlines, they were accompanied by comparable fiscal deterioration in several weak-performing EMU states. By 2010 these had become the international focus of attention as bond markets had taken fright at the scale of emerging deficits in Greece and other southern Euro states, and big interest differentials opened up in response to fears of sovereign default. The consequences of these dramatic developments and their implications for the fiscal policy regime in EMU will be discussed in later chapters.

The Japanese predicament

The fragile global environment near the end of the 20th century brought worries that deficient domestic demand had become a chronic problem in a number of developed and emerging economies seemingly characterised by persistently high saving rates, principally in Asia. The problem was particularly serious in Japan, where growth had stalled around 1990 as a result of the banking crisis following the collapse of Japanese equity and property prices; a consequence of rapid financial liberalisation without adequate regulation. (The roller-coaster profile of Japanese equity prices in the 1980s and 1990s was shown in Figure 5.3.) The asset-price collapse in 1990 led to a wave of insolvencies in the Japanese banking system and a subsequent credit crunch which damaged investor and employee confidence and necessitated substantial government bailouts of over-exposed banks. Through the 1990s the Bank of Japan made a series of attempts to stimulate economic recovery by reducing its lending rates to historically low levels, and eventually to zero under the 'zero interest rate policy' (ZIRP). But this policy proved largely ineffective in the face of the chronically high domestic saving rate and massive capital losses on financial assets, even when short-term interest rates became negative in real terms (see Chart A of Box 1.1), until inflation also turned negative for a time. Even when the Bank of Japan finally resorted to unorthodox modes of monetary stimulus – forerunners of the quantitative easing seen in Western regimes during the recent crisis – the economy responded only sluggishly. Observers agree that the Bank of Japan's huge liquidity creation in the mid-1990s helped the banking system to avoid the credit crunch when the dot com boom collapsed, and reduced long-term interest rates, but neither bank lending nor investment seemed to respond. (See Spiegel 2006 for a review and bibliography.)

Economists of a Keynesian persuasion have seen the Japanese predicament as a modern example of one of the most intractable problems experienced in the 1930s: the liquidity trap identified by Keynes in the *General Theory* (Keynes 1936: ch. 13, sec. II) – a situation in which central-bank efforts to drive down interest rates by increasing the money stock result in accumulation of private liquidity rather than extra investment spending.[5] On this view monetary policy is virtually powerless to stimulate aggregate demand when investor confidence is low and interest rates are near zero. Fiscal policy must then step into the breach, even if it means running substantial government deficits and accumulating large government debt stocks (Krugman 1998).

Others have seen the Japanese problem more as a failure by the authorities to deal effectively with the asset-price collapse and associated structural weaknesses, the remedies for which should lie in restructuring banks and industrial firms to improve productivity and profitability. (This was the view of IMF staff economists; see Callen and Ostry 2003.) Yet in the early 1990s many international organisations (including the IMF) supported calls for fiscal stimulus in Japan, and the government there responded with fiscal expansion of unprecedented proportions (visible in Chart B of Box 1.1). By the end of the century there was an erratic recovery in

Japanese GDP, though this was due partly to strong export growth, thanks to the buoyancy of the US and EU economies. Meanwhile by the mid-1990s the IMF and OECD had become concerned about the heavy burden of Japanese public sector debt and argued that the recovery provided an opportunity for fiscal consolidation and tax reform (IMF 1996: 55–6). In the event, the recovery faltered after a few years, leaving unemployment much higher than before the 1990s, and the economy especially vulnerable to global recession.

Japan's predicament illustrates the argument that rigid, uniform fiscal targets may not be appropriate for all economies or in all situations. Overall fiscal balance is unlikely to be a suitable objective for an economy with a secular private-sector saving ratio as high as that of Japan. Instead fiscal targets should take account of institutional circumstances and behaviour patterns in different economies, as well as factors like the stock of public debt in relation to international norms and whether action is needed to reduce it. Yet the 1990s synthesis prescribes budget balance as virtually an article of faith.

The separation of monetary and fiscal policy

For many adherents to the 1990s synthesis, its strong commitment to central-bank independence is an essential principle, without which few central banks might have been capable of maintaining price stability for so long. But some critics expressed worries about the division of responsibility for macroeconomic policy implied by the new settlement.[6] In particular, the separation of responsibilities for monetary and fiscal policy was thought to be at odds with the interdependence that exists between these two branches of policy. There is a danger that if monetary and fiscal decisions are taken separately they will conflict, leading to problems like the 'crowding out' of private investment, which is liable to occur when an expansionary fiscal stance is accompanied by a non-accommodating monetary one.

Defenders of the 1990s synthesis believe that it deals adequately with such problems by relegating fiscal policy to a passive role in support of monetary policy and introducing rules to ensure this. The fiscal limits adopted for EMU exemplify such rules, and comparable constraints have been adopted elsewhere. Yet, as has been suggested above, it is questionable how robust such rules will be when they are put under serious pressure, as has manifestly happened in the recent global recession. These questions are especially relevant for the EMU regime, where the Excessive Deficits Procedure introduced under the Maastricht Treaty (subsequently the EU Treaty) has turned out to lack teeth despite appearances. Even the Stability and Growth Pact agreed by Euro participants has failed to achieve the intended degree of fiscal discipline, as will be seen in Chapter 8. Lack of fiscal policy cohesion in EMU is hardly surprising given that fiscal decisions, unlike monetary ones, are still in the hands of national authorities, most of which still face somewhat different economic situations despite the nominal convergence achieved through EMU, and all of which are subject at times to strong domestic political pressure. The European Commission tries to encourage fiscal policy cooperation between member states and it is practised to a limited extent through information exchanges and peer group pressure in the ECOFIN (finance ministers') Council and the officials' committees that serve it, but efforts to strengthen it have met with little success.

Even in regimes where both monetary and fiscal policies remain exclusively under national control, as in the United States, Japan and UK among others, experience has shown that the fiscal rules are generally more elastic than their monetary counterparts. Above all, fiscal policy generally remains much more subject to political influence than monetary policy in these economies, as recent experience has shown.

If uniform and inflexible fiscal targets and limits are unlikely to offer the best way of coping with the divergent national trends and adverse shocks, as argued above, and if fiscal rules are made more diverse and flexible in various ways, or are simply overridden by political pressures, the case for more effective cooperation between monetary and fiscal policymakers at both national and international levels becomes hard to resist. The modalities of such cooperation will be discussed in Chapter 8.

Weak central bank accountability

The allocation of responsibility for monetary policy to independent central banks, though a much-prized feature of the 1990s synthesis, raises questions about accountability that could well become more prominent if serious dissatisfaction develops with the policy, or if tensions arise between the monetary and other branches of policy.[7] Inevitably, scrutiny of monetary policy is harder to exercise where the central bank is heavily shielded from political influence, as in the case of the European Central Bank, whose freedom from political interference is guaranteed by its Statute and enshrined in the EU Treaty. Accountability arguably works better in countries where there are well-established avenues for scrutiny, as in the United States and UK, where central-bank governors and officials are regularly and publicly interrogated by powerful congressional or parliamentary committees. Reflecting Bundesbank influence in drawing up the ECB constitution, the periods of tenure enjoyed by the president and directors of the ECB are long, their policy deliberations are highly confidential, and they have limited exposure to the Monetary Committee of the European Parliament and none to national parliaments. In addition the national central-bank governors who vote on the ECB Governing Council (its policymaking body) cannot be *required* to answer to their national parliaments (though they may choose to do so).

The ESCB Statute was incorporated in the Maastricht Treaty (subsequently the EU Treaty), as were all the other rules relating to EMU, and for that reason the ECB constitution and arrangements stemming from it can only be amended by consent of all EU member states, including states that have joined since EMU was formed, or will do so in future. This exceptionally strong legal underpinning was intended to be a bulwark protecting the ECB and the EMU regime from political tensions that might conceivably arise in the longer run among the group of sovereign states that comprise the Euro Area. Understandably, the ECB is a keen guardian of its policy autonomy, which contributes greatly to the Bank's authority and prestige. However, such inflexibility may in time inhibit the Euro regime's ability to adapt to shocks or change in the economic environment, and it cannot be ruled out that at some point this inflexibility may create difficulties for cohesion in the Euro Area, especially if and when more states adopt the euro and it becomes increasingly difficult to amend the rules.

In view of the Euro Area's weight in the global trading economy, no assessment of the durability of the 1990s synthesis in Europe can afford to ignore this issue. Outside EMU there seems rather less cause for concern about accountability, as few central banks in other regimes are accorded the complete policy autonomy found in EMU. Even so, the conduct of monetary policy is highly confidential in almost all jurisdictions, and policymakers other than central-bank governors are sometimes reluctant to reveal much about the reasons for their decisions, and from debating them in public. Moreover in most regimes based on the 1990s model, no monetary policymaker, from central-bank governor down, may be removed from office or even pressed to resign by an outside body (unless they commit a serious personal misdemeanour), even if they make important policy errors. While such a privileged official position may be beneficial in protecting an unwavering commitment to the objectives set by government or statute, it places heavy burdens on the individuals concerned, as well as giving them extraordinary economic power.

With a view to remedying the shortcomings of financial regulation in the wake of the recent crisis, central banks at the head of liberalised banking systems are being given more responsibility for overall financial stability, with macro-prudential powers and even new or revamped supervisory functions in some cases, to add to their acknowledged autonomy over monetary policy. As moves proceed in this direction in the major economies, the case for stronger central-bank accountability will become more pressing.

Exogenous threats

Since the turn of the century, the weaknesses inherent in regimes modelled on the 1990s consensus have been increasingly exposed by shocks and adverse trends coming from outside, whether in a geographical or a structural sense. Some of these threats are once-for-all events but others must be expected to persist or recur and increase in severity as the century proceeds, though their probability, extent, frequency and timing cannot be predicted with confidence. Moreover they may come in bunches, or their effects may be symbiotic to some extent, making them harder to cope with. It is now widely accepted that the global credit crunch of 2008 is a powerful example of such interaction, as will be reviewed later. Moreover some of the troublesome structural and environmental tendencies observable in both developed and developing economies, like ageing populations and climate change, will continue and accelerate. The former is a relatively predictable process but the latter is far from being so.

Commodity price shocks

Among the most troublesome events to buffet developed and developing economies in the first decade of this century, recalling those of the 1970s, has been the big
surge in world energy and food prices. These price shocks have been due mainly
to the rising, though at times erratic, pressure of global demand on the supply of
what are essentially finite natural resources. Output growth at or above trend in
the main developed economies for much of the 1990s was swollen after 2000 by a
sharp acceleration of industrialisation and output growth in emerging economies,
especially the two Asian colossi. These mounting pressures on supply have been
exacerbated by disruptions due to military and political conflicts in the Middle East,
reflecting that much of the world's oil reserves are located there; and by reductions
in the availability of agricultural resources for food production as a result of competition from environmental demands, as global warming has begun to affect crop
conditions and grain production has been diverted into bio-fuels as low-carbon
substitutes for oil.

The scale and timing of shocks to commodity prices over the past 50 years is
illustrated in Figure 5.6. As shown there, the recent surge was by no means confined
to oil prices, and was broadly comparable in real terms with what happened in the
1970s. It remains to be seen whether the large real-terms declines that followed the
1970s shocks will be repeated after the recent surges, or whether an early resump-
tion of fast output growth in the emerging world will prevent that from happening.
The sharp drop in commodity prices that occurred in 2008–9 (too recent to be
picked up here) was clearly due to the global recession, but it would be unwise to
interpret it as a return to normality on the scale seen after the 1970s shocks.

Despite the moderation of energy demand hoped for in time as a result of concerted international action to combat climate change, it is hard to be optimistic
about prospects for commodity prices in the longer term. The post-2000 trends in
GDP growth driving these demand pressures seem sufficiently rapid and robust to
outweigh the supply improvements being made from discoveries of new reserves
and more efficient extraction/cultivation techniques, and from the development of
alternative types of energy or foodstuffs. The outcome is likely to be a marked rise
in real prices of energy, foodstuffs and industrial materials in the medium and longer
term. After the oil price hikes of the 1970s and the stagflation of the 1980s, through
to the first few years of the present century, commodity prices were relatively subdued. This greatly assisted inflation control in the early life of the 1990s synthesis,
but these helpful influences have been rudely interrupted in recent years. For the
time being, the recession is masking what may turn out to be a rising secular trend
in real commodity prices, but this trend may well reassert itself as recovery becomes
established. There were already indications by mid-2009 that crude oil prices had
bottomed out, even though the global recession still appeared entrenched then.

Clearly oil price shocks are not a new development, and the latest fluctuation in
crude oil prices has not been much bigger in real terms than those seen in the 1970s.
But in future there will be less scope for replacing oil with other sources of energy,

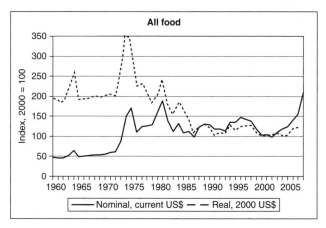

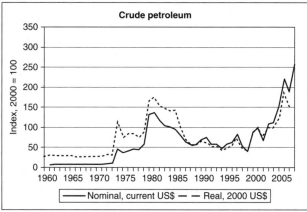

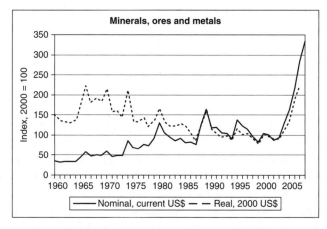

FIGURE 5.6 Commodity price indices, nominal and real, 1960–2008 (source: UNCTAD *Commodity Price Statistics* online database and author's calculations).

Notes: indices of free market prices in US dollars (2000=100). Real prices calculated by deflating nominal prices by an index of world manufacturing prices in US dollars.

unless and until the big investments in alternative energy sources and energy-saving currently under consideration begin to deliver results on a commercial scale. In the meantime, monetary policymakers in countries that rely heavily on imported energy and agricultural products may find that consumer price stability is harder to maintain than in the unusually favourable conditions of the 1990s.

Global warming

Global warming is a relatively new phenomenon which must be expected to have far-reaching economic effects if it occurs on anything like the scale and speed that most scientists now fear. As mentioned above, it is already contributing to higher commodity prices; other effects can readily be envisaged.[8] If the problem is to be addressed effectively, large resources will have to be devoted to production of alternative forms of energy with low carbon emissions and this will involve massive investments in the invention, development and large-scale application of new technology; and very large investments will also have to be made in energy-saving. These investments are unlikely to happen unless there are big and sustained increases in real energy prices (adjusted for general inflation). It will be important that these increases emerge as relative price changes with as little pass-through as possible into general price inflation, but this seems bound to pose difficult challenges for inflation control. Inevitably commodity price increases tend to be regressive overall, since on average poor countries and poor households spend much more of their income on food and energy than their richer counterparts, and this unfortunate feature will generate strong pressure not only for wage increases at the lower end of the spectrum but also for government assistance to maintain at least minimum living standards. This will doubtless translate into political pressure to raise public expenditure on benefits and subsidies for poorer households, and to raise tax rates on richer ones, though the increase in the overall burden of tax should be mitigated by revenues from taxes on carbon emissions.

Much investment in new energy technology is likely to be risky and to involve large external (non-market) benefits and costs. (BP's travails in the Gulf of Mexico through spring and summer 2010 are but the latest manifestation of the risks involved in developing deep-sea oil fields.) To some extent it should be possible to internalise the non-market effects (subject them to market mechanisms) through *emissions trading schemes* – schemes in which permits to emit greenhouse gases beyond limits set by governments are traded between high and low emitters. The largest multi-country example of such programmes is the EU Emissions Trading Scheme. Approaches of this kind should provide producers with incentives to invest in alternative energy sources or energy-saving technology, but they are still in their infancy and their effectiveness is still subject to debate. (See the assessment of the EU Emissions Trading Scheme in Ellerman and Buchner 2007.) However, investment in major new forms of energy generation, such as large-scale wind, wave and tidal power, and in the latest nuclear supply plants, are likely to be beyond the financial scope of such schemes. Instead the latter projects are likely to require substantial sponsorship, pump-priming and subsidy by governments, coupled with improved and probably tighter regulation. It may be possible to finance the associated expenditures to some extent by *emissions taxes*, which set uniform tax rates on carbon emissions and thus work though the price mechanism. One example is the UK Climate Change Levy, a tax on energy delivered to UK non-household users – though these too are subject to drawbacks. Nevertheless the net effect of global warming on general tax burdens in the developed economies will probably be appreciably upwards and this seems bound to create new problems for meeting responsible fiscal targets over the medium/long term. Without a high degree of flexibility in labour and goods markets, there must be a danger that downturns in activity caused by commodity-price increases and energy-tax hikes will turn into prolonged output stagnation and possibly depression. The recent global recession, to which surging energy prices were an important contributory factor, may be a harbinger of more serious problems.

Political instability in vulnerable regions

Among the most painful and intractable problems likely to be created by global warming, even on the most cautious climate-change projections that scientists have produced, is the economic hardship to be expected in regions of the world that stand to suffer from flooding when sea levels rise and droughts last longer as continental weather patterns change. The disasters foreseen in vast areas of low-lying territory and tropical desert-prone regions even in relatively mild climate-change scenarios will add greatly to the tensions that have arisen in the world's most vulnerable regions. Such events must be expected to add to the international and inter-racial tensions that came to prominence unexpectedly soon after the Cold War ended with the collapse of the Soviet empire around 1990. Even without global warming, the long-running Arab–Jewish conflict in the Middle East and the terrorism it has inspired, the two Gulf wars culminating in the US–UK occupation of Iraq after 9/11 in New York, and the NATO operations against the Taliban in Afghanistan and neighbouring parts of Pakistan are not only creating big demands on resources in themselves but also stoking up the ideological and faith-based differences that initially inspired them. Unless diplomacy and war-weariness resolve these conflicts fairly soon, they seem bound to generate increasing political instability, both in the affected regions and further afield. The modern techniques adopted by terrorists with causes to promote in these regions are posing new threats to security even in economies that had hitherto counted themselves among the most secure of the world's democracies.

A number of the largest emerging-market economies are playing important roles in these developments. The development of Iran as the most powerful economy in the Middle East, based on oil, the re-emergence of Russia as a territorially acquisitive power in the Caucasus, with newfound leverage as Europe's major oil supplier, and the arrival of China on the world stage with potential to surpass the GDP of the United States by about 2050 on some forecasts, are threatening to change the global balance of political and economic power. Over the long run, the prospect of such changes seems likely to weaken investors' confidence in the prosperity of the major developed economies, or at least puncture it at times – as evidenced by the fragility of the US dollar and US equity prices since around 2000. As the new century proceeds, developed economies' macro-policy regimes must learn to cope with a greater degree of global political change and instability than has existed since perhaps the deepest phase of the Cold War in the 1960s.

Ageing populations and the pensions time-bomb

For the past three decades a substantial ageing process has been evident in the populations of many developed economies and its continuation through the next half century and beyond is predictable with some confidence, given prevailing trends in birth and mortality rates. Its main cause is the increase in life expectancy due to improvements in public health and welfare, living standards, accommodation, etc., coupled in a number of countries with the effects of the end of the post-Second World War baby boom. While longevity is clearly a welcome development, it implies a persistent decline in the proportion of the population of working age. Although the consequences for the labour supply will also depend on future participation/activity rates, which are harder to predict, sharp increases in dependency ratios are expected in mature economies over the next 30 years. These will bring an appreciable decline in the growth of productive potential there, unless productivity accelerates for some other reason, which seems unlikely, or there is a marked increase in employees' normal retirement age, which seems more likely, and is already underway in economies facing intense fiscal pressures after the global recession. The adjustment burdens may also be mitigated somewhat by net immigration of people of working age from poorer countries, as will be noted later.

Despite these mitigating factors, the rise in dependency ratios seems bound to lead to a substantial increase in the overall burden of pension provision in developed economies, assuming that cuts in real pension entitlements will not be generally acceptable and that increases in the average retirement age will compensate only partially for the increase in life expectancy. Projections based on current real benefit commitments and retirement ages imply heavily increased fiscal burdens by 2050, particularly in regimes that rely heavily on government 'pay as you go' (PAYG) systems, as in many continental European countries.[9]

It used to be thought that the countries with relatively parsimonious state pension systems and the bulk of provision through voluntary private funded pensions, notably the United States and UK, would escape the worst effects of the 'pensions time bomb', but in the last ten years this has been recognised as too complacent a view. The underlying trend in private-sector employer pension contributions in the UK and similar regimes has been downward since the early 1980s, and for a decade or more until the late 1990s total private pension saving fell increasingly below the levels needed to fund many 'defined benefit' schemes (with benefits linked to final salary). Slowness to appreciate the implications of increasing life expectancy was partly to blame, but the under-provision was exacerbated in Anglo-Saxon economies by contribution holidays induced by the long unbroken equity price boom through the last two decades of the 20th century. Only when that boom was eventually punctured by the bursting of the Internet bubble in 2000–2 did the huge size of the funding gap in numbers of private pension schemes in the United States and UK become apparent. For example, an analysis by *The Times* newspaper in early 2006 estimated that 15 of the UK's largest blue-chip companies (the FTSE 100) had pension-fund deficits equivalent to more than 10 per cent of the market value of their shares (*The Times*, 12 January 2006). These funding gaps will have increased as a result of the stock market collapse in 2007–8. As a result, increasing numbers of defined benefit schemes are being closed to new members and a shift to less-generous 'defined contribution' schemes (with benefits determined by the fund's assets, sometimes termed 'money purchase' schemes) is now well underway in the UK private sector.

Solving the problems created by ageing populations, under-provision for rising life expectancy and the vagaries of stock markets in regimes reliant on private funding, will require hard political decisions on issues such as the acceptable level of state pension entitlements relative to earnings and increasing the state retirement age. Crucial also will be what happens to personal and company savings propensities as individuals and firms in the affected economies arrive at a more realistic appreciation of the need for greater private retirement provision. However, it seems clear that unless governments are prepared to impose much higher tax burdens on working households and firms in order to finance the increasing cost of state pensions, and to play a much bigger part themselves in investing the proceeds, private saving of one kind or another will have to play a bigger role in pensions provision in most developed economies. In that case governments will have to decide how far such provision can be left to be essentially voluntary, how far increased tax incentives can be afforded to encourage private provision, and how far participation by employers and employees in such schemes will have to be made compulsory (or semi-compulsory through automatic enrolment with opt-outs).[10]

Concerns about the risks and uncertain returns associated with private saving for pension provision have been heightened by the big collapses and only partial recovery in the world's major stock markets during the recent global financial crisis. Share-price instability has, understandably, come to be regarded as a serious problem by ordinary working households which depend on private funds for their future pensions. Moreover, a switch to greater reliance on funded pensions, if it implies greater share ownership by or on behalf of ordinary households, may contribute to greater instability of aggregate demand and activity in the economies concerned; so too may extension of share ownership to a wider section of the population. At present this is more a problem for Anglo-Saxon regimes than for their Continental European counterparts, but it will become more widespread there too as the pressures for privately funded pensions and wider share ownership spread.

Needs of the poorest economies

As the 21st century proceeds, there must unfortunately be a serious risk that economic and political tensions will develop between the world's poorer economies and the developed-market economies and that these will create demands on the latter's resources and goodwill which will add to their macro-policy problems. This seems too important a topic to be ignored in any policy review but there is insufficient space here to do more than touch on a few salient points.

If the adverse global trends outlined above continue even to only a mild extent, it is hard to avoid the conclusion that the poorest countries will suffer disproportionately. The combination of the rising pressure of economic growth on scarce material resources, adverse climate change due to global warming, emergence of highly competitive Asian economies to rival (and perhaps eventually surpass) the economic dominance of the United States and EU, and the further intensification of ideological differences between the existing superpower, the main emerging superpower China, and others that command large reserves of oil, water and other scarce commodities, will impinge hardest on the poorest countries of Africa, Asia and the Middle East, which are most lacking in natural resources, skills and education, and have vulnerable topographies and ecosystems. In these circumstances both humanitarian motives and the self-interest of the richer economies will generate strong pressures for them to provide greater investment and aid to the poorest countries as the century proceeds. Rising assistance to these countries is likely to be seen as a necessary condition for peace and harmony between developed and developing countries, which the former should be ready and willing to meet for both selfish and altruistic reasons, subject to the proviso that aid should be put to sustainable productive use, including civilised law and order and good governance.

It is hard if not impossible at present to attach even broad orders of magnitude to the likely volumes of assistance needed to address these needs in the medium/long term. However, it is unnecessary to do so in order to recognise that these needs will involve rising demands on donor economies' resources, and add appreciably to the policy problems faced by their monetary and fiscal authorities, as they strive to meet the objectives of the new policy consensus.

Over the past two decades a combination of circumstances has been leading to increased net migration from the developing to the developed world. Among the key factors behind this tendency have been: rising popular aspirations in the 'third world', generated by improved communications (the spread of television, the Internet and cellular telephones to developing economies, conveying perhaps an unduly favourable picture of living conditions in the developed world) and improved primary education in poorer economies; the removal of draconian restrictions on travel from countries previously in the Soviet or wider Communist sphere, and of sanctions against travel from places like South Africa; the emergence of repressive regimes backed by modern weaponry and technology (supplied by the developed economies) in many other parts of Africa, and of bitter military conflicts in the Balkans, Iraq and Afghanistan, which have led to increasing numbers of displaced persons seeking asylum or to escape large-scale hostilities and destruction; and finally the spread of globalisation in its various manifestations, including the relaxation of barriers to large-scale labour migration, for example within the expanding European Union and on the southern border of the United States.

International migration cannot of course be regarded as a new phenomenon after a century that saw the mass migrations from Europe to North America in the decades before the First World War and the relocation of displaced populations in Central and Eastern Europe after the Second World War. Those movements created large demands for transport, utilities and social overhead capital in the host economies, while providing much of the additional labour required for such investment, skilled as well as unskilled. But such investments would not have been possible without large increases in both private and public savings to finance them. The same is no less true of the wave of migration taking place in the present century. Net migration into the developed economies in the past two decades has led to an acceleration of population growth there. The acceleration is particularly marked in the UK, where population growth since 2000 has exceeded 0.5 per cent per annum compared with 0.3 per cent per annum in the 1990s and about 0.15 per cent per annum in the previous two decades (according to OECD data). Most of this increase has been due to net inward immigration. According to OECD data US population growth has also increased, from 1 per cent per annum in the period 1970–90 to nearly 1.25 per cent per annum in the 1990s, though it has fallen back a little since then.

Immigration is also raising the active labour force and thus productive potential in the developed economies, offsetting some of the effects of population ageing noted above, but it also seems bound to create extra demands for investment in housing, education, transport and social infrastructure there. It may also raise unemployment among older or less-skilled workers in the indigenous populations of the host regions. Such effects will add to pressures for increases in public expenditure and make it harder to observe the fiscal constraints in the 1990s consensus. Some of these pressures can already be seen in the UK and other recipients of net immigration, and they may well grow in the long run unless global warming and ideological conflicts turn out less serious than is widely feared.

Competition from emerging economies

Since around the turn of the century there has been rapid growth of highly efficient, low-cost industrial production in a number of large Asian emerging economies, notably China and India, and some of the region's smaller progressive economies like Taiwan and Singapore. The growth has been associated with a widespread process of urbanisation – movement of peasant populations from rural areas to industrial centres, attracted by the relatively high wages and job security offered by industrial employment. In some respects this process recalls the age of industrialisation in Europe and America in the 19th century, with its heavy reliance on the movement of cheap rural labour into industrial towns. The combination in emerging economies of low wages (relative to those in the developed world) and high productivity from the spread of best-practice technology means that producers there routinely outperform their developed-economy competitors in traditional or low-technology industries, where unskilled workers are particularly vulnerable to foreign competition.

This development was augmented by the recovery that eventually took place among the former South East Asian 'tiger' economies – South Korea, Thailand, Malaysia, etc. – from the financial crisis that swept through that region in 1997–9. Benefiting from the gains in competitiveness due to the large depreciations in their currencies during the crisis, these economies have managed to rebuild output and productivity in their traditional export industries. In addition their competitiveness has benefited from the global spread of satellite-based telecommunications in the past decade, which has meant that their comparative advantage as suppliers of abundant cheap and well-trained labour is increasingly felt in the high-technology and service industries of developed economies, which can now readily outsource their labour-intensive operations to remote locations (the 'call centre' syndrome). Moreover the strategy pursued by many emerging economies of linking their currencies to the US dollar has meant that their real exchange rates have fallen with the dollar against those of non-dollar developed economies, further boosting the former's competitiveness. As a result there was a sustained burst of export growth by the developing economies, small as well as large, from 2000 to 2007, as may be seen in Figure 5.7. The outcome was a sharp acceleration of export-based output

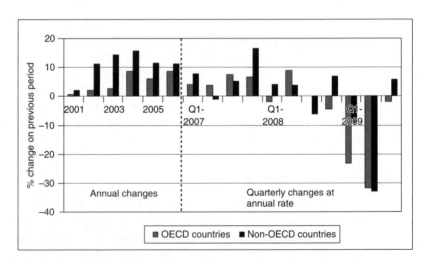

FIGURE 5.7 Export growth, OECD and non-OECD economies, 2000–9 (annual changes 2000–6; quarterly 2007–9) (source: OECD Stat online database and author's calculations).

Notes: changes in volumes of exports of goods and services in constant (2000) US dollars. Percentage changes on previous period, all expressed at annual rates.

growth in the emerging world which was an important contributor to the global boom of those years as will be seen shortly, and thus to the commodity price surge that followed.

The gains in export competitiveness made by emerging economies in the past two decades have led to debate about the cost-benefit implications for the developed world. Some economists have expressed concerns that the fierce competition from low-cost economies is creating 'dual economy' problems in the older industrial economies, implying widening income and employment gaps between professional and skilled occupations in sophisticated industries which are less vulnerable to emerging-market competition, and unskilled groups in low-technology fields that are highly exposed to external competition.[11] Others have argued that the abundant supplies of low-cost products from emerging economies are beneficial to the older economies and that the solution lies in industrial and occupational adjustment there over time. This will require more investment in high-technology industries and the R&D that creates them, and in workforce retraining and adult education, but even so political pressure is likely to emerge for measures to redistribute income from high-skilled occupational groups to supplement the pay of low-skilled indigenous groups.

In emerging economies the solution would ideally involve an improvement in the wage rates and working conditions of the industrialised labour forces there relative to those in developed economies. This would be beneficial not only for humanitarian reasons but also because it would narrow the competitive disadvantage felt by developed-world manufacturing and generate the purchasing power needed in emerging economies to absorb some of the output that presently goes into their burgeoning export surpluses. It would also generate long-term consumer confidence among households in Asian economies that seemed locked at the moment in a high-saving mentality. Without a marked strengthening of domestic absorption in these economies, it will be hard to achieve the much-needed adjustment in global saving and fiscal imbalances that have contributed significantly to the recent financial crisis, as will be explained later. Moreover, in the absence of adequate industrial and occupational restructuring in the developed world, and without reduction of wage gaps between the urban populations of the emerging and developed worlds, it may be hard to avoid rising pressure for trade protection which would be much more damaging for both types of economy in the long run.

Sovereign wealth funds and the 'global saving glut'

A notable consequence of the rise in crude oil prices and the burgeoning competitiveness of emerging economies since the turn of the century has been the growing presence on the international capital markets of entities known as sovereign wealth funds (SWFs). These are state-owned funds holding mainly foreign financial assets – bonds, equities, property portfolios, etc., issued in developed economies and denominated in their currencies. The earliest SWFs originated as foreign reserve holdings of oil-producing states in the 1970s, but in time their aims evolved to include long-term investment as well as liquidity management and currency stabilisation. The funds under their charge have grown rapidly since the early 2000s to reach $3.3 trillion in 2009 according to a City research agency (International Financial Services London 2009), equivalent to nearly one-quarter of US annual GDP. Over two-thirds of these holdings still derive from oil and gas revenues but the volume of non-commodity funds is also growing rapidly. A number of SWFs are known to have invested heavily in US and Swiss banks, and must consequently have made big losses in the course of the recent crisis. However, market commentators expect them to resume rapid growth when the global economy recovers. If so their holdings could overtake those of more traditional sovereign investors (public-sector pension funds, development funds and state-owned corporations) and official foreign exchange reserves, which are put at around $6 trillion and $5.3 trillion respectively (International Financial Services London 2009).

The expansion of SWF holdings in recent years has raised concerns in host economies where there are large elements of foreign ownership in strategic industries. The antitrust authorities and financial regulators of these economies have related concerns about inadequate transparency and compliance. Some governments are setting up procedures to limit foreign investments in sensitive industries, and the OECD is producing a code of conduct in this area. More importantly, however, the growth of SWFs is a manifestation of a much wider problem: the large flow of mobile capital to receptive developed economies as a result of high saving in emerging economies, and a few major high-income economies, since the late 1990s.

Attention was first drawn to the phenomenon of the 'global saving glut' by US Federal Reserve Governor (now Chairman) Bernanke in a speech offering a new explanation for the expanding US external current payments deficit (Bernanke 2005). He focused not on familiar domestic weaknesses like poor trade performance and weak household saving, but on the appearance of high saving rates among the fast-growing economies of Asia and South America, which had switched from being net importers to exporters of capital after recovering from the East Asian financial crisis and the associated crises in Russia, Brazil and Argentina. Governments of these economies began accumulating 'war chests' of foreign assets, partly in order to avoid their currencies appreciating against competitors and partly to secure the more attractive long-term returns available on foreign assets. Ageing populations were also a cause of high saving in some emerging economies (China) and high-income economies (Japan and Germany). Much of this mobile capital flowed into US securities and property via international banks, though several small developed economies with aggressive banks (notably Iceland) received proportionately much larger inflows.

In some cases the excess savings were generated through government budget surpluses, chiefly in the sparsely-populated oil-exporting economies of the Middle East. Otherwise the main source was high private saving in low-income, high-population economies, which was channelled by state agencies through the international capital markets to low-saving economies where long-term yields were higher and banking systems seemed to have the capacity to invest the funds securely.

The capital inflows depressed yields in host economies, boosting expenditure on imports and generating trade deficits as counterparts to the capital inflows. A contributory factor, less emphasised by Bernanke, was the one noted above – the large trade surpluses built up by low-wage economies able to avoid currency appreciation against the dollar.

Though the process offered some benefits for high-saving economies, as Bernanke admitted, the approach was unlikely to be sustainable indefinitely, as recent events have shown. The flows of cheap finance into the banking systems of low-saving economies fuelled the unsustainable credit booms and asset price bubbles of the late 1990s, creating the preconditions for financial crisis. At some point saving rates in the host economies will have to rise to provide the resources needed to service their rising external debts and to meet the needs of their own ageing populations, whereas most emerging economies, having younger and faster-growing workforces but being relatively capital-poor, are natural importers of capital.

The China syndrome

There can be no more dramatic illustration of the factors behind the global saving glut and the problems arising from it than mainland China's emergence as a major world economy since the turn of the century. As may be seen in Table 5.1, China's share of world output nearly doubled in the first decade of the present century (when measured in dollars of equal purchasing power). IMF projections put China's GDP at over 13 per cent of the world total in 2010, not far below that of the United States, and equivalent to over half of the combined GDP of the four major economies in our main tables. The Chinese economy has grown at around 10 per cent per annum in real terms since the early 1990s, with only a mild slowdown in the recent global recession, as may be seen in Table 5.2. Like many fast-growing emerging economies, much of China's output growth in the past

TABLE 5.1 China and four major economies: current-price GDP,[a] 2000–10 (trillions of US dollars)

	2000	2008	2010[b]
China	3.0	4.5	5.4
Share of world total %	*7.2*	*11.4*	*13.3*
United States	10.0	14.4	14.8
UK	1.5	2.2	2.2
Germany	2.2	2.9	2.9
Japan	3.2	4.3	4.3
Total, four majors	16.9	23.9	24.1
Share of world total %	*40.0*	*34.5*	*33.0*

Source: IMF *World Economic Outlook* online database.

Notes: [a] Valued in US dollars using PPP exchange rates.
　　　　[b] IMF projections.

TABLE 5.2 China: key economic indicators 1992–2010

	1992–2001 average	2002–6 average	2007	2008	2009	2010[a]
GDP growth, volume % p.a.	10.3	10.2	13.0	9.6	8.7	10.0
Consumer price inflation, % p.a.	6.9	1.5	4.8	5.9	-0.7	3.1
Central government net lending/borrowing, % of GDP	..	3.9	6.3	6.2	6.1	5.4
Current balance, % of GDP	1.4	5.1	11.0	9.4	5.8	6.2
Ratio of reserves to imports[b]	..	105	148	158	212	189
Exchange rate, yuan per US dollar	8.3	8.2	7.6	7.0	6.8	6.8

Source: IMF *World Economic Outlook* online database.

Notes: [a] IMF projections.
  [b] Official reserves at year-end as per cent of imports of goods and services.
  .. indicates that data is not available.

decade has been export driven. This has created a massive current-account surplus of some 5–11 per cent of GDP since the turn of the century, as also shown in Table 5.2.

China's formidable export performance has been attributable partly to the buoyant and open markets offered by developed economies through the past two decades, and partly to the competitiveness of its manufacturing output. China's remarkable competitiveness is due to persistently low labour costs and a relatively low exchange rate for its national currency the Renminbi (RMB) against the major currencies. As Table 5.2 shows, the RMB (or yuan) has been almost stable in nominal terms against the US dollar since the early 1990s (though appreciating somewhat in the past few years); even though Chinese inflation was significantly higher than US inflation on average until 2009, its costs and prices in dollars have remained well below those of many of the United States' other main competitors.

The near-stability of the yuan/dollar rate over nearly two decades has been maintained through an exchange-rate policy designed to maintain export competitiveness. This strategy has taken advantage of the dollar's substantial depreciation against most other major currencies since the early 2000s, which has meant that the RMB has depreciated significantly against most third currencies. The policy has involved regular and substantial exchange-market intervention by the Bank of China, selling yuan for dollars and adding them to the official reserves. As a result China's ratio of official reserves to imports has roughly doubled since the early 2000s (Table 5.2); its reserves now comprise over 40 per cent of the official reserves of all developing and emerging economies (Table 5.3). Without the intervention and the substantial other foreign investment undertaken by Chinese sovereign funds, the RMB would have appreciated much more than it has, and the economy's competiveness and its current external surplus would have been lower, other things being equal.

TABLE 5.3 China in the world economy: external current balances and reserves, 2008–10 (billions of US dollars)

	2008	2010[a]
External current balance		
China	426	335
All emerging and developing economies	709	420
United States	−578	−368
UK	−15	−13
Germany	296	235
Japan	170	159
Official reserves (end-year)		
China	1,951	2,706
All emerging and developing economies	5,961	6,133

Source: IMF World Economic Outlook online database.

Notes: [a] IMF projections.

China's policy of linking the RMB to the dollar has been subject to strong criticism from its competitors, especially the United States. The criticism has focused on the huge size of China's external current account surplus and the contribution it has made to the global payments imbalances in recent years. As Table 5.3 shows, China's external current surplus now accounts for the bulk of the combined net external balance of all emerging and developing economies, and it has more than matched the US external current deficit over the past few years. Although the US deficit cannot be attributed directly or solely to the Chinese surplus, the two imbalances are clearly related. In recent years these concerns have persuaded the IMF to introduce a new type of exchange-rate surveillance, to be conducted from the viewpoint of the *international* interest, not just that of the economy concerned (reported in the *Financial Times*, 19 June 2007); the triggers for this surveillance are large-scale currency intervention and 'fundamental exchange-rate misalignment'.

In a perceptive critique of this IMF initiative, the Australian economist Max Corden took issue with the emphasis on exchange-rate policy as the cause of China's persistent current account surplus. Instead he attributes the surplus to the excess of saving over investment in the domestic economy (Corden 2007: 2, fn. 2).[12] Much Chinese saving is undertaken by households, reflecting the absence of an adequate social safety net and limited access to financial markets, but Corden singles out the government's fiscal surplus for attention. (As may be seen in Table 5.2, Chinese central government net lending has averaged between 4 and just over 6 per cent of GDP through the past decade, and it seems clearly correlated with the current external surplus.) He argues that, in the absence of the fiscal surplus, sustained central-bank intervention to avoid RMB appreciation would have been inflationary, whether or not the impact on the domestic money stock would have been sterilised.[13] Had a stable nominal exchange rate been maintained for the RMB in the absence of a fiscal surplus, Chinese inflation would have been higher and that would have resulted in *real RMB appreciation* against other currencies, which would have removed much of the external surplus, other things being equal. That surplus was therefore due to the surplus of domestic saving over investment rather than to exchange-rate policy. Thus fiscal policy has been a basic cause of the 'China syndrome'.

Corden's focus on China's high saving rate as the main cause of its external payments surplus accords with the view taken in these pages. However, it did not lead him in 2007 to criticise China's fiscal surplus as a source of global financial imbalances, in the way voiced by the policy's US detractors. Instead he defended China's fiscal stance as a sensible way of 'parking' the economy's excess savings pending removal of the administrative obstacles and capital-market inefficiencies that hamper investment in China (2007: 7–8). He also saw China's surplus saving as being in the interest of developed economies, which benefited from the availability of cheap capital and low global real interest rates. The latter view was fairly typical of received economic opinion at the time. With hindsight it may seem remarkable that, even at that late stage, perceptive observers failed to anticipate the global financial cataclysm of 2007–8.

6

THE GLOBAL FINANCIAL CRISIS

The crash of 2007–8

The global financial crisis that broke with tremendous force in the late summer of 2007 has received wide coverage in the media and official reports, and only the main features need recapitulation here.[1] In many respects the crisis resembled a 'perfect storm' in that almost everything that could go wrong in innovative but over-exposed banking systems did go wrong: imprudent lending and faulty risk-management by bankers; destabilising activity by speculators; misjudgements by credit rating agencies; slackness and incompetence among financial regulators; and errors by central banks and finance ministries not only in the management of the crisis but also in the conduct of macroeconomic policy. A key question is whether the crash was a truly exceptional event – a massive stroke of bad luck, such as might occur once in a lifetime or even a century – or a disaster waiting to happen. If the latter is nearer the truth then macroeconomic policy, and indeed the policy regime itself (the 1990s synthesis) must be partly to blame.

The genesis of the crisis can be traced back to the exceptionally strong world economic boom which took off several years into the new century. The boom was exceptional not only in that world output growth rates of 4 per cent p.a. were well above previous averages, but also because it was led by fast growth in China, India and the large economies of South America and Eastern Europe, as can be seen in Table 6.1. Output growth in the emerging economies was substantially export-led (as shown in Figure 5.7), thanks to their competitive edge in world manufacturing markets and to developed economies' readiness to absorb rising imports. In contrast, growth in the developed economies, especially those with aggressive and lightly regulated banking systems, was driven by housing and consumption expenditure, fuelled by cheap finance from high-saving economies, as explained in Chapter 5. Credit creation in light-touch regimes was given extra leverage by

TABLE 6.1 Growth of real GDP, developed and developing economies, 1970–2007 (annual averages, per cent per year)

	1970–89	1990–9	2000–5	2006	2007
World	3.3	2.7	2.8	4.0	3.8
Developed economies	2.9	2.4	1.9	2.8	2.5
Developing economies	4.5	5.0	5.4	7.1	7.3
Asia	6.1	6.8	6.5	7.9	8.1
Of which: China	8.2	11.0	9.6	11.1	11.4
India	..	6.0	6.9	9.2	9.7
South America	3.4	3.5	2.8	5.3	6.5
Of which: Argentina	0.9	4.6	2.2	8.5	8.7
Brazil	4.9	3.0	2.8	3.7	5.4
Transition economies	4.2	−5.7	6.1	7.2	8.2
Of which Russia	..	..	6.2	6.7	8.1

Source: UNCTAD *Statistical Handbook 2008*, 'Development Indicators' database.

Notes: Growth of GDP at national base-year prices.
  .. indicates that data is not available.

relaxation of the lending criteria normally applied in mortgage finance and by the use of instruments like asset-backed securities (ABS) and securitised investment vehicles (SIVs) to transfer large bundles of mortgage loans off the books of specialist mortgage lenders and onto those of international banks and securities houses with little or no direct mortgage business.

The world boom generated a big surge in commodity prices, as also seen earlier (Figure 5.6). The shock to input costs fed quickly into developed economies' consumer prices and the inflationary pressure began to worry policymakers. Central banks responded by raising short-term interest rates, as may be seen in Figure 6.1: the US Federal Funds rate was pushed up sharply between 2003 and 2006; rather less aggressive tightening followed in the UK and the Euro Area, and eventually in Japan. Commercial bank lending rates and long-term rates responded in due course, though less than proportionately, reflecting the inertia in longer-term rates mentioned earlier.

The combination of soaring energy and food prices and sharp monetary tightening squeezed real incomes in developed economies from 2005 onwards. By early 2007 the effects of the squeeze began to show dramatically in the US housing market, where sub-prime mortgages had grown to comprise about 10 per cent of all variable-rate mortgages, and where higher mortgage interest costs and rising unemployment led to increasing debt-servicing difficulties for low-income households. Over the next 12 months the house-price bubbles that had developed in the United States, UK, and other property-oriented economies since 2000 finally burst. In the United States increasing numbers of sub-prime borrowers found they could not service their debts or sell their houses, and many were approaching foreclosure

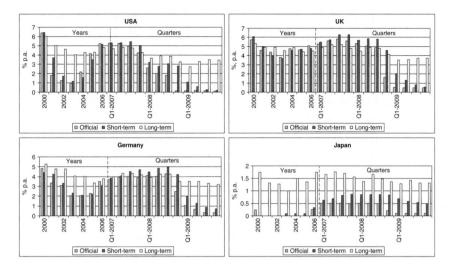

FIGURE 6.1 Official, short-term and long-term interest rates, four major economies (annual averages 2000–6; quarterly 2007–9) (source: OECD Stat, 'Financial Indicators' from 'Monthly Economic Indicators' online database).

Notes: 'Official': overnight or discount rates charged by central bank for advances to banking system; 'Short-term': three-month interbank, Treasury-Bill or CD rates; 'Long-term': ten-year government bond yields to residual maturity. Annual averages or end-quarters at annual rates.

by autumn 2007. In the year to September 2008, US median house prices fell by about 10 per cent, and by much more in problem regions.

What originated as a local crisis in heavily-mortgaged regions of the United States soon spread to the 'shadow' banking system there and abroad – investment banks, hedge funds and deposit-taking subsidiaries of financial conglomerates – as large swathes of mortgage-backed securities held by these institutions came to be regarded as nearly worthless. In the winter of 2007–8 there was a spectacular collapse of confidence in the main US and EU financial centres as interbank markets froze nearly solid and liquidity drained away from vulnerable banks. Nationalisation of one of the UK's largest mortgage lenders, Northern Rock, in February 2008 and the enforced takeover of the fifth-largest US investment bank Bear Sterns in March confirmed the seriousness and international character of the credit crunch.

Credit default swaps

The vulnerability of apparently well-capitalised and expertly-staffed investment banks to what seemed local problems in the US mortgage market was indicative of the spread of excessive risk-taking across a much wider area of banking business than mortgage lending. One of the chief props for such risk-taking, and arguably a major contributor to the difficulties of investment banks like Bear Stearns, was the growth of contracts known as 'credit default swaps' (CDS). These are a type of financial derivative in which the buyer makes a series of payments to the seller, in return for the latter's promise to pay the buyer a lump sum in the event of a designated bond or loan to a third party going into default. CDS are thus a kind of insurance, but unlike conventional insurance the buyer need not own the underlying security and the seller need not own reserves to cover the risk of default, or be regulated in any way. Moreover CDS are traded on over-the-counter markets rather than through organised exchanges with open information on deals and centralised clearing houses, and therefore lack transparency as well as regulation. Yet before the crisis they were widely believed to offer satisfactory protection against default, and probably contributed to a false sense of security among investors and banks. At their peak they reached huge magnitudes: the notional (book) value of the CDS market was officially put at $58 trillion by September 2008 (see US Securities and Exchange Commission 2008), though it was down to some $30 trillion by March 2009, perhaps 5 per cent of outstanding derivatives.

Some commentators have argued that CDS contributed disproportionately to the financial difficulties of investment banks because of the contracts' extreme sensitivity to speculative activity. Thus, as investor confidence in suspect banks waned in the weeks before their collapse, their CDS spreads (gaps between buying and selling prices) widened dramatically as buyers rushed to hedge against them. Admittedly the rush to secure protection against a Bear Sterns default may have been as much a symptom as a cause of the event (see Barr 2009). However, the US authorities were convinced that trading in CDS worsened the crisis and urged the Congress to act quickly to regulate them (US Securities and Exchange Commission 2008).

Policy responses

Central banks responded to the sub-prime crisis and the problems it created for the shadow banking sector by cutting interest rates further and pumping emergency liquidity into their banking systems, but these actions did not contain the crisis, partly because spreads between official rates and lending rates widened considerably on the way down, as was shown in Figure 6.1. The credit crunch and its attendant alarms caused industrial firms in the United States and UK to cut output in late 2007 and again, much more heavily, in the second half of 2008 (see Figure 6.2). The output cuts were especially severe in the automotive industry, and by late 2008 swingeing export cuts were felt by both developed and emerging economies (as Figure 5.7 shows). In contrast, as Figure 6.2 suggests, retail sales held up relatively well initially, as usually happens in recessions.

In an effort to combat the deepening recession, governments across the developed world applied fiscal stimuli according to their different perceptions of the downswing and their room for manoeuvre, and central banks cut their lending rates to historically low levels by late 2008. Despite these efforts at stimulation the credit crunch continued: by summer 2008 increasing numbers of banks in light-touch jurisdictions found themselves in difficulties, culminating in the bankruptcy of the

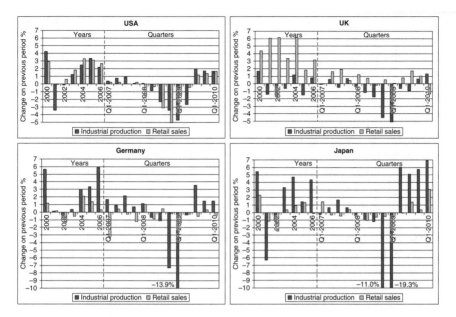

FIGURE 6.2   Changes in industrial production and retail sales, four major economies (annually 2000–6; quarterly 2007Q1–10Q1) (source: OECD Stat, 'Key Short-term Indicators' database).

Notes: percentage changes in volumes on previous period, annually 2000–6; quarterly (seasonally adjusted) thereafter.

fourth-largest US investment bank, Lehman Brothers, in September. Thereafter the recession deepened sharply in the United States, where unemployment rose from some 3.5 per cent in spring 2007 to 7.5 per cent in January 2009.

The decision of the US authorities not to rescue Lehman Brothers, a flagship international bank and one that had been widely thought too big to be allowed to fail, so alarmed the financial markets that other leading names came under serious threat and for a brief spell the banking systems of the United States and UK faced meltdown. It became clear in both economies that piecemeal efforts to rescue individual banks would not overcome the crisis and system-wide support was imperative. Both the US and UK Treasuries realised they had to mount emergency operations to remove large amounts of toxic assets from the balance sheets of loss-making banks, though opposition in the Congress delayed US action for several weeks. Finally, over a long weekend of frenetic activity at the start of October 2008 the UK Treasury launched a massive financial bailout to shore up the capital of the eight high-street banks by offering to purchase preference shares in any that required it (most did), and guaranteeing a large slice of the debt issued by them. The UK authorities confirmed by this drastic action that no major British bank would be allowed to fail, even if it meant that some would have to be effectively nationalised. Initially the US administration had hesitated to adopt this approach, but after a few weeks the US Treasury put in place somewhat similar provisions, including emergency share purchases of US banks if needed to restore liquidity.[2]

In tandem with these actions the Bank of England extended it special liquidity scheme to swap government bonds for banks' toxic assets. In early 2009, both it and the Federal Reserve stunned the markets by announcing their intention to undertake 'quantitative easing' – injecting large amounts of new money into the economy by purchasing outstanding securities from banks and other holders with the aim of reducing long-term yields. These bold and unconventional actions by the central banks in charge of the world's two largest financial centres appeared to calm the markets both domestically and abroad, and in due course confidence in their banking systems recovered somewhat. By spring 2009 there were signs that bank lending in the United States and UK had stabilised, though at a low level.

The financial markets appeared to draw further confidence from the London G20 Summit in April. At that meeting, G20 governments agreed to provide $1.1 trillion of extra balance of payments finance via the IMF and World Bank and $200 billion of extra trade finance, all aimed mainly at developing countries. When added to the $5 trillion of fiscal stimuli applied in individual countries in response to the crisis (reported in the *Guardian* newspaper, 3 April 2009), these provisions brought the total of emergency injections to approximately 1 per cent of OECD countries' GDP. But even if mobilised quickly these injections could hope to counter only part of the fall of some 4 per cent in developed economies' GDP forecast for 2009 by the IMF at the time of the Summit – the largest annual fall in these economies' output since the 1950s. A recovery of uncertain strength was expected to start some time in 2010, but unemployment in the majors was projected to continue rising through that year, to reach 10 per cent in the UK and over 10 per cent in the United States. (In spring 2010 the rises in unemployment in the major economies were turning out to be rather slower and smaller than forecast, but they were continuing.)

Lessons from the financial crisis

Much effort has gone into diagnosing the causes of the crash and prescribing remedies. Independent commentators largely agree that there was a widespread failure of business judgement at board and management levels in banks and shadow banks operating in light-touch jurisdictions. Many kinds of shortcomings are thought to have contributed, among which imprudence, greed, poor corporate governance, professional and technical incompetence and badly-designed incentive schemes have frequently been mentioned.

System-wide banking crises are not of course unprecedented. It has long been recognised in the literature that freely-functioning financial markets are prone to speculative bubbles and band-wagon processes which burst with damaging effect sooner or later. Explanations go back to Keynes' famous 'animal spirits' – the 'innate urge that makes the wheels go round', which is at the root of investors' unstable long-term expectations (Keynes 1936: ch. 12, sec. VII). Subsequent explanations in the Keynesian tradition include the 'financial instability hypothesis' put forward by Hyman Minsky in the 1960s, in which he argued that periodic financial crises are inherent in unregulated capitalist systems (see Minsky 1992 for a restatement of this idea). These themes have found more recent expression as 'irrational exuberance' (a term coined by Fed Chairman Alan Greenspan) in a best-selling study by Robert Shiller, who predicted that the sustained stock market boom of the late 20th century would burst sooner or later (Shiller 2000). Yet in the latest episode the post-crash plunge in equity prices was larger even than after the 1929 crash (see Bank of England 2009a: 13), and the downturn in the real economy after one year was broadly on a par with the Great Depression, though by autumn 2009 it was expected to be less prolonged.

Explanations of the exceptional severity of the 2007–8 crash identify a range of causes, most of which have already been mentioned: the root and branch liberalisation of financial institutions in the Anglo-Saxon economies from the 1970s onwards; the subsequent globalisation of capital markets and provision of financial services; and the hubris following the perceived triumph of free-market capitalism after the collapse of the Soviet system in 1990.[3] With hindsight some economists accept that major errors of macroeconomic policy also contributed to the crisis. In a discussion paper soon after the crash, John Llewellyn, former Global Chief Economist at Lehman Brothers, argued that it was interaction between multiple causes working at both the macro and micro levels that made the crisis so severe (Llewellyn 2009).

There is wide agreement among practitioners and in official reports that systemic weakness in the banking industry was due in part to a serious failure of prudential regulation in 'light-touch' regimes. The regulators themselves have been quick to acknowledge this and suggest remedies. Among the earliest to do so was the Financial Stability Forum, a network of central bankers, finance ministry officials and regulators founded by the G7 and based in Basel, whose report in April 2008 contained a detailed programme to strengthen regulatory and associated activities (Financial Stability Forum 2008). A summary of their main recommendations can be found in Box 6.1.

BOX 6.1 DIRECTIONS OF REFORM IN FINANCIAL REGULATION

In the wake of the US sub-prime mortgage crisis a number of detailed proposals to tighten-up financial regulation in global markets have been put forward by financial regulators from the major national jurisdictions. The following summary is based mainly on the report of the Financial Stability Forum (2008) and gives an indication of the content and range of the recommendations emanating from the official practitioners themselves. Many of them have been taken up in subsequent reports, for example the Larosière Report (2009) and the Turner Review (UK Financial Services Authority, 2009).

The main proposals:

- Raise capital adequacy requirements for most types of banking business, and especially for exposure to 'structured investment vehicles' (SIVs) like 'mortgage-backed securities' (MBS) beyond those provided in 'Basel II' (the second of the Basel Accords setting voluntary international standards on banking supervision, published in 2004).
- Adopt maximum limits on mortgage loan/value ratios.
- Improve and broaden risk assessment techniques, for example by adopting a greater variety of quantitative and qualitative approaches in risk assessments, and evaluating them more thoroughly using 'stress testing' techniques. Tighten the oversight of risk assessment by bank supervisors.
- Require banks to publish clear and timely information on their exposure to off-balance sheet liabilities, and step up other disclosure requirements, for example to make SIVs more transparent.
- Improve the assessment and management of firm-wide risks, including indirect as well as direct risks.
- Strengthen the settlement, legal and operational framework for over-the-counter derivatives.
- Set up an expert advisory panel to advise financial institutions on asset valuation when markets cease to be active, with a view to modifying the 'mark to market' approach.
- Securities market supervisors should work with market practitioners to set up a comprehensive information system on post-trade prices and volumes in secondary markets for SIVs.
- Credit rating agencies should make their ratings of structured credit products more realistic, and differentiate them from bond ratings. The agencies should communicate the assumptions and data underlying their ratings more clearly and re-examine the 'issuer pays' model, which may raise conflicts of interest over structured products. Supervisors should consider whether these ratings receive too much weight in prudential assessments.
- Establish an international 'college of supervisors' for each of the large pan-global financial institutions.

Many of these recommendations have been taken up in other official reports. The European aspects were addressed by the Larosière Group on Financial Supervision, a high-level expert group set up by the European Commission under the chairmanship of Jacques de Larosière, a former Banque de France Governor and IMF Managing Director. Their report concluded that regulation has been too piecemeal and insufficiently concerned with the financial system as a whole

(Larosière Group 2009). Among its main recommendations were the formation of a 'European Systemic Risk Council' under the auspices of the European Central Bank, with the task of bringing a 'macro-prudential' (system-wide) perspective to bear on the conduct of EU national regulators. More controversially, the Larosière Group recommended a 'European System of Financial Supervision', to harmonise national regulatory standards and coordinate the work of EU national supervisors in the fields of banking, securities trading and insurance.

The UK aspects have been addressed in a comprehensive review by the Financial Services Authority (FSA) under Lord Turner, who took over as chairman after the crash (UK Financial Services Authority 2009). The *Turner Review* recommended the end of light-touch (or 'principles-based')[4] regulation and put forward a wide range of measures for curbing excessive risk-taking in the banking industry. In particular, regulators should have power to set higher capital and liquidity requirements for higher-risk business and to vary minimum capital/asset ratios and maximum loan/asset ratios counter-cyclically (i.e. to counter asset-price fluctuations). However, the main impact of the review is likely to be seen in a toughening of regulators' attitudes rather than a tightening of the rules. In future the regulators will be expected to be less trusting of financial practitioners and more intrusive in vetting their business. For example they should use case-by-case judgement in raising capital requirements for firms with large off-balance-sheet exposures or bonus schemes that reward short-term risk-taking, and insist on greater transparency regarding hedge-fund and short-selling operations and the asset-composition of SIVs.

The *Turner Review* nevertheless endorsed the unified structure of financial regulation adopted in the UK in 1997, in which all financial institutions are dealt with by a single agency. It saw no reason to revert to segregated modes of supervision, with ordinary commercial banks supervised by the central bank and 'shadow' banks, hedge funds, private equity firms and insurance companies either regulated by specialist bodies or left unregulated, as has been the preferred approach in the United States. Despite the criticism levelled at unified regulation in the UK, the FSA was reluctant to break up the conglomerates that dominate much of the banking industry into commercial ('utility') and investment ('casino') banks, because of the scale economies and other synergies that characterise modern banking business. The FSA would prefer to deal with multi-function banks by creating clearer internal barriers between high- and low-risk business and adjusting capital requirements accordingly. It also recommended extending prudential supervision to hedge funds or other shadow institutions if their failure would damage the wider financial system.

However, in a considerable change of heart, the FSA bowed to the call for stronger international coordination of national regulators; it supported the Larosière Group's recommendation for a pan-European regulatory body while proposing that the approach be extended to all the main financial centres. Previous moves in this direction had been resisted by City interests but the FSA appears to have decided that London risks losing business unless the tougher regulation it is now proposing encompasses all national jurisdictions. This recommendation was endorsed at the London G20 Summit in April, along with the elevation of the Financial Stability Forum into a Financial Stability Board – a super-regulator with new powers to coordinate the work of national regulators (G20 Leaders' statement reported in the *Guardian* newspaper, 3 April 2009).

Although the reforms recommended in these reports are far-reaching in some respects, they clearly stop well short of the revolution that some critics have been calling for. They do not contemplate wholesale nationalisation of 'utility' banks, or the creation of state-owned 'people's banks' to compete in retail banking, or the outlawing of hedge funds, or the prevention of practices like securitisation or short-selling. Neither do they seek to transfer the work of day-to-day regulation from national authorities to international bodies. Banking supervision is still seen as an activity best left to experts with local knowledge and access to the national purse strings.

Even so it seems unthinkable, in the post-crisis climate of reform, that there could be a return to 'business as usual' in light-touch regimes, despite some accusations of backsliding. The days when free-market protagonists could confidently advocate minimal financial regulation are probably gone for the foreseeable future, if not permanently. The change in thinking on these issues has been remarkably rapid. As recently as spring 2008, even such perceptive free-market economists as Professor John Kay could still stoutly defend the minimalist approach. In his column in the *Financial Times* of 26 March 2008 headed 'More regulation will not prevent next crisis' he wrote:

> Banking supervision should then be limited to the weeding out of unfit persons. Capital requirements, liquidity provisions and risk assessments should be matters for the business judgement of the financial institutions themselves. We cannot prevent booms and busts in credit markets, but today's regulation of risk and capital – which is more reflective of what has occurred than of what may occur – does more to aggravate these cycles than to prevent them. Regulation in a market economy is targeted at specific market failures and should not be a charter for the general scrutiny of business strategies of private business. Banking should be no exception.
>
> *(Kay 2008)*

As the crisis recedes, the consensus among economists is probably closer to the view expressed by *Financial Times* commentator Martin Wolf, not previously an apologist for regulation, who wrote in April 2008:

> If regulation is to be effective, it must cover all relevant institutions and the entire balance sheet, in all significant countries; it must focus on capital, liquidity and transparency; and, not least, it must make finance less procyclical. Will it work perfectly? Certainly not. It is impossible and probably undesirable to create a crisis-free financial system. Crises will always be with

us. But we can surely do far better than we have been doing. In any case, we are doomed to try.

(Wolf 2008)

With hindsight Wolf's call for more systematic regulation seems to survive the fallout from the 2008 crash better than Kay's minimalism. Yet a number of important issues in this field are unresolved and may remain so for some time. Central bankers in liberalised regimes, notably Bank of England Governor King (2009), are very uneasy about the existence of banks thought 'too big to fail', and have called for new macro-prudential tools to deal with system-wide excesses. And the authorities in liberal regimes are concerned that moves to strengthen international coordination might damage their competitiveness. We will return to these questions in Chapter 7.

Global macroeconomic imbalances

Among other causes of the crash that have received attention in the expert debate and in official post-mortems has been the part played by the global macroeconomic imbalances, to which attention was drawn in the previous chapter. Keynesian economists have been in the forefront of this debate, notably Paul Krugman: in an op-ed column recalling Fed Chairman Bernanke's remarks on the global saving glut, he blamed the problems in 'wide-open, loosely regulated financial systems' on 'a world awash in cheap money, looking for somewhere to go' (Krugman, *New York Times*, 1 March 2009). On this view, the financial crisis and subsequent recession is partly attributable to excessive global saving, originating largely in the emerging economies but later compounded by the collapse of confidence in the developed world: a manifestation of Keynes' 'paradox of thrift' on a global scale. Similar views have been expressed by Martin Wolf, who has warned:

> It is going to be very hard to generate substantial net borrowing by households and non-financial corporations in the high-income countries with high internal debt. . . . Countries with large current account surpluses have long demanded an end to the profligate borrowing and spending of the customers upon whom they depended. They should have been careful what they wished for: they have now got it.
>
> *(Wolf, Financial Times, 27 January 2009)*

These themes also featured in the Larosière Report and the *Turner Review*, both of which regarded the persistent inflows of cheap foreign money into liberalised financial centres as contributors to the crash. The Larosière Group was particularly exercised by the regulators' failure to allow for these macroeconomic influences in their surveillance of individual banks, and blamed the lacuna on inadequate communication between the macro authorities and the micro regulators.

Errors in macro policy

In the sphere of macro policy, several prominent economists have criticised what they judge to have been an unduly expansionary stance of monetary policy in the major economies for several years before the crisis. A particularly trenchant critic has been Willem Buiter, a former member of the Bank of England Monetary Policy Committee and Chief Economist at the EBRD, who wrote as the crisis was breaking in summer 2007:

> The problems we are seeing today are the result of four to five years of (1) excessively low risk-free interest rates at all maturities in the US, Euroland and Japan, and (2) ludicrously low credit-risk spreads across the board (not just in the subprime mortgage markets).
>
> *(Buiter and Sibert 2007: 5)*

Others have focused on what were seen as belated and excessive responses by monetary policymakers to the commodity-price pressures that arose in 2005–7, when short-term interest rates were raised sharply in the United States and Euro Area, creating mortgage-servicing difficulties in the United States and elsewhere, as noted earlier. Having raised rates too late and too sharply, the central banks were then attacked for being too slow to lower them when the recession took hold. A noted critic of UK policy in this phase was David Blanchflower who, while a member of the Bank of England's Monetary Policy Committee, wrote an article implying that the Committee had been slow to perceive the seriousness of the recession (Blanchflower 2008). His willingness to criticise policy openly while still a member of the Committee surprised (and pleased) many commentators.

Economists have also been critical to varying degrees of the thrust of fiscal policy in major economies in the decade or so before the crash. By 2005 two independent UK research institutes (the National Institute of Economic and Social Research and the Institute of Fiscal Studies) were expressing unease that UK fiscal policy was not achieving all it should. However, their concerns at that stage were relatively mild; they related mainly to overshooting of the government's 'golden rule' (which required the budget balance on *current* account to be zero over the economic cycle) and to the UK's failure to improve its public finances as much as other countries during the period of economic buoyancy (National Institute of Economic and Social Research 2005: 6–7; Institute for Fiscal Studies 2007). But underlying the National Institute's concern was also the more serious worry that the UK economy was not saving enough overall to provide for long-term growth (Pomerantz and Weale 2005). One implication of this view was that the government should be saving more; budget current surpluses rather than deficits should have been aimed for. This was by no means the only remedy offered for low saving: taxes on the supply of credit and reforms in financial services and pensions provision were also considered part of the answer. But in time the recognition grew among professional commentators that if UK fiscal policy had been more cautious during the long period of buoyancy, more 'fiscal space' would have been created and the government would have been in a stronger position to combat the recession when it eventually came.

In the United States, criticism of what some economists saw as the profligate fiscal stance adopted by the Bush Administration had emerged somewhat earlier. A scathing attack on the Administration's tax-cutting policies was mounted by Krugman, who wrote in the *New York Times:* 'the simple truth is that the Bush tax cuts have utterly transformed our fiscal outlook, for the worse' (Krugman 2003). With hindsight similar views have subsequently become widespread among commentators on the US fiscal position.

If the diagnoses referred to above are broadly correct, the crash of 2007–8 cannot be dismissed as an unlucky mishap which policy could have done little to avert. It certainly seems true that the crisis was due to a range of causes, and in that respect it might be said to have been unfortunate. But in that case the appropriate response would appear to be remedial action on a number of fronts, and this indeed seems to be the conclusion of independent experts. Thus, now the dust is settling, there seems an emerging consensus on the main lines of reform to be taken, especially: that the bonus culture prevalent in liberalised financial sectors, with its rewards for short-term profit and its failure to penalise excessive risk-taking, should be moderated and redesigned; and that the light regulatory touch in Anglo-Saxon regimes should be toughened and made more responsive to macro-prudential and global concerns. Finally there seems growing recognition that the weaknesses seen in the design and conduct of macroeconomic policy before the crash are manifestations of serious flaws in the underlying policy model. With that conclusion in mind, the remaining chapters will suggest a programme of reforms in the 1990s synthesis, designed to reduce the risk of such a damaging crisis happening again.

PART II

The elements of a more durable regime

7
MONETARY POLICY

This chapter embarks on a series of proposals for reform of the 1990s synthesis, in light of the weaknesses and threats discussed previously. The focus will mainly be on policy at the national level in developed economies, but it will broaden to consider the international dimension where appropriate. The subject is inevitably a large and complex one, in which the devil tends to be in the detail. Since the relevant institutions and procedures differ somewhat between countries, there will inevitably be some tension between precision and generality. The discussion will address the UK regime first and then consider parallels elsewhere, and international cooperation where relevant.

Some of the exogenous threats outlined in Chapter 6 lie outside the conventional field of macroeconomics. For example, the banking excesses and asset-price aberrations at the heart of the financial crisis call mainly for regulatory improvements which are essentially microeconomic in character. Although these lie largely outside our ambit here, a number of macroeconomic steps designed to assist or supplement regulatory policy will be discussed. However, policy action of other kinds, such as government support for innovation or investment to tackle global warming or environmental pollution, or provision of training to cope with 'dual economy' problems, or better-directed aid for the developing world, will not be addressed here. Macroeconomic policy has little to contribute directly to these problems, though greater macroeconomic stability may well help with them in a general way.

Objectives and targets of monetary policy

Given that the 1990s synthesis was remarkably effective in overcoming the inflationary excesses inherited from preceding decades, it is hard to disagree that price stability should remain the primary objective of monetary policy. However, there are issues to be addressed in the design of inflation targets and making them internationally compatible. And there are reasons for including *output stabilisation* formally as part of the underlying price stability objective, and for thinking this could be done without compromising price stability.

Framing inflation targets

The price-stability objective assigned to central banks should preferably be expressed in terms of an explicit and uniform medium-term inflation target of, say, 0–2 per cent p.a., as now in the UK and Euro Area. It would be important for the international effectiveness of our reform package that similar targets should be formally adopted by the governments of all major developed economies, including the US and Japanese governments. In normal circumstances the targets should be the same for all the main economies, but some economies might opt for somewhat higher targets for transitional purposes or in exceptional circumstances, though only as temporary expedients. To this end the choice of target should be a subject for international consultation, preferably under the auspices of the IMF as part of its regular surveillance, under general guidance from the G20. (More will be said about the reasons for preferring uniform targets in the next two chapters.)

The precise framing of the inflation target – the operational target that guides the central bank in its pursuit of price stability – is not a straightforward matter. There is general agreement that the target should relate to the average price of consumer goods and services, but whether these should include housing, usually reflected in mortgage servicing costs, is more controversial. Preferably mortgage costs should be excluded from official targets, partly because the weight of these costs in household budgets varies between different economies, and partly because such costs move directly with the short-term interest rates that are the main instrument of monetary policy. Preferably a tightening of monetary policy should not lead to an immediate rise in the measured inflation rate. Although there is force in the argument that overall price stability should include the costs of home ownership because these are relevant to wage bargaining and living standards, this result can best be achieved by adopting house price stabilisation as a separate objective of monetary policy, as will be explained shortly.

A second question regarding the framing of inflation targets is whether such a target should cover import prices, particularly world commodity prices. In principle there seems a good case for excluding external elements in consumer prices from the target, especially where they lie outside the influence of monetary policy, as oil and food prices clearly do for most industrial economies. And even where the external components of domestic prices depend partly on monetary policy, as in the case of import prices that vary inversely with the exchange rate, there are grounds for excluding them from the target because they offer a deceptively easy option for using monetary policy to control inflation. Monetary policy can be expected to exert a direct and predictable influence only on the *domestic* component of consumer prices, and to that end the inflation target should if possible focus on that component only.

However, the available data are unfortunately far from ideal in this respect. National accounting data on home costs – measured by the 'GDP deflator' – are available only quarterly after long delays, and are often subject to significant revision. Data on unit labour costs in manufacturing and other major economic sectors tend to be more timely and less subject to revision, but they too are available only quarterly in most countries. Moreover their industrial coverage is wider than just consumer goods, and of course they omit profit margins, a strong cyclical element in consumer prices.

For these practical reasons, when setting an inflation target it is hard to improve on the measure of consumer prices known as CPI-X, the index of consumer prices excluding mortgage interest, which is the measure used by the ECB for monetary policy purposes. But policymakers should also monitor, and do more to publicise, other aggregate price indicators, among which whole-economy unit labour costs should rank high. Indicators of domestic costs should be helpful in avoiding a trap into which monetary policy in open economies fell in the early years of this century: a tendency to be too lax because the supply of manufactures from low-cost emerging economies kept inflation in importing economies artificially low. Now that China and other big emerging economies are themselves experiencing higher inflation, this prop to inflation control in the developed world may prove unreliable.

There are further questions as to the precise form that an inflation target should take, for example whether ranges or point targets are preferable, whether the periodicity should be short- or medium-term, and whether the target should relate to the price level or rate of change. (A non-technical discussion can be found in Svensson 2007.) In our view, simple targets are preferable to complex ones in order to facilitate international consistency and transparency. Nevertheless we agree with economists like Woodford who recommend that targets should be partly retrospective in order to recover past inflation slippage, as noted in Chapter 4. For that reason targets should be framed as medium-term averages with a backward-looking element.

Adding output to the price-stability objective

The theory of inflation control underlying the 1990s consensus (as for example in the NCM model discussed in Chapter 4) provides a rationale for broadening the price-stability objective to include output stability; and some of the macro policy mistakes made in the past decade suggest there is a strong case for doing so. More specifically, output stability should be adopted explicitly alongside price stability as the *joint* primary objective of monetary policy. The primary objective thus modified should be framed by government, approved by parliament, and enshrined in a formal and binding legal commitment for the economy concerned. To avoid misunderstanding, formal texts should always emphasise that action to stabilise output should be taken only if it does not jeopardise price stability.

Broadening the primary objective of monetary policy in this way would be both rational and highly desirable, for reasons that derive from the Phillips curve in its modern expectations-augmented form. According to this construct, price and output stability are entirely congruent objectives. If behaviour in labour and product markets conforms to a generally stable relationship of the accepted form, as seems broadly true if external price shocks and changes in labour-market institutions are allowed for, inflation and output (or at least capacity utilisation) are highly interdependent. As explained in Chapter 4, stabilising the general price level means keeping actual output at the unique level in relation to potential output that delivers zero or low inflation in the medium and longer term, i.e. the level implied by the NAIRU. Thus by stabilising output at that critical level the central bank would also be acting to stabilise the price level. Such a reform would reinforce and make explicit what monetary policymakers already do implicitly, or ought to do.

If inflation targets are re-framed to include output as recommended here, there are questions about which measure of output to use. The obvious candidate appears to be GDP, but there is alternatively a case for targeting *unemployment*, more specifically the unemployment rate necessary for price stability – the NAIRU itself. Data on unemployment are more reliable than those used to measure GDP, being more comprehensive and less subject to revision, and they are available more frequently (monthly not quarterly). Thus targeting unemployment would meet some of the objections of those who argue that output is too unreliable an indicator for inflation control purposes. Moreover, focusing on an unemployment rate for this purpose would reduce the onus on estimating links between unemployment and GDP (otherwise needed to convert the NAIRU into the 'output gap', another possible target) and yet be meaningful to the markets and the public generally, both as a measure of capacity utilisation and as a socially desirable objective in itself (employment stability).

However, there are also arguments against targeting unemployment. Causality in the short–medium term runs from output to unemployment and there tend to be long lags in the adjustment process: on average it may take 6–12 months for employment to respond to changes in national output, given the usual lags in hiring and shedding labour, and a further 6–12 months or more for registered unemployment to respond to employment, given the time taken for people to move in to and out of the active labour force. Since the monetary instruments bear directly on output (via expenditure) and only indirectly on unemployment – unless rational expectations operate powerfully enough to short-circuit the adjustment process – it may take one to two years for monetary action to affect unemployment fully, by which time new shocks may occur. For these reasons it seems best to accept GDP as the output measure rather than target unemployment. More specifically, monetary policy should target the *rate of GDP growth* needed to restore unemployment to the NAIRU over a horizon of, say, two to three years, allowing for the economic cycle and expected disturbances. Of course, the central bank should also monitor all relevant indicators, including leading indicators of expenditure and output, as well as lagging indicators like unemployment and other labour market indicators (vacancy rates, overtime and short-time working, etc.). And more prominence should be given to these ancillary indicators in communications to the markets and public.

More on the case for stabilising output

Introducing output stability as a formal objective alongside price stability is likely to make sense to ordinary people because they are likely to attach as much importance, if not more, to maintaining activity and jobs as to avoiding inflation. Moreover, unless proper account is taken of what is happening to output, the pursuit of price stability on its own risks being biased in economies that still experience wage and price rigidities. The risk arises from the existence in industrial economies of asymmetry in wage/price behaviour with respect to the pressure of demand. Despite liberalisation of labour markets and falling trades union membership in the UK and other EU economies over three decades, employee resistance to wage cuts is still apparent, so wage rates still tend to be stickier downwards than upwards in the short–medium term. And the continued dominance of oligopolies in industrial markets, despite the removal of restrictive practices in the Thatcher era and under the Single European Market (SEM) programme, means that goods prices still tend to be slower to adjust downwards than upwards over the short–medium term.[1] These economies may therefore experience quite long periods of rising unemployment without falling inflation, as shown by UK experience after the crash of 2008.[2] If so, policymakers may be slow to cut interest rates in periods of weak demand, while believing they are fulfilling their price-stability remit. The imposition of a formal duty to minimise downward as well as upward deviations in output and activity should reduce this risk.

A further argument for adding output to the inflation target is that it should assist both the conduct and the presentation of policy in the event of external *cost-push* shocks, such as those arising from world commodity prices. In theory a cost-push shock implies a rightward shift, temporary or permanent, in the expectations-augmented Phillips curve. A shock of this kind thus implies a *rise in the NAIRU*, other things being equal: price stability requires an increase, either temporary or permanent as the case may be, in the target national rate of unemployment. As our discussion of the Phillips curve showed, without such an increase, inflation expectations are likely to pick up unless the shock is quickly reversed, and the increase may be hard to reverse if allowed to persist beyond the short term. The appropriate response in such circumstances is to maintain a strictly non-accommodating policy stance, which in practice implies holding bank lending rates unchanged.[3] If that is done, the combination of higher input prices with unchanged flows of domestic money incomes and expenditure will reduce real aggregate demand and thereby raise unemployment. In that case the commodity price shock should not pass through to domestic wage rates and labour costs, and rising inflation expectations should not become established in collective bargaining or price-setting. The point of formalising the output target is that it would compel policymakers to focus explicitly on factors like the 'output gap' (the shortfall between actual and potential output), and thence the NAIRU; and it would assist in explaining the conduct of policy to the markets and the public.

Critics may object that a joint output-inflation target would confuse the markets and weaken the price-stability commitment, but such an objection misses the point of the change. In the case of demand shocks there should be no ambiguity in the policy signals coming from well-designed inflation and output/unemployment targets. If there is a positive shock to aggregate demand, both inflation and output are likely to rise above target in the short–medium term, both calling for a monetary tightening. And the converse should happen in the event of a negative demand shock, except that if wages and prices are sticky downward the fall in inflation may be sluggish, in which case output/unemployment provides the more dependable signal (calling for a policy relaxation). Admittedly the signals from the two targets are liable to be less clear in the event of a cost-push shock. Thus an exogenous increase in world commodity prices is likely to raise CPI inflation above target while depressing output below target, other things being equal. On its own, exceeding the inflation target would call for a tightening of policy, whereas undershooting the output target would call for a policy relaxation. In the face of these conflicting signals the stance of policy should be kept unchanged, unless the strength and duration of the shock suggests otherwise. Theory suggests that monetary policy should be non-accommodating of cost-push shocks, i.e. that (real) interest rates should be held unchanged in the event of a hike in oil or food prices, a fall in labour productivity, or some other supply-side disturbance.

Making financial stability a formal policy objective

As policymakers have now widely if belatedly recognised, the crash of 2007–8 highlighted the dilemmas faced by central banks at times of financial stress in reconciling what has been, for many, a new commitment to price stability under the 1990s consensus with their traditional role as guardians of banking stability. These dilemmas emerged more starkly in some regimes than others. Central banks in regimes where controlling inflation has been given top priority through formal targets, like the Bank of England and the central banks comprising the ESCB (European System of Central Banks) have struggled to square their traditional 'lender of last resort' roles with the overriding duty to maintain price stability; those for whom price stability is a less formal priority, like the US Federal Reserve and the Bank of Japan, have managed to walk this tightrope with less trouble.

The scope for policy conflict in this sphere underlines the need to clarify the responsibilities borne by central banks under the 1990s synthesis, and in particular to give greater weight to the pursuit of financial stability in regimes where price stability has been given top priority. It would help to resolve this dilemma if systemic financial stability were made a formal objective for central banks in major financial centres, subject to not jeopardising price stability. Like its price-stability counterpart, the financial-stability objective should be framed by government, approved by parliament and enshrined in statute.

In principle there should be no conflict between these two basic objectives: price and output stability can hardly be maintained in the long run unless the financial system also functions in a stable way, and vice versa. Nevertheless markets may worry that price stability will be compromised by bank-support operations and it would be important to address these. All parties involved must be clear that monetary policy is to be reserved for the price/output stability objective and can have no immediate or close role in securing financial stability. If central banks are also required to take on responsibility for financial stability they must have special tools for the purpose. These are likely to be of two kinds. First, some central banks may need new (or restored) powers to supply liquidity in the event of a systemic shortage, and to orchestrate takeovers of banks whose failure would threaten the system, where these are circumscribed at present, as appears to be the case for the central banks belonging to the ESCB. Second, in liberalised financial systems which are prone to big asset-price fluctuations, central banks should develop new *macro-prudential* instruments to deal with them.

Moves in the above direction have already been made in the two economies most affected by the recent financial crisis. In the UK, the Banking Act (February 2009) strengthened the Bank of England's responsibility for financial stability by putting this objective on a clear statutory footing, and gave the Bank new powers to intervene in the running of failing domestic banks when it judges the system's stability to be at stake, including a new 'Special Resolution Regime' to deal with failing banks and building societies. And in summer that year the government announced plans to set up a Council for Financial Stability comprising the Chancellor of the Exchequer, Bank of England Governor and FSA Chairman. However, as the Bank Governor Mervyn King pointed out, the 2009 Act did not provide it with specific instruments to cope with threats to financial stability (King 2009). As one of his first steps upon taking office in May 2010 George Osborne, Chancellor of the Exchequer in the newly-elected UK coalition government, announced that an independent Financial Policy Committee would be created in the Bank, with 'the tools and the responsibility to look across the economy at the macro issues … and take effective action in response' (Osborne 2010). But it remains to be seen how independent the new Committee will be and what tools it will use.

In the United States, the authorities are attempting to address corresponding problems by strengthening their powers to prevent banks from becoming overexposed in future. In 2009 the US Treasury developed a 'Financial Stability Plan' which includes a series of sweeping measures to strengthen banking regulation, with emphasis on increased transparency and disclosure by banks and near-banks, better coordination between the financial regulators, 'stress tests' to help assess capital adequacy in financial firms, and a 'special review process' for the largest firms (with assets over $100 billion). Banks that undergo comprehensive stress tests may have access to a 'capital buffer' facility provided by the Treasury to serve as a bridge for raising increased private capital (see US Treasury 2009). The US supervisory agencies, in step with their national counterparts on the Basel Committee, have raised the capital requirements for trading activities and securitization exposures, two areas of particularly high losses in the crisis. The Federal Reserve is especially concerned to minimise the systemic threats associated with affiliations of utility and investment banking, and is considering ways of reversing the trend towards such affiliations. Yet Fed Board Governors have expressed doubt that such a strategy would do much to limit the 'too-big-to-fail' problem, citing the Lehman Brothers' failure as an example to the contrary (Tarullo 2009). Notably, there seems little disposition (as of late 2009) to introduce macro-prudential measures in the financial field. Thus in both the main Anglo–Saxon regimes progress still needs to be made in the macro-prudential area, and we will return to this issue below.

Significant steps towards a formal financial stability objective are yet to be taken in other major economies, either because their authorities are not convinced such action is necessary or because their regimes are less receptive to such changes. This is especially so in the Euro Area, where the ECB and the national central banks under its wing are governed by statutory provisions that attach only subsidiary importance to financial stability as a central-banking goal. Thus under EMU rules the member banks of the ESCB are merely required to 'contribute to the smooth conduct of policies pursued by the competent authorities relating to the prudential supervision of credit institutions and the stability of the financial system' (Council of the European Communities 1992: Article 105.5). This provision is clearly insufficient to authorise ESCB members to intervene in the operations of failing banks or rescue them. In most cases the latter retain prudential powers and functions under their own national legislation, but some have largely given up their powers to finance bank rescues and these may need reinstatement. That may not be easy, given that compatibility between national banking legislation and the ESCB Statute is a condition for membership of the Euro Area, and some national central banks' powers were abandoned or weakened to meet that condition. Whether strengthening them would be permissible under the ESCB Statute remains to be seen.

Additional tasks for central banks

The giant house-price bubbles of the past decade in the United States and UK are acknowledged to have been important factors behind the crash of 2007–8 and action to minimise their chances of recurrence is clearly desirable. To that end, serious consideration should be given in these and other economies with heavily geared housing regimes – for example Ireland, Portugal and Spain – to adopting house-price stability formally as an additional policy objective. Such stability would be worth pursuing on its own merits, given the resource misallocation caused by house-price fluctuations and the misery they inflict on many thousands of households. Moreover, it should assist in maintaining overall price stability as well as financial stability, provided it can be pursued without interfering with the conduct of monetary policy proper. That would not be an easy task and it is probably one that should be assigned to central banks, given their macroeconomic expertise. The modalities will be discussed below.

Finally, in anticipation of the reforms in exchange-rate policy to be proposed later, we flag here our recommendation that exchange-rate stability should be adopted as a further policy objective by the major developed economies, again provided it does not jeopardise price stability. Such a step would be worthwhile on its own merits if it is accepted that long-period exchange-rate fluctuations are harmful to industry and trade, as argued earlier. Furthermore, far from conflict-ing with price stability as some critics will argue, exchange-rate stability should be entirely compatible with such stability provided the major economies align their individual price-stability objectives as recommended above, and central banks con-duct their monetary policies consistently with them. In the fullness of time the successful pursuit of exchange-rate targets could have big implications for monetary policy in an interdependent world, as will be explained in Chapter 9.

Instruments of monetary policy

Official interest rates and the transmission mechanism

There seems little reason to depart from the universal central-banking view in lib-eralised market regimes that in normal conditions it is best to use official short-term interest rates as the main instrument for conducting monetary policy. All central banks in developed economies rely on such instruments nowadays and seem bound to continue doing so. The Bank of England Bank Rate, the US Federal Reserve intervention rates, the ECB re-financing and fine-tuning rates, and their respective discount and deposit rates, are generally effective market-based tools and are widely understood by the markets. The precise ways in which open market operations are conducted differ somewhat between regimes – for example the extent to which they rely on 'repos' (repurchase agreements) rather than 'outrights' (outright sales or purchases) – but such differences reflect local conditions and it would be point-less to try to standardise them.

However, in setting official interest rates (or the Federal Funds target rate in the Fed's case), central banks should take more explicit account of variations in the links between their intervention rates and the lending rates that actually represent the cost of credit in the economies concerned. Policymakers need to assess, and communicate more clearly, the thrust of monetary policy not purely in terms of official rates but also with reference to the lending rates actually faced by firms and households. Experts may understand these links but others – especially the banks' main customers – need better guidance, especially in times of stress. Official rates tend to have a high profile in press reports, parliamentary evidence and briefings by central-bank officials. This emphasis may be appropriate in normal conditions but it ceases to be so when the financial system is under serious strain, as Figure 5.1 showed.

As explained in previous chapters, the normal links in the monetary transmission process may became so distorted by rumours and uncertainties in a severe credit crunch that changes in central-bank lending rates may have relatively little impact on the wider rate structure. In such conditions the key official rates and their imme-diate objectives – generally money-market rates (overnight or very short-term rates) – have increasingly tenuous links with commercial lending rates as they approach floors below which yields on very short-term assets cannot be driven; moreover worries about negative inflation in deep recession may convert low nominal rates into significantly positive real rates. These patterns were detectable in the Anglo-Saxon economies at times during the global financial crisis. As Figure 6.1 showed, action by the Federal Reserve to raise the Federal Funds rate through the boom period 2003–7 was immediately effective in raising medium- and longer-term rates. In that period the Fed was successfully 'pulling on the credit string'. In contrast the Fed's attempt to boost liquidity and credit in 2008–9 by lowering the Federal Funds target rate was relatively unsuccessful: bank lending rates and long-term rates fell little in that period; the Fed was unsuccessfully 'pushing on the credit string'. Yet ordinary borrowers and even sophisticated market commentators seemed largely unaware of these problems and received little enlightenment on them.

Quantitative easing

In basic respects, experience under the recent credit crunch resembled the liquidity trap identified by Keynes in the 1930s: market interest rates could not be reduced further by cutting official rates. The possibility that this problem might recur was foreseen by Fed Chairman (then Director) Bernanke, who suggested as early as 2002 that US inflation might give way to deflation at some point and that the Fed might then have to take unconventional action (Bernanke 2002). His concerns followed the experience in Japan, where falls in consumer prices since the late 1990s had produced 'debt deflation' – increases in the real value of capital-certain debt due to falls in the general price level, which created heavy repayment burdens for Japan's indebted firms and households. Bernanke predicted that if disinflation threatened the United States and conventional action to cut interest rates failed, the Fed would have to inject liquidity into the economy by purchasing securities from banks and private investors, or even through direct lending to firms. This suggestion surprised the markets at the time but it proved remarkably prophetic in due course.

The recent crisis has led to a wider acceptance that the normal working of the monetary transmission mechanism may be seriously disrupted in times of financial stress and in those circumstances the central bank should not shrink from unconventional action to stimulate the economy. Open market operations in government debt by central banks are not of course new. For decades central banks have routinely undertaken outright purchases or sales of long-term government bonds for structural purposes – for example to meet changing demands for low-risk assets on the part of life insurance and pension funds, or to provide extra liquidity for faster growth when judged appropriate – to supplement the much larger and more frequent repos (repurchase agreements) which generally provide overnight or one- or two-week loans to offset temporary liquidity fluctuations. But since the 1960s open-market operations in longer-term debt have tended to be modest in size and designed to meet revealed private-sector demands at prevailing interest rates rather than changing the maturity structure of rates. However, in periods of recession central banks may have to use open market operations to change the shape of the official yield curve (the time-structure of interest yields on government debt with maturities from three months up to 50 years). In extreme conditions such tactics may have to be pursued proactively even if it means accumulating large debt holdings on their balance sheets.

Unconventional action of this kind is one of the few tools available to central banks for combating recessions caused by acute disjuncture of the financial system, as in the recent crisis. In such exceptional situations central banks may have little choice but to provide liquidity by purchasing financial assets from commercial banks, including even assets of suspect quality where these represent particular concentrations of risk in the banking system, creating extra 'high-powered' money in the process. Such expedients should of course be no more than temporary, carry a moderate interest penalty ('hair cut'), and be unwound as soon as the relevant asset markets recover. Yet in recessions the power of such action to stimulate bank lending is likely to be limited, as shown by the earlier Japanese experience, as discussed in Chapter 5. It is more liable to be effective in reducing longer-term interest rates but that is unlikely to stimulate investment as long as firms see few profit opportunities and house-purchasers fear unemployment. The main short-term benefit is more likely to be restoration of bank liquidity and capital without intensifying the credit crunch.

There are certainly risks in resorting to large-scale quantitative easing. Injections of cash on the scale undertaken in the UK and United States in 2008–9 seem almost bound to be inflationary eventually if the cash is left in place after the recession ends. Such actions should be reversed as demand recovers, even if it entails capital losses for the central bank by selling debt into a falling bond market, creating eventual burdens for the taxpayer. A particular risk for an economy with a high proportion of debt held by non-residents is that the cash injections will flow abroad, causing an exchange-rate depreciation which could be inflationary in due course. Market commentators felt that the Bank of England's announcement of quantitative easing in 2008 contributed to sterling's sharp depreciation in that year. Given these risks, it would clearly be preferable that debt purchases should be aimed at resident investors so far as possible.

Public debt management

Quantitative easing by the central bank is not the only technique by which policy-makers might seek to strengthen the monetary transmission mechanism during a recession. More controversially, there is also a case for government debt managers in developed economies to be more proactive in influencing the shape of the yield curve, if and when monetary policy calls for it. In previous eras when the Bank of England was responsible for managing the government debt, activity to influence the term structure of rates by varying the maturity of gilts issued and redeemed was fairly routine (Geddes 1987: 79). But this practice was abandoned with the switch to CCC in the 1970s, and debt management was finally removed from the Bank in 1998, after it had been given responsibility for monetary policy. The UK Debt Management Department created at that time is an agency under the wing of the Treasury and has in its terms of reference the key duty of minimising the cost of government borrowing, subject to the legitimate needs of the main debt-holding institutions. The department is also required to take the needs of monetary policy into account but it is unclear how far this happens at present or how it could be done, given the department's agency status, which means that it operates at arm's length from both government and the Bank. In the light of the credit crunch there is a case for re-involving the Bank in debt management. Corresponding steps might be taken in other regimes where debt management is detached from the central bank.

Even if the foregoing suggestions are taken up, and even assuming that policy actions in these fields are well-judged, they may not be enough on their own to cope with the recessionary effects of a credit crunch as severe and widespread as the recent one. At such times the risk premiums in bank lending rates may become so large that feasible modifications in the yield curve could hardly restore normality to the transmission process. And even if they could, firms and households may be so lacking in confidence that they fail to respond to cheap finance. In short the liquidity trap may be hard to overcome in such conditions and, if so, the arguments for resorting to fiscal policy become harder to resist.

The interface between monetary policy and financial regulation

A controversial institutional issue arising from the financial crisis concerns how responsibility for the stability of the financial system should be allocated between the relevant policy authorities, especially the regulatory agencies and the central banks. It is widely agreed that mistakes by both financial regulators and monetary policymakers in financially-liberalised regimes contributed to the crisis. In the UK, some commentators have argued that the three-way division of responsibility between the FSA, Bank of England and Treasury was partly to blame. In Europe, inadequate communication between regulators and central banks was one of the chief criticisms in the Larosière Report.

In the nature of the exercise, financial regulation is unlikely to be a straightforward task which can be safely put on automatic pilot. As the recent crisis has amply demonstrated, liberalised financial regimes contain elements that are liable to interact and create systemic problems: the exceptional susceptibility of banking systems to contagion, stemming from information asymmetries between borrowers and lenders; the ease with which problems in traditional banking business may spread to 'shadow' and foreign banks, given the growth of integrated, international banks; the huge sums needed to rescue such banks if they get into trouble; and the many different types of expertise needed to address these problems. Governments are inevitably drawn into major banking crises because only they have the resources and law-making capacity to take effective action if things go wrong, but few Treasuries are equipped with the skills and knowledge to deal with the practical work of regulation. In the past, many central banks have practiced banking supervision and maintained the necessary in-house expertise, but a number have moved to shed such activities under the influence of the 1990s synthesis with its heavy emphasis on price stability, especially in EMU. Some central banks outside the EU (notably the Federal Reserve) still retain direct supervisory responsibilities, but even there the potential conflicts with monetary policy are greater in an era when inflation control has top priority.

There are persuasive reasons for thinking that the day-to-day work of financial regulation is best done in specialist agencies rather than central banks. The skills needed for day-to-day supervision of banks and other financial firms lie mainly in the fields of accounting, commercial-banking law and practice, corporate finance and business management. These differ from those found nowadays in mainstream central banking, with its focus macroeconomic analysis and forecasting, money-market and foreign exchange operations, and compilation of money and banking statistics. Admittedly there are links between the latter activities and prudential supervision, and to that extent central-bank experience may provide good training for supervisors. But few central banks collect data outside the banking system and few of their staff have expertise in investment banking, securities trading, company finance, etc. Regulators deal with individual firms whereas central bankers are concerned with aggregates and system-wide effects. The professional divide between macro and micro specialists is thus deep and pervasive.

Moreover there are likely to be tensions between the central-banking commitment to price stability and the financial regulators' commitment to commercial-bank viability, as many observers have pointed out. In the debate about reform, senior officials of the ECB have been quick to warn about such conflicts and have urged that financial stability be left primarily to the regulators, though with guidance and support from central banks (Bini-Smaghi 2008; Papademos 2009).[4] They fear that if conflicts over these issues arise within the institution that is responsible for price stability its credibility will be weakened. 'Reputation' is vital for policy credibility and yet financial regulation is notoriously a field where only failures, not successes, are publicised. Senior central bank officials tend to be overstretched at the best of times; they can hardly be expected to devote their full attention to price stability if they are regularly concerned with supervisory issues. There may also be competition for staff resources, recruitment and training in an organisation that attempts to bridge several expert disciplines.

Pursuit of systemic financial stability falls somewhere between these different but overlapping spheres, and regulators and central bankers both clearly have a stake in it. The challenge is to bring both types of skills and experience to bear in the middle ground. There seems official agreement in the UK, following the *Turner Review*, that the regulators should discriminate more clearly between types of financial business when setting capital requirements, as noted earlier. There are also recommendations in the *Review* and elsewhere that such requirements should be varied counter-cyclically. Experience suggests that a much stronger input is needed from central banks in this respect: one of the latter's main tasks should be to guide the regulators in actions to vary prudential requirements across broad spectrums of financial business, with a view to countering excessive asset-price fluctuations or other system-wide aberrations.

This puts a heavy onus on closer collaboration between central-bank officials and regulators, involving stronger chains of command and a clearer division of labour between the two groups. In some regimes the central bank might acquire new powers to vary system-wide prudential requirements when the macroeconomic situation requires it; in others the emphasis should be on guidance and coordination through formal consultative machinery. That was the approach favoured by the Larosière Group and lay behind its recommendation for a European Systemic Risk Council. Somewhat similar arrangements might operate elsewhere in the EU.

In the UK the creation of a high-level Financial Stability Committee within the Bank of England, announced by the coalition government in June 2010 as noted earlier, will provide a much-needed interface between regulatory and monetary policy, to be led by the Bank though with participation by regulators and, presumably, the Treasury. It thus represents a continuation of reforms announced by the previous government (see UK Treasury 2009a). However, the new government's decision at the same time to transfer financial regulation entirely to the Bank is a much bolder step which departs abruptly from the previous government's intentions and from the advice of the *Turner Review*. By abolishing the FSA and the tripartite regime and creating a 'new prudential regulator, which will operate as a subsidiary of the Bank of England' (Osborne 2010), the new Chancellor is placing sole responsibility for financial regulation firmly with the Bank. In so doing he hopes to bring the Bank's 'broad macroeconomic understanding' directly to bear on regulatory decisions, but he also intends that the Bank 'must also be responsible for day-to-day micro-prudential regulation as well' (Osborne 2010). This represents a significant departure from one of the central tenets of the 1990s synthesis, in that it transfers functions to the central bank that potentially conflict with its price-stability commitment. It will also enlarge the Bank's economic power to an extent that could raise questions about its accountability, its reputation for conducting monetary policy, and its ability to ensure the viability of individual financial firms across the entire financial spectrum, 'including banks, investment banks, building societies and insurance companies' (Osborne 2010).

Adherents to the 1990s consensus can hardly be comfortable with such a radical change of tack, for the reasons outlined above. There must be considerable risks in plunging the Bank of England back into the detailed conduct of prudential supervision, and it seems doubtful that other countries where central banks have shed their supervisory activities will wish to follow the UK example in this respect. At the very least, it will further increase the onus on developing new tools to cope with systemic financial instability.

Macro-prudential instruments for central banks

As explained earlier, official views are divided on whether central banks should have specific new macro-prudential tasks, for example to stabilise asset prices. The Larosière Group advised against doing so, arguing that monetary policy should not be diverted from its principal task; on this view, action to stabilise asset prices should be a regulatory responsibility, though with inputs from the central bank. This view has been firmly endorsed by ECB officials, as noted above. Yet in regimes where asset-price fluctuations are a long-standing problem, explicit targets would give much-needed precision and transparency to countervailing action; and central banks are best placed through their macroeconomic orientation to set and pursue such targets.

Among economists there seems general agreement that new operational approaches are needed to address financial instability but opinion is somewhat divided on the case for introducing additional targets and instruments. Most who have addressed the subject resist any idea that asset prices should be targets for monetary policy proper, whether by giving them specific weight in the official inflation target or including them as formal objectives to be factored into official interest-rate decisions. Some in this school nevertheless suggest that asset-price mis-alignments should be taken *informally* into account, along with the normal inflation-unemployment calculus (see for example Wadhwani 2008). They have in mind a process of 'leaning into the wind', in which monetary policymakers' customary responses to goods-price inflation would be adjusted systematically to allow for asset-price aberrations. Others doubt the efficacy of such a strategy, on the ground that interest-rate hikes sufficient to puncture asset-price bubbles would materially slow the whole economy and thus affect the basic thrust of monetary policy.

If modifying central-bank intervention rates to resist asset-price fluctuations would imply an unacceptable weakening of price-stability commitments, an alternative course would be to take such fluctuations into account when setting the regulatory standards routinely applied in prudential supervision, particularly those designed to ensure capital adequacy. This approach is advocated by Goodhart, among others, who favours the systematic application of counter-cyclical adjustments to Capital Adequacy Requirements under the Basel Accords (Goodhart 2010: 17–26). The effect would be to mitigate the strong pro-cyclical influence hitherto exerted on banking and financial intermediation by existing prudential rules, which has been 'exacerbated by a combination of Basel II and mark-to-market accounting' (Goodhart 2010: 17–26).[5] Goodhart believes that the principle of counter-cyclical regulatory requirements has been broadly accepted in Europe, though less so in the United States. However, he stresses that problems lie in the detail, and research in the field is in its infancy.

An unresolved issue in such approaches is whether asset-price stabilisation can be made more transparent to markets and the public generally, and in particular whether it should be governed by explicit targets. The potential problems involved in pursuing formal targets for equity price indices or other relevant magnitudes (such as the growth of aggregate bank lending, a suggestion floated by Goodhart in a paper before the crisis, as mentioned in Chapter 4) admittedly seem daunting. However there is one asset price which is both amenable to such treatment in our view, and highly deserving of it, namely house prices. House prices are the obvious candidate for targeting in mortgage-oriented economies because they have a very strong influence on the real economy – much stronger than that of equity prices:

they affect many more households and are known to have strong effects on consumer credit through equity-release in housing, and thence on consumer spending; and they have a powerful influence on wage demands through mortgage servicing costs. Moreover mortgage lending is determined by financial factors which are relatively well understood and documented in the literature, and familiar from experience over decades in the affected economies.

There accordingly seems a strong case for central banks in Anglo-Saxon regimes to adopt and publish explicit targets for house-price stability and develop instruments to pursue them. More specifically the Bank of England, and possibly some regional Federal Reserve Banks of the United States, and even some national central banks in the Euro Area, should target the *long-term trend value of real house prices, as measured by average house-price/income ratios* in their jurisdictions. As instruments for this purpose they should set maximum loan-to-value ratios and loan-to-income ratios for mortgage lending, and vary them to counter house-price fluctuations.[6] Such actions would certainly call for expert judgement and forecasting, as do conventional monetary-policy actions, and they would need to be undertaken in close consultation with the regulators, and monitored by them as part of their routine supervision. If necessary they should be supported by system-wide variations in mortgage lenders' capital and liquidity requirements, determined by the central bank in consultation with the regulators. All such instruments would be market-based, in harmony with the 1990s synthesis, and would helpfully reinforce the business judgements that prudent lenders should be making in any case.

A related but less obtrusive task for central banks in the macro-prudential field should be to devise and publish *early warning indicators* of stress in the financial system. Most official reports on the crisis have advocated this kind of measure. The indicators might comprise an amalgam of data covering asset prices (with house prices a principal component), credit and monetary aggregates, liquidity and gearing of banks and other financial firms; and they might extend to broader aggregates like household and national saving rates and the external current balance – on which we will focus later. Transparency and accountability would be enhanced if they became the subject of regular assessments published jointly by central banks and regulatory agencies.

The global interface

Corresponding improvements in the macro–micro prudential interface should be carried up to the global level. While few expert commentators have called for hands-on supervision to be transferred from national to international bodies, there are frequent demands for stronger cross-border coordination of such work as we have noted, especially in relation to the operations of the largest international banks; and for harmonisation of high prudential standards across all major financial centres. The Financial Stability Forum, Larosière Report and *Turner Review* all recommended the setting up of international colleges of supervisors for each of the largest global banks and this is already happening, building on arrangements that have been in existence for some years but strengthening features like information-sharing and links with macro-policy. Thus although prudential responsibility for global firms will continue to lie with regulators in the *home* regime, supervisors in *host* regimes should gain unrestricted access to relevant information on firms with operations in their territory, and should be able to communicate any worries they have to the lead supervisors and to their own policy authorities quickly and privately.

A more controversial issue in this field is the international harmonisation of prudential standards. Although there is wide support for greater harmonisation, some governments fear that the imposition of uniform regulations will reduce legitimate international competition, or result in uneven application owing to laxity in some regimes and 'gold-plating' in others. The Basel Accords provide a generally acceptable model for standardisation of prudential rules, though their codes will doubtless undergo extensive revision in the light of the crisis. However, they have not so far comprised a fully global solution because some regimes are not members of the Basel network and the coverage of the Accords is largely confined to banking business, reflecting the central banking influence on their work. Instead the international harmonisation of regulatory rules will probably lie with the new Financial Stability Board (FSB), which though still Basel-based will have global and industry-wide coverage. All post-crisis reports advocate this way forward, the G20 governments have endorsed it, and the new Board was set up in April 2009 with a wide mandate to promote international financial stability.

It remains to be seen how the FSB will pursue its remit and how transparent its actions will be. The important requirements are a strong macro-prudential role for the new Board and an active interface with macroeconomic policymaking at global level. In this context the FSB's government backing and global membership should enable it to work closely and on equal terms with the IMF, and this is the direction in which it should go. The IMF is the one institution with the financial and staff resources and competence to provide the FSB with the necessary macroeconomic guidance at global level. By virtue of its in-house economic and statistical resources and expertise in central banking and financial markets it should be well-equipped to compile the early-warning indicators of global financial stress on which the FSB will depend. And the IMF alone has the scope and authority to conduct the comprehensive national and multilateral surveillance needed to check that appropriate macro-prudential standards are being adequately observed in all the main regimes.

8

FISCAL POLICY

This chapter turns to reforms in the design and execution of fiscal policy. The first part will suggest a new long-term role for fiscal policy, aimed at achieving a sustainable rate of national saving, thus helping to maintain financial and external balance in the economy as a whole. The second part will recommend a more active short-term role for fiscal policy in stabilising aggregate demand in the face of cycles and shocks, subject to not jeopardising the longer-term objectives, in particular the 1990s commitment to price stability. The final part will call for reunification of fiscal and monetary policymaking in a single process so far as possible, thereby repairing the separation prescribed by the 1990s consensus; and suggest practical ways of achieving this.

Objectives and rules of fiscal policy

A long-term role for fiscal policy

If fiscal policy is to make an effective contribution to overcoming the problems discussed in Chapters 5 and 6 it should be given a more positive role than the one assigned by the 1990s synthesis. This would entail changing its long-term objectives and rules and making them compatible across the major economies, while allowing greater flexibility to respond to abnormal shocks in the short–medium term.

A particular challenge would be to adapt the fiscal targets and rules to the circumstances of individual economies, and especially to distinguish between the needs of low-saving and high-saving economies. Fiscal policy has a vital role to play in strengthening the saving performance of chronically low-saving economies, notably the United States and UK among others. The experience of the past two decades suggests that many of the problems confronting these economies stem from the long-run decline in private saving, mainly by households. The causes of this decline are not fully understood but they seem to lie in a combination of myopia regarding provision for old age, ill health, obsolescence of skills and other contingencies, and the aggressive promotion of personal credit following the financial liberalisation of the past few decades, which has induced large numbers of households to become increasingly indebted. The boom in property prices generated by this credit bonanza has also contributed to lower household saving in the Anglo-Saxon economies, and the exceptionally low and negative real interest rates experienced in the United States in the early 2000s further discouraged household saving there, as official studies have shown. So long as these tendencies persist, governments in these economies have a duty to compensate by increasing their own saving.

The chief blueprint for fiscal orthodoxy in the 1990s model comprised the uniform and inflexible rules adopted for EMU. Progress in the direction recommended here would require the redesign of these rules, together with the even tougher limits and the financial penalties in the Stability and Growth Pact. As explained earlier, these were introduced largely on the insistence of the German government in the negotiations before the Maastricht Treaty. Even though the worst of the fiscal excesses and associated inflationary problems observable among EU economies had been largely overcome by the start of EMU in 1999, fiscal discipline is still viewed as fragile there, and the escalation of budget deficits in Greece and other southern Euro states during the global recession has raised concerns about the integrity of the monetary union. Although the rules have been largely bypassed by Euro national governments in efforts to overcome the recession, uniform constraints on fiscal deficits are still seen by the European Commission and the ECB as essential to preserving EMU. The challenge here would be to modify the rules without jeopardising the hard-won commitment to fiscal discipline.

The key elements of a more positive role for fiscal policy are essentially threefold:

- Over the medium and longer term, fiscal policy should aim to achieve *sustainable objectives for national saving and investment*, where sustainability involves providing for future population growth and an ageing population as well as maintaining price stability, while leaving as much freedom as possible within effective prudential rules for private agents to exercise their own choices over saving and investment. The new fiscal objectives should be as clear and compelling as those of monetary policy under the 1990s consensus, despite the admitted difficulties of measurement and evaluation in the fiscal field.
- Explicit fiscal targets should be adopted to give conviction and clarity to these objectives (see the next section).
- Subject to meeting these new targets over the longer term, fiscal policy should be used more actively in the short–medium term to assist monetary policy in the pursuit of price and output stability, but only if circumstances clearly require it.

Long-term fiscal targets

Under the proposed approach, government saving would be set to deliver the official objective for national saving over the course of the economic cycle, taking account of saving in the private sector. More specifically the 'general government balance on current account' (the balance between current expenditure and revenue of central, regional and local governments) should equal target national saving *minus* expected saving by households and companies. The saving and fiscal targets should be expressed as percentages of gross national income (GNI)[1] on a cyclically-adjusted basis, i.e. averaged over the medium and longer term.[2]

The target for the customary measure of 'budget balance', namely the government's *net financial balance* (government net lending to, or borrowing from, the rest of the economy) would then be given by target government saving *minus* government capital expenditure. More specifically the government net financial balance (the surplus or deficit of general government on current and capital account – the usual definition of the budget balance[3]) should equal target saving minus its physical investment in the domestic economy and net capital transfers to the private sector and abroad. All these target magnitudes, and performance against them, would be expressed in cyclically adjusted terms.

The broad objective for national saving, and the criteria for setting the associated fiscal target, should be set by government, approved by parliament and enshrined in legislation, not merely in a code like the former UK Fiscal Stability Code (UK Treasury 1998). In trans-national systems like the European Union the broad objectives should ideally be backed by a treaty, not just a pact or intergovernmental agreement. As with most such objectives, there should be provision for temporary suspension by governments in the event of serious national or international emergencies. But any such suspension should not be permitted to weaken the commitment to the underlying objectives, by providing transparency and effective accountability. The targets should relate to the medium term (five years ahead) and longer, but should be capable of periodic revision to suit changing economic circumstances (such as persistent changes in private saving rates), subject to achieving the national saving objective.

Implicit in any national saving target, and indeed equivalent to it, would be a target for national investment, since the two are equal by definition, if national investment is defined to include all (net) investment abroad as well as physical investment in the domestic economy.[4] Thus choosing a target for national saving would also imply choosing one for national investment. The practical task of setting national saving and investment targets would be far from straightforward. Difficult issues surround the estimation of an economy's aggregate production function (the technical relationship between output and inputs of capital and labour) and its aggregate rate of time discount (the economic relationship expressing the optimal rate of substitution between present and future consumption). And difficult statistical issues would arise over the measurement and valuation of net wealth (non-financial capital). Yet these difficulties have not deterred economists from speculating as to what might constitute optimal saving rates in the major economies. A simple estimate is presented for the UK in Box 8.1. It concludes, predictably enough, that actual saving in the UK in the past ten years has been at least 3 per cent and perhaps up to 8 per cent of GDP *less* that it should have been on the assumption that saving should at least maintain the prevailing stock of net wealth in relation to trend GDP. More will be said about the orders of magnitude of national saving targets and implied government budget balances in the next section.

BOX 8.1 HOW MUCH SHOULD THE UK AIM TO SAVE?

For at least the past two decades the UK national saving rate has been one of the lowest among the main developed economies. A low saving rate in the UK is sometimes defended on the ground that the population is projected to age less rapidly than in other industrial countries, but the burden of pensions financing is set to rise substantially in the UK in coming decades. Is it possible to assess how much the UK economy ought now to be saving?

The table below offers a broad-brush estimate using national accounting aggregates. It follows a simple approach that has been used in the *National Institute Economic Review* (see NIESR 2003: 5–6). The method is based on the assumption that an economy should be saving enough on average at least to maintain the outstanding stock of physical wealth – essentially fixed assets, inventories and land – in relation to national income through time. Since the trend rate of growth of UK real national income (and GDP) is close to 2.5 per cent p.a., this assumption implies that saving should provide for growth of net wealth – the value of land and physical capital net of depreciation (or capital consumption) – at that rate.

UK national wealth and required saving, 1998 and 2008
(*£ billion at current prices*)

	1998	2008
Net national wealth, end-year	3,354	6,953
Required net national saving (2.5% of net national wealth)	83.8	173.8
Plus capital consumption	99.0	162.3
Required gross national saving	182.8	336.1
Ditto, % of GDP	20.8	23.2
Actual gross national saving	158.3	219.0
Ditto, % of GDP	18.0	15.1
Shortfall of gross saving, % of GDP	2.8	8.1

Source: UK Office of National Statistics online database.
Note: GDP is at current market prices.

According to these estimates, the shortfall of actual gross national saving below the amount needed to maintain a constant wealth/GDP ratio rose from nearly 3 per cent of GDP in 1998 to a huge 8 per cent of GDP in 2008. The estimates should be viewed with caution. The wealth data value business sector capital (and the capital consumption deducted to arrive at its net value) at current replacement cost, so these values should not be much affected by short-run fluctuations in stock-market prices. However, land and house prices are valued at current market prices, so the value of wealth in 2008 will be inflated by the recent property boom (even though house prices had fallen back then from the mid-2007 peak). For that reason the saving shortfall in 2008 may be somewhat exaggerated here, though the true shortfall in that year was probably significantly higher than in 1998.

On the face of it the above proposals might appear to be at odds with economic orthodoxy in this field: many free-market economists would argue that physical investment is not an appropriate subject for macroeconomic targeting in modern market economies, since well-functioning markets should deliver sustainable levels of investment in normal conditions over the medium and long term. This is the accepted view under the 1990s synthesis, at least for investment in the private sector, and increasingly in the modern era public investment also tends to be based on market criteria, moderated to allow for external and social effects in some fields. Accordingly, regimes modelled on the synthesis generally accept prevailing levels of aggregate capital formation, averaged over the cycle. In that case, setting a national saving target would mean aiming to ensure that aggregate saving provides the resources needed to sustain prevailing rates of physical investment without undue stress over the medium and longer run. Nevertheless even highly non-interventionist governments might wish to set higher saving targets if they judged prevailing national investment rates to be insufficient for long-term sustainability, provided efficient ways of stimulating investment could be found.

Although the idea that fiscal policy should be used to target national saving did not feature in the 1990s consensus, it has a highly respectable neoclassical lineage. In the 1960s a distinguished neoclassical economist, James Meade, suggested that fiscal policy should be dedicated to targeting national wealth as part of a new pattern of policy assignments designed to promote growth and stability. In the 1990s he repeated the recommendation in the context of policy for EMU (Meade and Weale 1995). But the notion did not appeal to traditional Keynesians, who were mostly preoccupied with fiscal policy's counter-cyclical role: it was not taken up in the era of Keynesian management; nor did it resurface in the 1990s consensus. However, the idea is now being revived in the light of concerns about ageing populations and inadequate saving for retirement. Among its exponents is Martin Weale (a former associate and protégé of Meade) who, with his colleagues at the National Institute of Economic and Social Research, have been addressing the role of fiscal policy in relation to *fairness between generations* and the implications for national saving. Although their concerns differ somewhat from ours with macroeconomic stability, their conclusions are consistent with our recommendations here, in particular that fiscal policy should target national saving as a long-term objective, rather than mere fiscal balance. A fuller account of their arguments can be found in Box 8.2. The fiscal policy aspects of pension provision will be discussed near the end of the chapter.

BOX 8.2 FISCAL POLICY, INTER-GENERATIONAL FAIRNESS AND NATIONAL SAVING

This box outlines the analysis and findings of economists at the National Institute of Economic and Social Research who have been assessing fiscal policy from the perspective of fairness between generations, and its relationship with national saving. It draws particularly on a recent paper by Ray Barrell and Martin Weale (2009).

The authors start by surveying earlier thinking on the nature of the national debt and whether it is different from other forms of debt. The message is that the national debt is indeed a burden on future generations if government borrowing finances more consumption overall than would occur in the case of equivalent tax financing, and if output is largely supply-determined (as the paper assumes, see below). They also report some new empirical evidence on whether governments can actually change the national saving rate through changing the amount they save themselves. A regression analysis using pooled annual data for 26 OECD economies (Korea and Norway are excluded because they are outliers) for 1987–2007 finds that on average a 1 per cent increase in government saving as a proportion of GDP raises national saving by about 0.5 per cent of GDP. This provides helpful corroboration of our view that governments can influence national saving by changing the aggregate stance of fiscal policy.

The main part of the paper uses an 'overlapping generations' model to investigate the consequences of differences in national debt levels and certain other key exogenous factors on transfers of consumption between two temporarily coexisting generations or cohorts in a simple two-cohort economy, the first comprising old and retired property-owners and the second, young actively-employed workers. The analysis examines differences between alternative long-run steady states and is thus highly relevant to the choice of long-run objectives for fiscal policy. It employs a standard neoclassical framework including, importantly, the assumption that national productivity and its growth are given purely by long-run supply factors, and are therefore wholly independent of fiscal policy and other demand-side influences. Most Keynesians would of course question that assumption in a short- and medium-term context, but we think few nowadays would see it as ground for rejecting the broad conclusions of an analysis so focused on the long term.

A chief finding of the model when put through its paces is that, other things being equal, high levels of national debt will indeed transfer resources from the younger to the older generation, and in the process permanently reduce the national saving rate; the model also shows that precisely similar transfers and reductions in national saving will occur through pay-as-you-go benefit systems, which create no government debt but which create tax burdens that are equivalent to the interest burdens created by a high-debt policy. Fairness between generations then requires government action to redistribute income from the older (retired) cohort to the younger (employed) cohort, thereby raising the national saving rate. The obvious response would be to switch policy from budget deficits towards surpluses.

The latter conclusion depends somewhat on which of several alternative notions of fairness are thought relevant. The case for remedial fiscal action is clearest if fairness is interpreted to mean that each age-cohort is required to pay its own way, without net transfers between parents and children; the case is less clear if a social planner opts to allow transfers from younger to older generations on the ground that productivity growth raises consumable income in favour of the former cohorts successively through time.

The potential equivalence of the inter-generational transfer effects found in this analysis, when comparing pure government debt-creation policies and pure pay-as-you-go systems, is a particularly helpful result for us because it demonstrates the importance of adopting national saving rates rather than fiscal balance as long-term targets for fiscal policy. As the authors point out, 'the budgetary position is, on its own, not a useful indicator of whether future generations are being burdened or not' (Barrell and Weale 2009: 10). Moreover, although these authors focus mainly on inter-generational fairness rather than the questions of economic sustainability that concern us, there is clearly a degree of congruence between the two approaches which leads to similar conclusions. In Weale's analysis the sustainability aspects arise with particular force from the finding that large changes in property prices (resulting for example from changes in demand for housing, given the inelastic supply of residential land) will lead to resource transfers between the older generation of retired property owners and the younger generation of active wage earners that are qualitatively similar to those from high government debt. The underlying rationale for this, recalling Meade earlier, is that big property-price changes are akin to exogenous wealth effects (positive or negative windfalls) that influence property-owners' consumption and saving, and thence the national saving rate. On this reasoning, the property-price boom in Anglo-Saxon economies during the early 2000s transferred wealth to the older generation and led to a surge of consumption that that was clearly unsustainable. The subsequent fall in property prices brought about by the 2008–9 credit crunch has only partially eliminated this windfall gain. As the authors conclude, the long-term resolution of these problems will involve some combination of higher government net saving in the Anglo-Saxon economies, reduced government transfers to property-owners, and increases through time in the working lives of the younger, employed, generations.

Pursuing a national saving target is unlikely to be an easy task in an era when private saving rates diverge a long way from historic averages, as among major economies in the past decade. Nevertheless, with such vital issues at stake it should be possible for governments to find an approach that would overcome most of these difficulties and offer a common-sense solution that would appeal to markets and electorates. Reasons for optimism regarding this task turn on the links that exist in all economies between national saving and the balance of payments, as should become clearer in a moment. The failure of fiscal policy to allow for the vagaries of private saving behaviour has led to the emergence of massive international payments imbalances between the major economies since the late 1990s, which in turn represent substantial net foreign investment or disinvestment (the latter largely unintended, and regretted by some in the countries concerned). These net international capital flows are a component of national investment alongside domestic physical investment, and should be taken into account when setting national saving targets. A novelty of our approach is that by including net foreign investment alongside domestic physical investment as an element in national investment, it would imply setting explicit *targets for net external current payments* alongside those for national saving and the budget balance.

To restate the argument slightly differently: if an economy's national saving falls below its domestic expenditure on physical investment, and market forces do not close the gap somehow, the result will be an *external payments deficit* – a deficit on the current account of the balance of external payments. Conversely if an economy's national saving exceeds its domestic investment the result will be an external payments *surplus*, as seen in the context of the 'global saving glut'. The national accounting links which underlie these propositions are set out in Annex 8.1 at the end of this chapter. They are a commonplace of macroeconomic theory and expositions can be found in standard textbooks (for example Miles and Scott 2005: sec. 19.6; Blanchard 2003: sec. 19-6).

Accordingly, setting a national saving target would require governments to take a view not just about the adequacy of their economy's domestic investment performance but also about the desirability of generating resources for (net) foreign investment. For some developed economies this might amount to setting a national saving rate that merely matches their economy's physical investment rate over the long run, which would mean aiming at zero external balance on current account. For others a more ambitious national saving objective would aim to finance persistent net external investment or aid in addition to sustaining prevailing levels or trends in domestic physical investment, which would mean targeting an external current account surplus. Only a few might opt freely for persistent net external *disinvestment* and might have to be subjected to strong international persuasion, or inducements, before doing so.

It would be sensible to regard the 'default' position under our approach as one in which most or all major economies would set fiscal policy to target *zero* balance on current external payments.[5] This would nevertheless imply a distinctly more ambitious saving target than, for example, the UK's 'golden rule', which merely aimed at a government saving rate of zero over the cycle and permitted the government to borrow to finance investment regardless of saving in the private sector.[6] Under the approach proposed here, governments of economies with chronically low private saving rates, like the United States and UK, would aim to be *net savers* over the medium and longer term, preferably to the extent of reducing net external debt as well as domestically-held government debt steadily in the long run. On the other hand, governments of economies with chronically high private saving rates, notably Germany and Japan, would aim to be dis-savers over the medium and longer term, so long as high private saving persists. Such compensatory patterns of government saving have generally not materialised in recent decades, as will shown below.

Sceptics may question the technical feasibility of the balance of payments targeting proposed here. No correlation is apparent between fiscal and balance of payments deficits in major economies over the past decade, as Bernanke (2005) has pointed out. However, this is hardly a surprise in an era when fiscal policies were generally passive, aimed at achieving budget balance or small deficits, so that national saving rates (and thus external current balances) were dominated by the disparate movements observed in private saving rates. There is no disagreement about the close link between *total* national saving and the balance of external payments in most economies, for the accounting reasons referred to earlier. A key issue in this field is the response of private saving to changes in government saving, and there the evidence seems encouraging. For example a recent study of 26 OECD economies by Barrell and Weale (2009; see Box 8.2) found that a change of 1 per cent in government saving as a proportion of GDP raises national saving by 0.5 per cent of GDP over the long term. But other studies imply smaller effects in the United States (see Bernanke 2005: 11). Much may depend on the time horizon of the study, the openness of the country concerned, the response of monetary policy to shifts in fiscal stance, and policy responses in the rest of the world.

Finally the role proposed for fiscal policy here does not claim to be a complete response to the low saving rates seen in Anglo-Saxon economies. A full response would include better financial regulation to discourage imprudent borrowing – to which new monetary instruments should make a contribution, as argued in Chapter 7. Another remedy would lie in the provision of stronger incentives for private saving, including preferential tax treatment of pension contributions and probably an element of compulsion for employees to participate in approved pension arrangements, perhaps in the context of a nationally sponsored scheme, as will be explained later. If stronger incentives and better regulation are put in place, and the uncertainties created by the present financial crisis subside, private savers may regain confidence and normal household saving (as distinct from the panic saving created by the recession) may eventually recover to a more sustainable rate. But it would be optimistic to count on that occurring to the full extent needed for long-term sustainability, or on its happening soon.

Orders of magnitude

An indication of the relevant orders of magnitude is offered in Table 8.1. The table observes the equality that must hold in all economies between the combined

TABLE 8.1 Saving, investment, net lending and external current balance: four major economies, 1985–2008 (per cent of GDP at current prices, five-year annual averages)

		1985–9	1990–4[a]	1995–9	2000–4	2005–8[b]
United States						
Saving:	Private	17.8	16.8	16.2	15.1	15.1
	Government	−1.9	−2.3	1.2	0.2	−1.0
	National	15.9	14.5	17.4	15.2	14.1
Investment:	Private	17.0	14.7	16.9	16.6	17.0
	Government	2.3	2.4	2.4	2.5	2.5
	National	19.4	17.1	19.2	19.1	19.4
Net lending:	Private	0.6	1.9	−1.0	−1.7	−1.4
	Government	−4.1	−4.5	−0.9	−2.2	−3.6
	National	−3.5	−2.6	−1.8	−3.9	−5.0
External current balance		−2.7	−1.0	−2.1	−4.9	−5.9
(Of which, net income from abroad)		(0.5)	(0.5)	(0.3)	(0.5)	(0.8)
UK						
Saving:	Private	16.0	17.1	16.9	14.6	15.4
	Government	1.3	−2.0	−0.3	0.6	−0.7
	National	17.3	15.2	16.6	15.2	14.6
Investment:	Private	17.7	15.1	16.1	15.7	15.8
	Government	2.1	2.2	1.4	1.5	1.7
	National	19.8	17.3	17.5	17.2	17.5
Net lending:	Private	−1.1	3.2	1.4	−0.6	1.0
	Government	−1.2	−5.2	−2.3	−1.3	−3.4
	National	−2.3	−2.1	−0.9	−1.9	−2.4
External current balance		−2.4	−2.1	−1.0	−1.9	−2.7
(Of which, net income from abroad)		(−1.2)	(−1.1)	(−0.2)	(0.9)	(1.4)
Germany						
Saving:	Private	..	20.6	20.5	20.4	23.5
	Government	..	1.2	0.2	−0.3	1.2
	National	..	21.8	20.7	20.1	24.6
Investment:	Private	..	20.3	19.6	17.0	16.6
	Government	..	2.7	2.0	1.6	1.4
	National	..	23.0	21.5	18.6	18.0

TABLE 8.1 *Continued*

		1985–9	1990–4ª	1995–9	2000–4	2005–8ᵇ
Net lending:	Private	..	1.3	3.0	4.1	7.8
	Government	..	<u>−2.7</u>	<u>−3.9</u>	<u>−2.6</u>	<u>−1.2</u>
	National	..	<u>−1.3</u>	<u>−0.9</u>	<u>1.5</u>	<u>6.6</u>
External current balance		..	−1.2	−0.9	1.4	6.5
(Of which, net income from abroad)		..	(0.1)	(−0.8)	(−0.6)	(1.7)
Japan						
Saving:	Private	28.0	27.7	27.3	27.4	27.3
	Government	<u>4.1</u>	<u>4.7</u>	<u>1.5</u>	<u>−1.5</u>	<u>−0.4</u>
	National	32.0	32.4	29.0	25.9	26.9
Investment:	Private	25.3	25.5	21.4	19.2	20.3
	Government	<u>4.7</u>	<u>5.5</u>	<u>5.9</u>	<u>4.6</u>	<u>3.3</u>
	National	29.9	31.0	27.4	23.8	23.7
Net lending:	Private	3.3	2.8	8.7	10.0	7.5
	Government	<u>−0.1</u>	<u>−0.4</u>	<u>−6.6</u>	<u>−7.2</u>	<u>−3.5</u>
	National	<u>3.2</u>	<u>2.4</u>	<u>2.1</u>	<u>2.8</u>	<u>4.0</u>
External current balance		3.3	2.4	2.3	2.9	4.1
(Of which, net income from abroad)		(0.5)	(0.8)	(1.2)	(1.7)	(2.8)

Source: OECD Stat, 'National accounts' and 'Economic Projections' online database; and author's calculations (see below).

Notes: ª   For Germany, four-year annual averages 1991–4.
   ᵇ   Four-year average, except for Japan (2005–7).
   ..   indicated that data is not available.

All percentages relate to income and expenditure at current market prices. GDP, saving and investment are all measured 'gross' (before deducting capital consumption).

Saving: the residue of gross income after deducting tax, net current transfers to other sectors, and final consumption.

Investment: expenditure on physical capital (fixed assets and inventories), before deducting capital consumption; alternatively 'gross capital formation'.

Net lending: the balance of saving *minus* investment and net capital transfers to other sectors (e.g. investment grants); alternatively, 'net acquisition of financial assets'.

Private net lending: the sum of net lending by households and non-profit-making institutions serving them, and financial and non-financial firms (corporations). Calculated as the balance of net national lending *minus* government net lending.

Government includes national, regional and local governments; alternatively 'general government'.

National net lending: equivalent to the economy's net financial balance with the rest of the world (alternatively 'external' sector). In principle, national net lending is also equal to the economy's balance of external current payments, except that the latter is arrived at before deducting net capital transfers to the rest of the world (whereas national net lending is net of such transfers).

External current balance: the balance of exports *minus* imports of goods and services, *plus* net income and current transfers from abroad. In principle it equals national net lending before deducting net capital transfers to the rest of the world (see Annex 1 of Chapter 8). However because the data sources for external payments differ from those for domestic income and expenditure, statistical errors may arise between them. These contribute to the discrepancies between national net lending and external current balance in the table.

Net income from abroad: residents' receipts of property income (interest, profits and dividends) and labour income from the rest of the world, net of the corresponding payments abroad; alternatively 'net primary income'.

net lending (or net financial balance) of domestic sectors – essentially the sum of saving minus investment by the private and government sectors, which may be negative (implying net external borrowing) – and the economy's balance of current external payments (which equals the *external sector's* net financial balance with sign reversed). As explained above, this equality is an identity if statistical errors and omissions are ignored: it holds by definition and must therefore always be true.

The main features from the late 1980s until the recent global recession are as follows:

1. Gross national saving (the balance of gross national disposable income not spent on current consumption) has tended to be a much lower proportion of GDP in the United States and UK than in Germany and Japan. The two Anglo-Saxon economies have become chronically low savers by international and their own previous standards.

2. Gross national saving rates have tended to fall markedly in three of the four major economies (Germany is an exception). As will be seen shortly (Table 8.2), the falls have occurred mainly in the household sector. However, in Japan and Germany, increases in company saving have compensated for much of the fall in household saving, unlike in the United States or UK.

3. National physical investment (gross capital formation in fixed assets and inventories) in the United States and UK has been within a band of 15–20 per cent of domestic output (GDP), though subject to fairly shallow cyclical fluctuations. In contrast, investment has been on a marked downward trend in both Japan and reunified Germany, having started higher.

4. In all four majors the great bulk of physical investment has been, and continues to be, undertaken by the private sector (firms and households). Government investment amounts to about one-tenth of national investment in three of them, though rather more than that in Japan.

5. The United States and UK have consequently experienced a substantial shortfall of national saving below investment, and the gap has increased considerably in the past few years. This is reflected in high and generally rising levels of national net borrowing (negative net lending) since the turn of the century. In contrast, Japan has recorded substantial and generally rising net national lending in the past decade and Germany has re-established its traditional position as a net national lender in the same period.

6. This contrasting experience is reflected in these countries' external payments balances. The shortfalls in domestic saving below investment in the United States and UK have resulted in net external borrowing via regular, and latterly rising, current external deficits for both. In contrast the excesses of national saving over investment in Japan and, recently, reunified Germany, have created rising external payments surpluses.

7. So far, the impact of the implied increase in US and UK net external debt on their net income from abroad has been muted. US net income from abroad

TABLE 8.2 Gross and net saving, four major economies, 1985–2008 (per cent of GDP at current prices, five-year annual averages)

	1985–9	1990–4[a]	1995–9	2000–4	2005–8[b]
United States					
Gross national saving	15.9	14.5	17.4	15.2	14.1
Less capital consumption	−11.3	−11.1	−11.1	−11.7	−12.0
Net national saving	4.6	3.4	6.3	3.5	2.1
Of which: Households	5.7	4.9	2.8	1.6	0.6
Firms	2.1	2.3	3.8	3.4	3.9
Government	−3.3	−3.8	−0.3	−1.4	−2.4
UK					
Gross national saving	17.3	15.2	16.6	15.2	14.6
Less capital consumption	−12.9	−13.0	−11.6	−11.3	−11.1
Net national saving	4.4	2.1	4.9	3.9	3.6
Of which: Households	4.8	6.9	5.7	3.4	2.6
Firms	−0.5	−1.6	0.6	0.8	2.6
Government	0.1	−3.2	−1.4	−0.3	−1.6
Germany					
Gross national saving	..	21.8	20.7	20.1	24.6
Less capital consumption	..	−14.4	−14.7	−14.9	−14.8
Net national saving	..	7.4	6.0	5.1	9.8
Of which: Households	..	8.1	6.6	6.5	7.0
Firms	..	−0.1	0.9	0.7	3.3
Government	..	−0.6	−1.6	−2.0	−0.5
Japan					
Gross national saving	32.0	32.4	29.0	25.9	26.9
Less capital consumption	−15.4	−17.3	−18.9	−20.4	−20.8
Net national saving	16.6	15.1	10.0	5.5	6.1
Of which: Households	8.8	8.6	6.7	3.1	2.1
Firms	3.7	1.8	3.9	6.7	7.5
Government	4.1	4.7	−0.5	−4.3	−3.5

Source: OECD Stat, 'National accounts' online database and author's calculations (see below).

Notes: [a] For Germany, annual average 1991–4.
  [b] Four–year average except for Japan (2005–7).
  .. indicates that data is not available.
Net saving: gross saving minus capital consumption.
Firms' net saving here was calculated by deducting net saving of households and government from net national saving.

has averaged around 0.5 per cent of GDP for two decades, though US net property income (profits, interest and dividends) has been falling steadily. The UK's net foreign income has been relatively resilient in recent years but has nevertheless averaged little more than 1 per cent of GDP since 2000. In contrast there have been significant rises in German and Japanese net foreign income in recent years.

Table 8.1 focuses on gross saving and thus begs the question of how far differences in saving rates may reflect different rates of capital consumption, as opposed to differences in net wealth creation. Gross national saving rates may differ because more physical capital is used up in producing output in some countries than others. Table 8.2 addresses this question by distinguishing between gross and net saving in our four major economies, and between net saving by the main sectors in each.

The main features since the late 1980s until the global recession are as follows:

1. Annual capital consumption has been markedly higher in relation to GDP in the high-saving economies than in the low-savers: of the order of 15 per cent increasing to 21 per cent in Japan and nearly 15 per cent in Germany, compared with 11–13 per cent in the United States and UK. The trend has been flat in three of the four majors, Japan being the exception.
2. Accordingly the gap in saving rates between the high and low-saving economies in recent years has been less marked on a net than on a gross basis. Yet the gap has remained appreciable even on a net basis: since the late 1990s, net national saving has fallen to an average of about 3 per cent of GDP in the United States and UK, well below the average of around 6 per cent in Japan, while it has risen to nearly 10 per cent in Germany.
3. The fall in net national saving in the United States and UK since the mid–late 1990s has been accounted for mainly by lower household net saving; if anything net corporate saving has risen there somewhat, though remaining low in relation to GDP. Household net saving has also been on a falling trend in Japan since the 1990s, but it has been accompanied there by strongly rising corporate net saving, while much of the fall in net national saving in Japan in the past ten years has been accounted for by the substantial government dis-saving. Household net saving has remained fairly robust in Germany, and corporate net saving there has been strong in the past few years.

In short, the trends in net saving in our four majors conform to the broad picture shown by Table 8.1. Weak and falling net private saving in the two Anglo-Saxon economies, attributable largely to falls in household saving since the early 1990s, have generated net borrowing which has been allowed to spill over into rising external current deficits; robust net private saving in the other two economies, to which strong corporate saving has latterly made a strong contribution, has generated the financial counterpart to rising external current surpluses for both economies, despite the large Japanese fiscal deficits of the past decade.

To see what our fiscal proposals might imply in practice, consider the US experience in Table 8.1. Between 2000 and 2008, gross physical investment in the US economy averaged about 19 per cent of GDP. Under our proposals, and assuming the US government would have been content with this as a sustainable rate of investment, it would have set a national saving objective of 19 per cent for this period, implying an external current balance of zero. In fact US private saving averaged only around 15 per cent of GDP since 2000, so government saving should have averaged some 4 per cent of GDP to achieve the national saving objective, rather than the small average deficit actually recorded. On the admittedly questionable assumption that US private saving and investment would have been unaffected by the tighter stance of fiscal policy, the higher government saving rate would have resulted in a US budget surplus (government net lending) averaging around 1.5 per cent of GDP, rather than the average deficit of 2.75 per cent actually recorded. Alternatively the US government might have chosen a higher national saving rate in order to reduce external debt, in order to aim at an external current payments surplus, other things being equal. For example, if an external payments surplus of 1 per cent of GDP had been aimed at (to reduce US net external debt by 1 per cent of GDP annually), a government budget surplus averaging 2.5 per cent of GDP would have been required.

These are of course no more than mechanical calculations and make no allowance for the effects of a different stance of US fiscal policy on private saving and investment. Those questions will be revisited in a moment.

Are persistent external deficits a serious problem for developed economies?

A balance of payments deficit may not mean that the economy is living beyond its means (as is sometimes said), because some foreign borrowing may finance productive investment at home, indirectly if not directly. But a large and persistent payments deficit does raise questions about sustainability which no responsible government can ignore. The prospect of a number of the world's wealthiest economies regularly importing capital from the rest of the world is at odds with the view, well supported in economic theory, that rich economies should be capital exporters. Rich economies should aim not only to generate resources for investment in, and aid to, poorer economies but also to finance the creation or acquisition of business stakes (foreign direct investments) abroad. It is widely accepted that multinational firms are effective vehicles for international transfer of the knowledge-based products and technologies in which advanced economies generally have a strong comparative advantage. As things stand, both the United States and UK continue to undertake substantial direct investment abroad, but much or all of it has to be financed, indirectly if not directly, by short-term foreign borrowing rather than by domestic saving. The result is a persistent increase in these economies' net external short-term debt, which tends sooner or later to raise exposure to exchange-rate volatility.

As explained in Chapter 5, financial assets issued in the Anglo-Saxon economies have long been regarded as a safe haven for the excess savings of emerging economies, especially the big oil exporters. This motivation appears to have survived the recent global financial crisis but it must eventually decline if the long-term prosperity of the host economies comes into serious question; indeed the dollar's big depreciation in recent years suggests that this is now happening. Admittedly the United States and UK, more than most other majors, have experienced high net

immigration since the turn of the century, and they might be thought to be importing capital temporarily to provide for the rise in population. However, doubt is cast
on that view by the continuing long-run decline of physical investment as a share of
GDP in both economies. If external borrowing were being used to finance exceptional additions to the capital stock in order to accommodate population increases,
their rates of capital formation should be rising, not falling as in Table 8.1. Moreover, external payments deficits were an established feature of both economies well
before net immigration began to rise.

Economists have long debated the question of optimal rates of investment and
saving in market economies and there is an extensive literature on the subject. The
standard neoclassical models assume that factor prices are flexible in the long run
and respond freely to excess demand, that investors and savers have perfect fore-
sight, that industrial goods are homogeneous and that most markets are freely competitive in all other respects. They often also assume a closed economy, with some
possibility for interest rates to differ between economies. On these assumptions the
real interest rate adjusts freely to bring the rate of investment into equality with the
rate of domestic saving at full-capacity output.[7] However, many of these assumptions are questionable in a real-world context, especially the assumption of a closed
economy. If saving rates at comparable levels of income and real interest rates differ
markedly between economies, capital will tend to flow from high- to low-saving
economies. Provided markets are efficient and flexible, low-saving economies will
invest the capital flows in ways that will generate income sufficient to service the
external debt and eventually repay it. But if markets are prone to inefficiencies and
excesses of the kind described earlier, the outcome may be much less sustainable.
In particular, if resources borrowed abroad are not invested in operations capable
of producing exports profitably, but are instead consumed in the capital-importing
economy, or invested in non-tradable goods, the share of domestic incomes payable abroad will eventually rise and disposable national income will be progressively
squeezed, and the share of the low-saving economy's capital stock owned abroad,
net of foreign assets owned by residents, will rise commensurately. In the long run,
if nothing happens to reverse these trends, the bulk of the economy's productive
assets in tradable goods industries will eventually be owned abroad, and the bulk
of profits arising from them, payable abroad. And if the tradable goods are poor
substitutes on world markets, and/or domestic factor prices are not flexible enough
to deliver the changes in relative costs needed to restore international competitiveness, these trends may be hard to reverse. Sharp and protracted movements in real
exchange rates may then be the only feasible adjustment mechanism, damaging
though they may be.

The impression in Table 8.1 that persistent US and UK external deficits have led
to no more than a mild squeeze on net income from abroad is of only limited com-
fort in this context. These net income flows are the outcome of much larger gross
flows inward and outward, which tend to be both cyclical and erratic. Much of this
volatility is due to exchange-rate fluctuations, given that inflows tend to be fixed
in foreign currency and outflows in domestic currency. Moreover, the figures omit

capital gains or losses on overseas asset holdings, which may be substantial when large swings occur in corporate profits and stock markets fluctuate widely. Even so, the fact that these two economies with large foreign direct investments now receive only small net foreign incomes should concern their governments.

For all these reasons it is hard to avoid the conclusion that the long-run decline of private saving in the Anglo-Saxon economies needs to be urgently addressed and that fiscal policy has an important part to play. Admittedly the long-term rule suggested here – that fiscal policy should target the balance of payments – is a rather limited solution to the low-saving problem; preferably microeconomic measures should also be taken to address myopia and misinformation among private savers, like better education and stronger incentives for long-term saving. But the rule's simplicity has merits in terms of transparency and accountability. Balance on external payments is a straightforward objective, offering advantages in terms of steady trading conditions and exchange-rate stability that should have strong business appeal in open economies. Balance of payments targets could be readily monitored and should be easily understood by the markets and the public generally. And the principle that fiscal policy should be assigned to securing external payments balance should have wide intuitive appeal.

Potential problems under the proposed approach

Nevertheless the proposed approach would not be without problems. The main and obvious drawback would be that, in the transition, it would imply a significant tightening of fiscal stance in low-saving economies, which would be deflationary over the short–medium term, other things being unchanged. Without an offsetting stimulus from some other source, low-saving economies could be subjected to lengthy recession. For example consider the figures for the UK in Table 8.1. On the face of it, and ignoring feedbacks induced by the change, a fiscal target aimed at balancing total UK saving and physical investment over the period 2000 to 2008 would have required a government budget in approximately zero average balance, instead of the average annual deficit of about 2.25 per cent of GDP actually recorded. Such a target would have called for significantly higher tax rates or lower government spending, which would have markedly reduced national disposable income and private investment, other things being equal.

One way of compensating for such a fiscal tightening would be to apply an offsetting stimulus via monetary policy. Had fiscal policy been significantly tighter on average in the low-saving economies in recent years, the effects on aggregate demand might have been countered by relaxing monetary policy enough to leave national income and investment unaffected. But lower interest rates might have further depressed private saving and the target for government saving might then have had to be raised further. It would be important not to allow more ambitious long-term fiscal targets in low-saving economies to slide into a permanently deflationary policy stance. Much would depend on the strength and timing of spontaneous recovery from the current global recession. Even in favourable circumstances, a shift in fiscal policy to target sustainable national saving rates in the United States and UK might have to be stretched over around five years to avoid prolonging the recent recession.

A policy approach of this kind, involving as it would a substantial change in the *mix* of fiscal and monetary policies in low-saving economies, should take account of the international linkages that exist between interest rates in conditions of high capital mobility. Under free international markets the conventional closed-economy argument that higher government saving will reduce the cost of capital for domestic investors might not apply, even if it were accompanied by an offsetting relaxation of monetary policy. When financial capital can flow freely across national boundaries, a fiscally-induced boost to national saving might simply reduce the economy's reliance on cheap foreign funds to finance its external borrowing requirement, rather than reducing the cost of finance to domestic industry. In short, a fiscally-inspired boost to national saving would not necessarily reduce domestic interest rates under globalised capital markets. (A fuller explanation of this argument is offered in Annex 8.2 at the end of this chapter.) On the other hand, the feared disincentive to private saving from lower long-term interest rates, mentioned above, might not materialise either in these conditions.

Apart from merely attenuating the policy change, two other ways of countering the short-/medium-term deflationary effects of a fiscal tightening in low-saving economies might be considered. If domestic bank lending rates failed to respond to a cut in official intervention rates, central banks might turn to quantitative easing, in the manner described earlier. In compensation for a fiscal tightening, the central bank could inject money into the economy on a large scale through open-market operations in order to drive down long-term interest rates, hoping to stimulate credit in that way. If this tactic were insufficient to counter the deflationary influence, the fiscal authority might seek to offset the negative effects on private investment by raising public investment or subsidising worthwhile private projects. Under our proposed long-term rule, the additional government investment would need to be financed either by cutting government current expenditure or raising taxes, leaving the government net financial surplus at its post-shift level. If tax increases were chosen, the deflationary effects would be partly mitigated through the 'balanced budget multiplier' postulated by Keynesian theorists, under which an increase in public investment will stimulate aggregate demand even if it is fully matched by tax receipts, since the whole of the expenditure increase represents extra demand, whereas part of the tax increase would be financed by cutting private saving rather than consumption. The latter fall in private saving (as compared with the situation before fiscal tightening) would be unwelcome, but it would be more than offset by higher government saving.

International fiscal cooperation

Some problems that might be encountered by our fiscal proposals lie in the international field and it would therefore be vital for the approach to have an international dimension, in at least two respects. Firstly and crucially, any sustained fiscal tightening in low-saving economies should be accompanied by corresponding fiscal relaxation in their high-saving counterparts. Although an overall rise in developed economies' saving should reduce international real interest rates and so stimulate global investment, other things being equal, there can be no presumption that the investment response would compensate for the expenditure cuts or tax increases required by higher government saving. Moreover, since individual countries' external current balances must sum to zero globally (after allowing for statistical errors and omissions), there is a risk that fiscal pursuit of higher national saving and external payments surpluses in low-saving economies would initiate a 'pass the deficit' process, in which high-saving economies responded by tightening their own fiscal stance. Unless countered in some way, this process could initiate a downward spiral of activity and incomes worldwide. The surest way of avoiding that damaging outcome would be for governments of high-saving economies, acting together, to reduce their saving, and thence their external surpluses, commensurately with the increase of saving in low-saving economies.

Ideally therefore our fiscal proposals call for the adoption of compatible national saving targets in *all major economies*. In the absence of a marked reduction in private saving in the high-saving majors, government saving there would need to be significantly below the average levels of recent years. For example the data in Table 8.1 suggest that, ignoring feedbacks, annual government budget deficits since 2000 should have been higher by some 3–4 percentage points of GDP on average in Japan, and by a broadly similar margin in Germany. A test of the success of such a policy rebalancing would be that the massive external payments imbalances seen among the major economies in recent years would steadily fall and eventually disappear, while maintaining output and price stability overall.

The second area calling for international cooperation under our proposals is that of exchange rates. There is a risk that the long-term fiscal rebalancing we envisage would be frustrated by exchange-rate changes, if it is accepted that the huge and rising trade imbalances seen between the major economies in recent years have been due at least partly to inappropriate exchange rates, as argued in Chapter 5. At times over the past two decades, phases of substantial overvaluation of the dollar and sterling have contributed to US and UK trade deficits by worsening their international competitiveness. Although these influences have fluctuated, the dollar has become increasingly undervalued against most other key currencies (until the recent decline in the euro), and sterling suddenly became so in the recent crisis. But serious difficulties would emerge if the dollar and pound strengthened appreciably in the event of fiscal tightening in the United States and UK. Whether this would happen is hard to judge. In principle countries with an established record of tight fiscal policy (like China) should enjoy competitive exchange rates, because their domestic interest rates tend to be below global rates, but this abstracts from the influence of risk premiums in determining exchange rates, especially when policy stances change unexpectedly. An unexpected shift from budget deficit to surplus in low-saving economies might have the reverse effect, generating sharp real appreciations in their currencies as international investors regained confidence in them. Big upswings in the dollar and sterling cannot be ruled out in those circumstances, given the propensity of floating exchange rates to overshoot in response to unforeseen policy changes; though any appreciation might be moderated by lower US and UK interest rates if fiscal tightening were accompanied by monetary relaxation. A lurch back to overvaluation of the dollar and sterling would make reduction of the US and UK trade deficits by fiscal tightening harder to achieve; indeed that result might not then be possible without deep recessions in these economies.

Correspondingly, the task of reducing Japan's national saving rate and large external payments surplus through fiscal expansion would be even more difficult than it has been if relaxation pushed the yen down further, for that would boost Japan's trade surplus in due course. A similar outcome would be less likely in Germany because German fiscal relaxation on its own might not weaken the euro much, though it might do so if other Euro-Area members followed the German lead and euro interest rates fell significantly.

The best hope for avoiding these problems would lie in cooperation by the major economies to stabilise the key exchange rates at sustainable levels over the medium and longer term, as part of the wider reform programme. Ideally, therefore, international cooperation should cover not only compatible targets for national saving, budget balances and external payments balances but also sustainable exchange-rate targets for the major currencies. The modalities of such cooperation will be addressed in Chapter 9.

Fiscal cooperation in the Euro Area

The fiscal tensions evident in the Euro Area in the wake of the global crisis illustrate only too compellingly the problems that can arise when a group of countries merge their currencies and adopt a single monetary policy but fail to cooperate on fiscal policy. It is worth reflecting on the nature of these tensions and the remedies implied by the fiscal policy reforms proposed above.

As explained in Chapter 5, economists warned well before the formation of EMU that countries with different industrial and financial structures should hesitate to join a monetary union without a central fiscal authority or mechanism to provide stabilisation and income transfers, unless they have highly flexible labour and goods markets. It is now clear that although the structural convergence and market flexibility required for secure economic integration may exist at the core of the Euro Area, they do not extend across its economic periphery. The big fiscal deficits and associated sovereign debt difficulties faced by Greece in spring 2010, and their potential to spread to other economies outside the core of the Area, suggest underlying problems whose solution lies beyond the scope of the temporary financial assistance now being offered, reluctantly and belatedly, by richer Euro states, sizeable though it looks. Among these problems are persistent differences in rates of national saving and investment, resembling those among the major economies observed above.

Key orders of magnitude for eight of the 16 Euro states can be found in Table 8.3, which are grouped into four 'high-saving' and four 'low-saving' economies. The

TABLE 8.3 Private and government net lending and external current balance, eight Euro-Area economies, 2000–10 (per cent of GDP at current market prices, annual averages)

Four high-saving economies	2000–4	2005–7	2008–10[b]	Four low-saving economies	2000–4	2005–7	2008–10[b]
Germany (26.7%)[a]				**Italy (17.3%)**[a]			
Private net lending	3.9	8.1	7.9	Private net lending	2.1	0.8	1.8
Government net lending	–2.6	–1.6	–2.8	Government net lending	–2.8	–3.1	–4.6
Gross public debt[c]	62	67	73	Gross public debt[c]	106	105	113
External current balance	1.4	6.5	5.0	External current balance	–0.7	–2.2	–2.8
France (19.4%)[a]				**Spain (13.2%)**[a]			
Private net lending	4.1	2.0	4.6	Private net lending	–3.4	–10.4	1.1
Government net lending	–2.8	–2.7	–6.7	Government net lending	–0.5	1.6	–7.4
Gross public debt[c]	60	65	76	Gross public debt[c]	53	40	51
External current balance	1.3	–0.6	–2.1	External current balance	–4.0	–8.8	–6.2
Netherlands (6.1%)[a]				**Greece (2.9%)**[a]			
Private net lending	5.1	8.3	9.3	Private net lending	–1.6	–6.9	–1.8
Government net lending	–1.1	0.1	–3.2	Government net lending	–5.2	–4.2	–10.1
Gross public debt[c]	52	48	64	Gross public debt[c]	101	98	110
External current balance	4.0	8.4	6.1	External current balance	–6.8	–11.0	–11.9
Austria (2.9%)[a]				**Portugal (2.3%)**[a]			
Private net lending	2.8	4.2	5.9	Private net lending	–5.1	–5.4	–5.2
Government net lending	–1.8	–1.4	–3.5	Government net lending	–3.3	–4.2	–5.7
Gross public debt[c]	66	62	69	Gross public debt[c]	55	64	74
External current balance	1.0	2.8	2.4	External current balance	–8.4	–9.6	–10.8

Source: OECD Stat, 'National Accounts' and 'Economic Projections' online database and author's calculations (see below).

Notes: [a] Country shares of total Euro–Area GDP (16 States) at current market prices, converted using PPP exchange rates, in 2007.
[b] OECD projections for 2010.
[c] Maastricht criterion.

Private net lending was estimated in this table by deducting government net lending from the external current balance (see the accounting links set out in Annex 1 to this chapter). It thus includes errors and omissions in the external current balance data. For fuller definitions see the notes to Table 8.1.

high-savers comprise just over 55 per cent of Euro-Area GDP, and the low-savers, nearly 36 per cent, so the sample is fairly representative of the area as a whole. The high savers were chosen because their private sectors are estimated to have been in *net financial surplus*, with net lending (saving minus physical investment) averaging comfortably above 2 per cent of GDP since EMU was formed in 1999; whereas the low savers have been in (or close to) *net financial deficit* in their private sectors, with private net lending negative or below 2 per cent of GDP through most of the time since EMU was formed (Greece was admitted in 2001). Italy's categorisation as a low saver is perhaps debatable but its economy clearly qualifies in other respects (persistent fiscal and external deficits and a high public debt/GDP ratio).

A predictable feature is that all the low-saving economies have been in persistent and generally rising external current deficit since the formation of EMU, whereas the high savers have been in persistent and (except for France) generally rising external surplus. Thus the low savers have become heavy net external debtors, and much of their government debt is held externally: about 70 per cent in the case of Greece and over 50 per cent in that of Italy (see Bank for International Settlements 2010: 68).[8] This feature, together with their heavy government debt/GDP burdens (less heavy in Spain), explains why the international capital markets have become so concerned about the possibility of default on sovereign debt by Greece and other deficit states, or at least substantial debt rescheduling. It is hard to escape the conclusion that if these economies are to survive the disciplines of EMU they must start to reduce their external deficits soon and continue reducing them until near-balance is established.

Three kinds of policy changes will be required, in some combination, if the weakest Euro economies are to survive on a firm basis: first, provision of regular income transfers to these economies from high-income economies. Ideally the transfers should be automatic and semi-permanent, and administered by a central fiscal authority, much as happens in existing federal states. Preferably they should supplement rather than replace the EU's existing regional aid policies. However, none of the wealthy states that would be the main paymasters for such transfers have been prepared to contemplate them in the past, and it is questionable whether any would do so now, even if it were seen as necessary for EMU's survival. Only time will tell whether the political cohesion necessary for such assistance can be summoned up in the monetary union. Second, along with this central transfer mechanism there is an urgent need in the low-saving economies for improved incentives for household saving via tax concessions and pension reform, on lines to be outlined later in this chapter; and, third, for a substantial though carefully phased shift into cyclically-adjusted fiscal surplus over the long term, on the lines proposed above. As the magnitudes in the table imply, the scale of long-term fiscal tightening required in Greece, Portugal and Spain is likely to be substantial: of the order of 5–10 per cent of GDP on a cyclically-adjusted basis, unless their private-sector saving rates rise appreciably.

Crucially, however, the above changes should be part of an exercise to pursue compatible targets for national saving and external payments balances in *all* Euro economies, taking account of their private saving and investment rates. As a 'quid pro quo' for fiscal retrenchment in low-saving economies, their high-saving neighbours should undertake counter-balancing fiscal expansion. The magnitudes in the table imply long-term fiscal relaxation of the order of 5 per cent of GDP or more on a cyclically-adjusted basis by Germany and the Netherlands – unless their private saving rates fall appreciably.

Fiscal retrenchment by the peripheral economies will entail considerable belt-tightening and a substantial, though hopefully temporary, rise in unemployment there, and hence carries serious political risks, but the uncomfortable message appears to have been accepted by their governments. Budgetary tightening commenced in Greece and Ireland in 2009 and by early summer 2010 most low-savers had announced tough austerity measures. Yet, simultaneously, fiscal cutbacks are also being announced by the Area's high savers, notably Germany and France, following the pattern being adopted elsewhere in the developed world (except the United States). According to political leaders in these economies, this action is being taken in order to 'set a good example', though other reasons, including concerns about infringing EMU's fiscal rules, may weigh with them. As Table 8.3 indicates, gross public debt ratios in Germany and France already exceed the Maastricht limits significantly and are projected to rise further on present policies. Yet fiscal cutbacks by high savers are wholly contrary to the remedies put forward in this chapter. If they are carried out as planned there is a serious risk that, in conjunction with the fiscal cuts by low savers, they will lead to a deepening recession in the Euro Area from 2011 onwards. If so the external financing difficulties faced by low-saving economies would seem bound to recur despite their tough fiscal action.

In short, a sustainable solution to the cross-border financial imbalances now evident within the Euro Area calls for cooperative action by Euro governments to rebalance the existing pattern of fiscal surpluses and deficits between low-saving and high-saving states. In the absence of significant compensatory movements in private saving rates, this rebalancing would require fiscal tightening by low savers to be largely offset by fiscal stimulus on the part of high savers. Without such countervailing action there must be serious doubts that the monetary union will survive with its present membership intact beyond the next few years.

Abandon limits on government debt stocks?

As should be evident from the above discussion, the international fiscal rebalancing envisaged in our reform package would not fit easily within the 1990s synthesis, especially the limits on stocks of government debt which are prominent in the EMU blueprint. If sustainable targets are adopted for government saving and budget balances as proposed, meeting the mandatory debt limits (or at least moving steadily down towards them) should not be a problem for low-saving economies, as their government borrowing would be significantly below what it has been for several decades, and their government debt/GDP ratios would fall over time. But there would almost certainly be problems sooner or later for high-saving economies like Germany. Unless the debt limits are modified to allow for different private saving rates, high-saving economies would doubtless exceed them substantially in time and the limits would eventually bear little relation to reality. That would send further confusing signals to the markets and be counterproductive for interest rates and fiscal policy generally. Yet it could not be predicted with confidence how private saving would actually respond to persistent changes in the stance of fiscal policy, or how long such changes would need to last in order to achieve their objectives, and so it would be difficult to devise more suitable limits without experience of the reformed policies. It seems clear that mandatory debt/GDP ratios do not suit a situation in which long-term fiscal targets differ substantially between economies.

There are accordingly strong grounds for removing or at least de-emphasising the fiscal limits in EMU, and corresponding though less formal limits elsewhere, as part of a cooperative international move towards a more rational fiscal regime. Mandatory limits may have had a role to play in securing fiscal retrenchment during the preparations for EMU, and they may have a continuing role as convergence criteria for EU states preparing to join EMU in future. But they lacked a convincing economic rationale when introduced, and were accordingly attacked by economists who were otherwise strong EMU protagonists, for example Buiter *et al.* (1993) as noted earlier. In recent years they have been massively breached by a number of EU governments, latterly in efforts to combat the global recession. The European Commission has had little choice but to sanction these infringements, as will be seen later. This does not mean that the behaviour of government debt stocks should be ignored; they will always contain useful information for markets and policymakers and should continue to be monitored along with other relevant indicators, but uniform and rigid limits should be quietly abandoned.

The foregoing recommendation applies especially to the uniform limits on *gross* stocks of government debt (before deducting government assets) imposed under the Treaty's 'excessive deficit procedure', which all EU governments are expected to observe. It is certainly arguable that persistent borrowing to finance government consumption or physical investment tends to raise interest rates and crowd out private investment in the long run, and nationally-selective constraints on net debt are perhaps justifiable on those grounds, if differences in national saving rates are properly allowed for. But if governments borrow mainly to acquire financial assets which generate rates of return in excess of the post-tax interest cost, constraints on gross debt stocks seem hard to justify on macroeconomic grounds.

An active stabilisation role for fiscal policy

As explained earlier, regimes based on the 1990s consensus confine fiscal policy to a passive stabilisation role: the automatic stabilisers implicit in most national tax and social security systems are allowed to operate freely and in that respect fiscal policy has a useful if limited counter-cyclical role, but more active use of the fiscal instruments has been ruled out for the reasons discussed. For many adherents to the 1990s synthesis these concerns still carry a lot of weight. On the whole, the passive fiscal approach seemed to work tolerably well for more than a decade after its adoption. Economic growth proceeded fairly steadily at or moderately above trend in most of the majors for over ten years, with the notable exception of Japan. Elsewhere the real-economy cycles and shocks experienced by developed economies seemed comparatively benign and monetary policy was sufficiently stabilising to keep inflation well under control.

This comfortable view was overturned by the recent global recession. The latter's origin in a severe credit crunch meant that monetary policy has not been well placed to deal with it, given policy's preoccupation with inflation. The drying-up of the wholesale money markets necessitated huge emergency lending by central banks, and recapitalisation of ailing banks and emergency loans and guarantees to other big financial institutions created big financial commitments by governments in economies where international banks are based. The exceptional depth of the recession in liberalised economies meant that even near-zero official interest rates and the monetary injections applied by central banks did not suffice to restore bank lending or aggregate demand to pre-shock levels; and yet little scope was left for further monetary action. Even committed neo-liberals accept that a degree of emergency fiscal stimulus was necessary. The serious debate has been about the size and composition of the action needed, its likely effects, and the extent and timing of subsequent action to restore fiscal balance in due course. It is widely agreed that the limited 'fiscal space' left in many economies after 15 years under the 1990s synthesis has constrained the scope for fiscal action.

In the light of these events some basic re-thinking of policymakers' attitudes to fiscal stabilisation seems in order. Although the crash of 2007–8 was comparable in severity with the pre-First World War banking crisis and the stock market crash of 1929, and for 12 months the global recession was more serious than anything experienced in the major economies since the 1930s, it is unlikely to be an isolated event without recurrence in future decades. Given the uncomfortable geopolitical environment emerging in the new century, other types of shocks must be expected sooner or later, as argued in Chapter 5. They may not resemble the recent crisis; hopefully better regulation will prevent repetitions of the recent banking excesses. But there can be no presumption that they will be less severe or pervasive. Unless violent commodity-price instability is moderated in some way, growth of the emerging East Asian giants steadies to a more sedate pace, and the global saving glut recedes soon, future booms and slumps on a comparable scale may be hard to avoid.

Although serious, these concerns do not warrant a retreat from our foregoing proposals that the fiscal instruments should be set to achieve sustainable levels of national saving over the long term. But in abnormal circumstances it may be advisable to adjust them temporarily to assist monetary policy in its primary task – keeping GDP as close as possible to the level consistent with price stability; indeed that qualification might define the difference between normal and abnormal circumstances. However, this flexibility should be conditional on a number of important reforms in the conduct and institutions of fiscal policy:

1. Any substantial departure from the long-term fiscal objective should require a declaration of *fiscal emergency* by the fiscal authority, which would be subject to government approval. Reasons for such a declaration would include a systemic crisis in the national or international banking system, a breakdown in world oil supplies, a collapse in business confidence due to large-scale terrorism or military conflict, or a serious global recession arising from these or other sources.

2. The fiscal authority should then pre-announce an emergency programme of fiscal changes to stabilise the economy, together with a firm and credible commitment to return the economy back to its saving target in the medium term. The programme should be updated if circumstances change, but in any case at intervals of not more than a year.

3. In reaching these judgements, the fiscal authority should operate within the framework of statutory objectives for price and output stability and sustainable national saving set by government.

4. Finally, so far as possible, fiscal policy should operate independently of political interference, and be seen to do so.

The fourth of these reforms – greater autonomy in the conduct of fiscal policy – would be beneficial in most developed economies, but far from easy to achieve in modern liberal democracies. It would entail distancing macro policymaking from the other fiscal tasks normally performed by finance ministries, probably by setting up a new authority somewhat apart from the established machinery of government. The new authority would distinguish clearly between normal and abnormal circumstances and communicate that judgement to the markets and the public. It should preferably be capable of addressing the entire range of issues thrown up by macroeconomic policy, including the *mix* between fiscal and monetary policy; the latter questions tend to be overlooked in existing regimes, with fiscal policy deemed to be on automatic pilot and attention focusing on monetary policy's active role. Finally, the new authority would need to be fully and effectively accountable to government and parliament.

Reforming the fiscal policy institutions

The arguments for shielding fiscal policy from short-term political interference are similar to those that inspired the drive for monetary policy autonomy in the 1990s, more especially in the run-up to EMU. Indeed it can be argued that protection from political influence is even more desirable in the fiscal than the monetary field because electorates are thought to be more sensitive to fiscal than interest-rate changes, even in the era of widespread mortgage borrowing. The architects of EMU sought to overcome this problem by introducing mandatory fiscal rules, but if these are modified to recognise national differences in private saving rates, as recommend above, the arguments for fiscal autonomy become at least as strong as those for monetary autonomy.

Reforms in this direction are likely to be controversial because they could be seen as undermining the constitutional safeguards to which tax and public spending decisions are subject in liberal democracies. Fiscal actions are liable to have bigger and clearer redistributive effects than monetary actions, and so generate strong if sectional opposition. For this reason fiscal decisions normally require detailed parliamentary consent and their design and implementation often require extensive prior consultation; the legal and administrative procedures involved make it hard to distance them from political influence. Any move to exempt fiscal changes from parliamentary approval would doubtless (and rightly) be viewed with suspicion by everyone concerned with hard-won democratic rights and freedoms. Moreover much more administrative time and effort is needed to change tax and benefit rates and public spending programmes than is needed to change central-bank interest rates. For these reasons a complete transfer of responsibility for fiscal policy from finance ministries to bodies as detached from the political process as the ECB would require a constitutional and administrative upheaval unthinkable in most democracies outside wartime. Any move towards fiscal autonomy would therefore have to be more circumscribed than in the monetary field. Yet ways of distancing the key fiscal decisions from short-term political influence can and should be found.

Institutional reform in the UK

The UK presents a particular challenge in this respect. The arguments for passing responsibility for UK fiscal policy to a more independent authority are similar to those behind the transfer of monetary policymaking from the Treasury to the Bank of England in 1997. For that purpose a new Monetary Policy Committee (MPC) was set up as the decision-making body within the Bank. The MPC comprises nine voting members, of whom five are officials from the Bank (including the Governor and the two Deputy Governors) and four are professional economists, selected for their expertise in monetary policy.[9] The rationale recognised not only the need for independence from political and sectional pressures but also the importance of bringing independent expertise – analytical skills and knowledge of the macroeconomy – to bear on monetary policy. It was felt that the inclusion on the MPC of a number of highly respected economists without political ties would improve the quality of decision-making. Somewhat similar reasoning has applied with respect to the few independent economic advisory bodies found in other major economies, notably the Council of Economic Advisers (CEA) in the United States, which is the leading and longest-standing example (see Feldstein 1992 for an insider's account of the CEA's role).

There are also other reasons for creating new institutions in the fiscal field. As argued earlier, macroeconomic policymaking calls for a *synoptic* approach because there are important interdependencies between its main branches. In particular there can be powerful and sustained feedbacks between fiscal and monetary policy, and serious mistakes may be made if they are not taken properly into account. Thus the effects of a change in the stance of fiscal policy depend on whether monetary policy is *accommodating* or not. For example, a given cut in tax rates will have a larger impact on aggregate demand if the money stock is allowed to respond freely than if it is closely controlled: the induced changes in interest and exchange rates will be less restrictive on aggregate demand in the former case. The expansionary effects of a tax cut may be crowded out if the central bank prevents the money stock from rising in response to the induced rise in disposable income. Such linkages may also work in reverse: a given monetary stimulus will have much larger effects if fiscal policy is accommodating than if it is restrictive. Many of the misapprehensions about the likely effects of fiscal or monetary actions which are common in popular debate arise from failure to take account of these feedbacks. Our earlier concerns about fiscal tightening in low-saving economies illustrated the importance of considering whether or not the action is accompanied by monetary relaxation.

The merits of a synoptic approach to policymaking also arise from the simple but sometimes overlooked need for policy aims to be common to both fiscal and monetary arms. This should be easier to ensure if both arms were joined to a single independent and expert body, and subject to the same process of reporting and scrutiny. Unfortunately, complete institutional unity in macroeconomic policymaking would be impracticable in liberal democracies for the reasons given earlier. Probably the best that can be achieved in the UK and similar regimes is a degree of unification, not of the two institutions in question – Treasury and Bank of England – which would recall the failures of Keynesian management, but of the information, analysis and forecasting that underlies them. This would require close collaboration between the two groups of policymakers.

In the UK, responsibility for fiscal policy lies almost exclusively with the Chancellor of the Exchequer and his senior officials in the Treasury, where supporting forecasts and policy simulations are carried out using a large econometric model of the national economy, together with off-model studies and projections. Nowadays many Treasury officials (probably a large majority) are trained in economics or a related quantitative discipline, leaving generalists to work principally as administrators, though there is some movement between these categories. Considerable efforts are made to keep the policy process secret, though it is subject to a degree of retrospective parliamentary scrutiny by the House of Commons Treasury Select Committee. Thus although fiscal policymaking in the UK is generally characterised by high standards of technical competence and professional integrity, it is a highly secretive process and very subject to day-to-day political pressures on the Chancellor and his colleagues.

While it would be difficult and hardly desirable to remove much of the administrative work involved in tax and expenditure changes from Treasury hands, it should be possible to make fiscal policymaking more independent and open to public scrutiny. A worthwhile innovation would be the creation of a high-level Fiscal Policy Committee (FPC) alongside the Treasury (though not physically within it) to be responsible for strategic decisions, on a par with the MPC in the Bank. The FPC might comprise the Chancellor as chairman, four senior Treasury officials, including the First Permanent Secretary and the Chief Economist, and *four independent professional economists*, all appointed by the Chancellor for renewable terms, as in the case of the MPC (though all such experts should be subject to parliamentary confirmation). Since the main fiscal instruments are less flexible and slower-working than the monetary ones, the FPC would need to meet less often MPC; perhaps six times a year, plus ad hoc meetings in emergencies. Decisions would be by majority of the nine voting members, with the Chancellor having a casting vote.

The FPC's main task would be to determine the overall budget judgement which sets the annual public-sector borrowing requirement and encapsulates the overall stance of fiscal policy. In doing so the committee would assess the need for 'proactive' action and if necessary initiate a state of fiscal emergency, as suggested earlier. The FPC would also take decisions on the broad budget structure – the mix between tax and expenditure changes, and between direct and indirect taxation, and their timing. It would also give guidance on the main expenditure aggregates and tax rates, but the details of these should be left for ministers to decide. The committee would thus need to be in step with the annual rhythm of the official budgetary process, starting with the review of expenditure plans in late autumn through the planning of tax changes in early spring to the production of the budget proper in the spring, and any supplementary budgets later in the summer. Its proceedings would be confidential, but its expert members would be subject to regular parliamentary scrutiny in the same way as Treasury ministers and officials.

The FPC's independence should be strengthened, and a synoptic approach to macro policymaking facilitated, by creating a new, politically independent, expert body outside the Treasury and Bank but with strong links to both. Named perhaps the Economic Policy Council (EPC), it would be a high-level advisory body to government, on the lines of the CEA in the United States. But crucially, it should also have decision-making influence via direct links with the FPC and MPC. To this end EPC membership would comprise *the eight independent members of the FPC and MPC*, so bringing the independent experts from both committees together in the new Council. Its main functions would be to monitor progress on meeting the government's macroeconomic targets – price and output stability and a sustainable national saving rate and to report on these annually to the Chancellor and Parliament. In order to do this it would make and publish (with a delay) independent forecasts and assessments for both the short and long term. It might also publish interim or occasional assessments of chosen aspects of macro policy. Its annual reports would be published, but certain other documents could be confidential (for the Chancellor and Bank Governor and their officials) by mutual agreement.

The EPC would be moderate in size and resources but high in prestige and influence. Its chairman would be elected by the eight members from among themselves and it would generally operate by consensus, though minority reports would be permitted. It would have a small secretariat and a support staff of perhaps 20 to 25 highly qualified researchers, who would be employed full time on renewable short-term contracts from universities and research institutes, as in the case of the CEA, or on secondment from the Treasury or Bank. They would undertake and publish some research of their own, but the Council would not collect data or maintain its own large forecasting model. Instead it would rely on existing information and resources in the Treasury, to whose work it would have unrestricted access and over which it would exercise the kind of authority that the MPC commands in the Bank of England. (To this end the FPC should meet at on or near the EPC's offices.) For some purposes (like world economic forecasting) the Council might also use the big econometric models maintained by independent research institutes.[10] It might meet occasionally in public to consult on policy issues if it wished, and its members would be required to give evidence in public hearings of the relevant parliamentary committees.

In summary the EPC would exert a synoptic, independent and expert influence on macro policymaking both confidentially via its members' participation in the FPC and MPC, and publicly through its reports and open meetings. Bringing together the expert members from the FPC and MPC in the Council's sessions would facilitate a dialogue between the two arms of policy which is missing at present. The Council would also provide its members with an independent resource base for research and personal briefing, which the MPC lacks at present.

Accountability would be exercised over the Council through its documents and open meetings, and through attendance at parliamentary hearings. Its periodic public meetings would give members a legitimate platform to communicate their views to professional peers, the media and the concerned public. Yet it would be important for it to exert genuine influence on policy and avoid spreading its focus too thinly. Otherwise it might meet the same fate as the UK's National Economic Development Council, the last vestige of the Labour government's 'industrial strategy' of the 1970s, which was disbanded by the Conservative government in 1992. The regular involvement of EPC members in policymaking should help it avoid that fate.

A tentative move in the direction of greater fiscal independence has already taken place in the UK. Upon assuming office in May 2010, Chancellor of the Exchequer Osborne set up an independent Office for Budget Responsibility (OBR) to publish information and make forecasts in preparation for the budget, with unrestricted access to official data. The Office quickly reported to the Chancellor and its inputs have guided the new government's first budget. The new Chancellor has confidently avowed that 'Budget making in Britain has been changed for ever' (Osborne 2010). Yet this is only a timid first step compared with the reforms proposed above. The OBR has soon run into strong criticism for being insufficiently independent – it started life inside the Treasury and was very dependent on cooperation by Treasury officials – and under-resourced – its expert group initially comprised just three members, with only a temporary chairman and a very small support staff. It has no decision-making powers and its freedom to communicate publicly is unclear, beyond attendance by its members at the Treasury Select Committee. It remains to be seen whether and how the new body will develop in due course.

Institutional reform in the United States

Steps to distance fiscal policymaking from short-term political influence seem desirable in other economies too, though any institutional changes would of course need to suit national circumstances. Arguably moves in this direction would be beneficial even in the United States, notwithstanding the valuable role played there by the CEA. Our main reservation regarding the United States in this context is that the role of independent advisers does not go far enough. The CEA should be given a stronger and more formal role in fiscal decision-making than its present advisory role. This might be done by passing responsibility for the strategic fiscal decisions to a top-level committee within the Administration, on which CEA members would have a vote, somewhat on the lines of our proposed FPC for the UK. That would imply some broadening of responsibility for US fiscal policy, which at present seems to reside too heavily with the President and his officials in the White House.

Another reservation about the US regime relates to its virtually complete separation of responsibilities for monetary and fiscal policy. At present there seems about as little connection between monetary and fiscal policymaking in the United States as there is in the UK. The autonomy of the Federal Reserve Board and the Federal Open Market Committee (FOMC) in conducting monetary policy is jealously guarded, while fiscal policymaking is conducted largely behind closed doors in the White House. The CEA is expressly required to advise the President, and though it may do so on all aspects of economic policy, its main duty is to comment on programmes and activities originating within the federal government itself. In the era following the Council's creation in 1946 it focused primarily on Keynesian-style fiscal policies, but when those went out of fashion in the 1970s it broadened its scope to cover supply-side and structural issues, and also external trade and investment, and more recently it has turned to market structures and deregulation, and other microeconomic issues. But it has not ventured far into monetary policy, and would probably feel constrained from doing so.[11] Its remit should therefore be broadened to allow more dialogue between fiscal and monetary policymakers than takes place at the moment.

Institutional reform in the Euro Area

As pointed out earlier, there are likely to be serious obstacles to implementation of our fiscal-policy reforms by the 16 member economies of the Euro Area. While there is nothing in the Treaty or the Stability Pact to discourage participants from pursuing tighter fiscal limits than EMU rules require, the rules if interpreted strictly would prevent pursuit of the generally more expansionary stance we recommend for high-saving economies. The German Finance Ministry might well feel duty bound to shelter behind the Treaty limits on public debt stocks and the constraints on deficits in the Stability Pact, even if some politicians felt disposed to exceed the rules if it seemed necessary to preserve harmony in the monetary union. Accordingly the rules would probably have to be amended or attenuated if desirable reforms are to be made the Euro Area.

For political reasons, changing EMU's fiscal rules would be far from easy. EU Treaty amendments have to be agreed by all member states and ratified through national constitutional procedures, which involve parliamentary approval and in some cases referenda. Amending the Stability and Growth Pact should be less difficult, as it is an intergovernmental agreement (not subject to ratification) and involves only EMU members, but its revision would hardly be easy, given successive German governments' strong attachment to it. In addition, the Treaty criteria for judging eligibility to join EMU require observation of the fiscal rules for stated periods before admittance, and existing members might object to relaxing the entry tests for future applicants. On the other hand, the EMU authorities have been willing to bend the fiscal rules during the recent recession, and the largest member states have always done so with impunity when it has suited them.

Although EU countries' fiscal institutions differ somewhat, most would stand to benefit if fiscal policy were distanced from national political pressures and if co-operation between the national fiscal authorities were strengthened. In the negotiations leading to EMU there was little support for such cooperation, and none for the creation of a central fiscal authority. It was this lacuna at the heart of the new regime that led German officials to insist on mandatory fiscal rules. Thus there is no fiscal counterweight in EMU to the ECB in the monetary sphere. Yet the macroeconomic case for having a central fiscal authority in a monetary union is strong, as argued earlier, and from time to time EMU's academic protagonists have called for one. Yet, after ten years of living with the fiscal stresses created by monetary union, there is little sign that more than a few of the smaller member states are becoming more amenable to fiscal cooperation, much less the coordination that a central fiscal authority would bring.

On the other hand, all governments that have joined EMU have been prepared to sign up, not only to the Treaty's fiscal rules but also the tougher ones, and even financial penalties, in the Stability Pact, for the sake of harmony in the union. Now that EMU is firmly established, some members might be willing to align their fiscal policies more closely if it offered an escape from such a potential straightjacket, and if it were believed necessary to keep the present membership intact. Along with this type of concession might come greater flexibility in applying the rules, if weaker-performing states made it a condition for accepting the tough policies needed to reduce their deficits. Moves in the direction of flexibility have been officially sanctioned for some time, as the Commission itself admits (European Commission 2009: ch. 2). As early as 2005 the Stability Pact was modified to allow member states with 'excessive' fiscal deficits more time to implement corrective action. Later, as the global recession deepened, the Commission and the Ministers' Council felt obliged to suspend the full force of the Excessive Deficits Procedure. By mid-2009 almost all EU member governments were running excessive deficits as defined in the procedure (European Commission 2009: 30) but no sanctions had been taken against them. The Commission has however called for firm action by members to achieve their medium-term budgetary objectives as and when activity recovers.[12]

Some proposals to improve the institutions and procedures for cross-border fiscal cooperation and unify macroeconomic policymaking in EMU are outlined in Box 8.3. They involve streamlining the Finance Ministers' Council (ECOFIN) and strengthening its presidency and its links with the ECB, and new tasks for the European Commission and the European Parliament in the fiscal field. These steps would clearly fall well short of the creation of a central fiscal authority in EMU, but they would represent useful progress towards a more flexible regime. Without such flexibility there are always likely to be tensions within the Euro Area as the single monetary policy struggles to reconcile member states' diverse situations with the common interest in economic stability. There are wider interests at stake here too, for without such moves by the major EU economies it would be hard to carry through the cooperative international programme outlined here, especially the international monetary reforms in the next chapter.

BOX 8.3 REFORMS TO PROMOTE FISCAL POLICY COOPERATION IN THE EUROPEAN UNION

Listed below are the minimum institutional reforms required to give our fiscal policy proposals a reasonable chance of being implemented through cooperative action in the European Union, more especially in the Euro Area. Some of them have been canvassed by the author and others in the academic literature:

1. Strengthen and streamline the Finance Ministers' Council (ECOFIN) by reducing its size through merging national representation among the smallest countries and converting its presidency into a long-term personal appointment, thus ending the present rotating system. This would offer greater continuity and independence in fiscal policymaking and allow a much needed longer-term focus. The new-style president would be a trusted figure with high credentials, possibly a former finance minister or central banker with a proven track record, elected by qualified majority of national governments. He/she would represent the interests of EMU as a whole rather than a particular country. Such a figure would enjoy greater credibility in international forums like the G7, one of the chief ambitions of EMU's architects. The case for this kind of change will strengthen as EMU membership grows.

2. Set up regular consultative links between ECOFIN, thus reconstituted, and the ECB. ECOFIN's president or his/her deputy would be invited to participate in meetings of the ECB Council (but not vote) and there should

be reciprocal provision for the ECB president at ECOFIN meetings. This should facilitate a more synoptic approach to macroeconomic policy and greater collaboration between EMU's monetary and fiscal policymakers.

3. Assign to the European Commission the task of recommending and publishing indicative fiscal targets for all EU members, based on the long-term objectives we have outlined. This would add focus and weight to the research and forecasting already undertaken by the Commission services. Peer group-pressure on individual countries to observe these targets should then be exercised through the reconstituted ECOFIN; this would be a more effective route than via the Excessive Deficits Procedure at present.

4. In pursuing this remit the Commission should strengthen inputs from independent experts by creating an advisory body somewhat on the lines of the CEA in the United States.

5. Improve the European Parliament's scrutiny of fiscal policy at EMU level by strengthening the powers of its relevant committees to question the President of ECOFIN and the Commission on the setting of fiscal targets and performance under them and require the provision of written evidence. This would provide much-needed accountability for a branch of policy that tends to escape public scrutiny at present.

A sustainable approach to pensions financing

Pensions provision is not usually regarded as a macroeconomic issue, and yet the financing of pensions clearly has important implications for fiscal policy, because of the dominant part played by governments in pensions provision in many economies, the concerns about the 'pensions time-bomb' referred to earlier, and the difficult choices between private and public provision in this context.

As pointed out in Chapter 5, one of the fundamental questions in this field is the relative merits of *pay-as-you-go* (PAYG) arrangements, in which pensions are essentially paid for out of current tax revenues, versus *funding* approaches, in which pensions are financed by accumulating funds specifically earmarked for the purpose. Experts in this field believe that both approaches have their merits and drawbacks, and both have a role in economies with developed financial markets and a strong tradition of equity financing, as Davis (2002) has argued. In most market-based economies, sustainable solutions will require a judicious combination of a PAYG-based safety net, involving lower state entitlements and a higher pensionable age than currently found in most regimes, and greater reliance on private-sector schemes to provide the bulk of pensions above the basic level, supported by well-targeted concessions and probably an element of compulsory participation. It seems inevitable that most such funding will work on 'defined contribution' (money-purchase) principles, under which the investment risks are borne by savers, not by the pension providers.

Now that the big boost to pension-fund assets from the sustained boom in US and European equity prices towards the end of the last century has been seen to be impermanent and partly reversible, final salary schemes are proving too costly and risky for most employers. In the private sector, pension schemes are increasingly switching from the 'defined benefit' (final salary) basis that had been customary previously to a 'money purchase' basis, at least for new employees. Employers and trades unions are seeking to negotiate acceptable, cost-effective, ways of compensating existing employees for loss of defined benefits. This shift of approach will probably spread into the public sector, where governments will also have to bite the bullet of switching to money purchase principles, although it may be expedient to compromise by combining the two approaches for a transitional period.

However, if money purchase schemes are to be a generally acceptable alternative for private savers, the great majority of whom are likely to be both risk-averse and uninformed about investment for retirement, ways will have to be found of protecting them at reasonable cost from the risks that attach to investment in unstable securities markets, even for long-term investors. Otherwise the outcome in troubled times is likely to be large numbers of discontented individuals who feel that they have been cheated of their pension rights and, in conjunction with that, enhanced instability of aggregate demand due to big equity-price fluctuations in economies where share ownership is widespread. This is one of the chief unsolved questions in the pensions sphere confronting governments at present.

Reform of the UK pension system

A thorough review of pension policy was launched in the UK around the turn of the century. It was undertaken by the Pensions Commission, headed by Lord Turner (before he became Chairman of the FSA), whose first report was referred to in Chapter 5. The Commission's second report recommended wide-ranging changes in UK pensions arrangements (Pensions Commission 2005). Although the Commission has now been disbanded, its proposals seem likely to shape UK pensions policy over the next few decades. After wide public debate they received general acceptance and eventually broad government endorsement in two White Papers in 2006, and their implementation is due to take place under the Pensions Act 2008.

In summary, the Commission recommended two main reforms: the streamlining and simplification of direct pension provision by the state and a much greater role for personal saving in earnings-related pension provision via a new national funded scheme, to be administered and strongly encouraged by the state. Under the first reform, the state will move to provide a single, universal, flat-rate pension, paid for out of taxation and designed to provide the minimum income needed by retired people. This basic pension would be indexed to earnings (restoring a much-prized feature withdrawn by the preceding Conservative government) and would in due course absorb the existing State Second (earnings-related) Pension, which should be gradually phased out. Although the costs to the taxpayer would be contained by phasing-out the earnings-related element in the existing state scheme and steadily raising the state pension age to 68 by 2050 to reflect increasing life expectancy, there would be a moderate increase in the tax burden over coming decades.

Under the second reform, a comprehensive National Pension Saving Scheme (NPSS) will be set up to promote private funded saving. Government intervention was felt necessary in the private field because the Commission found in its first report that 'the current voluntary private funded system, combined with the current State system, is not fit for purpose looking forward' (see the 'Foreword' in Pensions Commission 2004). The failure of the voluntary system was attributed to 'irrational equity markets' and to 'delayed appreciation of life expectancy increases', which had brought about a significant decline in the trend of private-sector pension contributions (Pensions Commission 2004: 'Key Conclusions'). On present trends many people – perhaps seven million, on subsequent government estimates – would face inadequate pensions unless they delayed retirement beyond the current average. The system was found particularly unsatisfactory for 'low income, low premium, customers' who need encouragement and advice to make rational decisions about long-term saving, and yet face providers' charges that can absorb 20–30 per cent of an individual's private saving (Pensions Commission 2004: 'Key Conclusions').

For these reasons the Commission recommended that participation in the NPSS should be near-compulsory up to a certain contributory level (around 8 per cent of earnings), in that enrolment should be automatic for all employees, subject only to an opt-out into a high-quality employer scheme. Participation would involve contribution to one or more of a range of commercial funds approved by government and selected by the individual, with a 'default fund' available for those who make no selection. Voluntary participation in the NPSS would be allowed up to double the required contribution level.

It is hard to disagree with the broad thrust of these recommendations for simplifying the UK state basic pension and restoring the earnings link, and the proposed national scheme to promote private funded saving. The tax implications of retaining the present two-tier system of state provision through coming decades are exceedingly daunting, given prevailing trends in life expectancy, and voluntary saving through funded schemes is unlikely to deliver adequate pensions for the majority of households unless there is strong government encouragement, supported by action to centralise and standardise the contribution and funding processes. For these reasons the elements of compulsion in the NPSS seem hard to avoid, as do the proposals to simplify the choice of fund and to administer the scheme at much lower cost than the fees for management and financial advice typically charged by private schemes, which is one of the chief drawbacks of the present entirely market-based system.

On the other hand it is hard to accept that, if there is to be an element of compulsory participation in the national funding scheme, individual contributors should be expected to bear the associated risks unless they strongly wish to do so (in pursuit of higher returns). Preferably there should be more effective provision within the

NPSS to protect risk-averse participants from the possibility of loss of pension rights due to stock-market fluctuations or failures of commercial fund management, and that such risks should be borne by the state (or perhaps the employer in the case of a company pension fund). Such protection could be achieved by offering a guaranteed *real* (indexed) rate of return on assets held in the national scheme's 'default fund', to be available only on pensionable savings held in the fund until retirement; the cost of providing which guarantee should be met by the state. Protection of this kind would of course involve a cost to taxpayers, and it would be important that the guaranteed rate would be as fair as possible between present and future generations of pensioners. This might be achieved by setting the guaranteed real rate equal to the *long-run rate of per capita GDP growth*, perhaps averaged over the relevant retiree's working life. So far as we are aware, no such guarantee is to be available under the UK proposals.

Although pension reform is mainly aimed at social and political objectives, the measures planned in the UK are likely to have important implications for macro-economic policy in that, if successful, they should significantly raise the underlying rate of long-term saving by households and firms. Moreover they should have their strongest appeal in the very economies that have experienced historically low private saving rates in recent decades – financially liberalised economies with highly developed securities markets. These are the economies where easy personal credit and erratic equity prices have contributed most to under-provision for retirement among other problems, and where schemes like the NPSS have most to contribute. Accordingly their adoption should help greatly in the formidable task of achieving sustainable national saving targets in low-saving economies, which would otherwise fall heavily on fiscal policy under our proposals.

ANNEX 8.1

Saving, investment and the balance of payments: accounting links

This annex sets out the accounting links that exist in all economies between aggregate saving, physical investment and the balance of external payments. All the equations here are accounting identities, based on standard national accounting principles. They all hold by definition and are therefore always true. All items relate to the same time period, generally a year or calendar quarter. Some details are omitted for the sake of simplicity but no matters of principle are affected.

For simplicity here the economy is divided into just three broad sectors, comprising the private sector (firms and households); government (all forms of government – central, regional and local); and the external sector (the rest of the world). However, corresponding conclusions hold regardless of the degree of disaggregation.

The following equations express three key national accounting definitions; first, national output in terms of its broad expenditure components:

$$GDP = C + I + G + X - M \tag{1}$$

Equation (1) states that the value of an economy's national output (gross domestic product or GDP) is the sum of expenditure on private consumption C (expenditure on consumer goods and services by households), physical investment I (gross capital formation in fixed assets and inventories by firms, households and general government), government consumption G (current expenditure on goods and services by 'general government', i.e. central and local governments) and exports X (expenditure on national output by non-residents) *minus* imports M (residents' expenditure on foreign output). All expenditure is on currently-produced output valued at current market prices. Output and investment are gross in that they are measured before deducting consumption of physical capital used up in producing output, often termed 'depreciation'.

Second, the definition of national income, which includes income and transfers from abroad, less payments due abroad:

$$\text{GNI} = \text{GDP} + \text{NITA} \tag{2}$$

Equation (2) states that an economy's gross national income GNI is the sum of income from producing national output GDP *plus* net income and transfers from abroad NITA (residents' property income from abroad – interest, profits and dividends from foreign investments – and income from employment and entrepreneurial activity abroad, *plus* current transfers (gifts and aid) and tax receipts from abroad, all net of the corresponding payments abroad). Like output, national income here is 'gross' in that it is measured before deducting capital consumption. It is also 'disposable' in that it is net of taxes and other transfers payable abroad.

Third, the definition of the balance of current external payments:

$$\text{CB} = X - M + \text{NITA} \tag{3}$$

Equation (3) states that the current balance of payments CB (the balance of external payments on current account) is the sum of exports X *minus* imports M *plus* net income, taxes and current transfers from abroad, NITA.

Combining equations (1) and (3) with (2):

$$\text{GNI} = C + I + G + \text{CB} \tag{4}$$

Equation (4) states that national disposable income GNI is the sum of household and government consumption ($C + G$) and investment I *plus* the current balance of payments CB.

Now for private-sector saving:

$$\text{PRS} = \text{GNI} - C - T \tag{5}$$

Equation (5) states that private-sector saving PRS (the gross saving of households and firms before deducting capital consumption) is the residue of GNI after deducting household consumption C and net tax payments T (taxes receivable by general government *minus* government transfers to the private sector, which include state pensions, social security payments and net interest on government debt). It is assumed for simplicity here that all corporate businesses are in the private sector, so all company profits or 'gross operating surpluses' arise in the private sector; but this does not affect the main conclusions.

Next, the definition of government saving:

$$\text{GS} = T - G \tag{6}$$

Equation (6) states that government saving GS (the gross saving of general government) is the residue of net tax receipts *less* government transfers T, *minus* government current expenditure G.

Private and government saving are then combined to arrive at national saving:

$$NS = PRS + GS \tag{7}$$

Equation (7) states that gross national saving NS is the sum of private and government saving.

Substituting equations (5) and (6) in (7), and cancelling the Ts:

$$NS = GNI - C - G \tag{8}$$

Equation (8) states that national saving NS is the residue of national income GNI after deducting household and government consumption.

Substituting equation (4) into (8), cancelling the Cs and Gs and taking CB to the left-hand side, reveals that:

$$CB = NS - I \tag{9}$$

Equation (9) states that the balance of external current payments is equal to the difference between national saving and physical investment, both measured gross of capital consumption. Thus if $NS = I$, $CB = 0$. In other words if national saving equals physical investment, the economy must be in zero external current payments balance.

Finally consider net lending or borrowing by the various sectors and by the whole economy. A sector's net lending (alternatively called its 'net acquisition of financial assets') is defined as the balance between its *saving and its physical investment*. If a sector saves more than it spends on physical investment, it is a net lender to other sectors; if it saves less than it invests physically, the sector is a net borrower.[1] Note that the financial balance of the whole economy as a whole is then its net lending to, or borrowing from, the rest of the world (the 'external sector')

First, NS and I in equation (9) are split into private-sector and government components:

$$CB = (PRS + GS) - (PRI + GI) \tag{10}$$
$$= (PRS - PRI) + (GS - GI) \tag{11}$$

where PRS and GS are gross private and government saving as before, PRI is private-sector gross physical investment, and GI is government gross physical investment. Bearing in mind that $(PRS - PRI)$ and $(GS - GI)$ are the net lending of

---

[1] Strictly, a sector's net capital transfers to other sectors should also be deducted in arriving at its net lending, but we omit these here for simplicity.

the private sector PRNL and the net lending of government GNL respectively, it follows that:

$$CB = PRNL + GNL \tag{12}$$

Equation (12) states that an economy's balance of external current payments is the *sum of the net financial balances of the private sector and government*. Thus, for example, if private net lending exceeds government net borrowing, the economy as a whole must be in surplus on its current external payments. Alternatively, if the private sector is a net borrower while the government is a net lender, but the former's financial deficit exceeds the government's financial surplus, the economy must be in external payments deficit; or if private net borrowing is exactly matched by government net lending, the economy must be in zero external current balance.

Note that the net financial balance of the external sector is defined as $I - NS$. It equals both the net lending of the economy concerned *with sign reversed*, or alternatively the economy's balance of current external payments. This follows because the net financial balances of all an economy's sectors must sum to zero by definition: the economy's net external lending must therefore equal the external sector's net borrowing with sign reversed. It also reflects that the balance of external payments on *current* account must equal the external balance on *capital and financial* accounts with sign reversed: *total* external payments must always sum to zero, by definition.

ANNEX 8.2

Saving, investment and the balance of payments: a loanable funds analysis

The behavioural links between flows of saving, investment and external payments are explored below using an approach based on the 'loanable funds' theory of the interest rate, a standard piece of neoclassical analysis. The analysis relates to the long-run steady state and so abstracts from adjustment to cycles or temporary shocks. It also largely avoids questions of money and its influence on the interest rate. In these respects it is a distinctly un-Keynesian approach, but it helps to explain our proposed long-run role for fiscal policy under conditions of high international capital mobility. All the arguments here observe the national accounting identities in Annex 8.1.

Assume a highly simplified two-economy world, in which each economy has a domestic capital market through which saving flows are channelled into physical investment. Both economies have a single financial asset (in addition to money) with uniform characteristics. This could be a long-term bond carrying interest at a fixed rate or, more realistically, a representative basket of fixed-rate bonds of unchanging risk and maturity composition. Firms and governments issue these bonds to finance physical investment (capital formation) and savers (generally households and other firms) acquire them as wealth-holding vehicles. All private physical investment is financed through bond sales (all profits are distributed) and all private saving goes into bonds or money balances; governments are assumed to finance some expenditure by issuing money but private savers acquire money and bonds in the same fixed proportions regardless of the interest rate. The analysis thus abstracts from monetary policy; the interest rate is determined solely by the supply and demand for loanable funds. It also abstracts from inflation, or at least assumes that inflation occurs at the same low rate in both economies.

The two economies are identical in all respects except that one (called Low-saver) saves a smaller proportion of its GDP than the other (High-saver) at all possible interest-rate levels. Both are represented in Fig. A, where the horizontal axis measures saving and investment flows as percentages of GDP in each economy and the vertical axis measures the real interest rate R. The upward-sloping lines

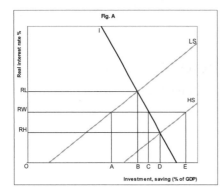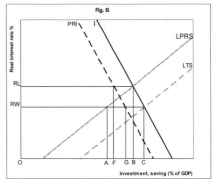

FIGURE 8.2　Saving and investment in a two-economy world

labelled LS and HS represent the supplies of loanable funds (in per cent of GDP) as positive functions of R in Low-saver and High-saver respectively, LS indicating a lower saving rate at all values of R. Their positive slopes indicate that the share of GDP saved tends to rise in both countries as R rises, other things being equal. This reflects rising time preference on the part of households at higher levels of income: most consumers prefer present to future consumption, so the interest rate must rise if they are to be induced to save more, other things being equal. LS and HS are parallel straight lines, implying that the two economies' *marginal* rates of time preference are constant and equal. This assumption is purely for ease of exposition; the lines could alternatively be curved and one could be steeper than the other, without affecting the main conclusions.

The downward-sloping line I represents each economy's 'investment function' – its demand for loanable funds as a percentage of GDP, or equivalently the rate of physical investment, as a negative function of R. Line I's negative slope reflects that the returns from additional investment tend to fall as investment rises in relation to GDP, a feature known as the 'diminishing marginal efficiency of capital'. Thus the real cost of capital must fall to encourage more investment, other things being equal. Line I is assumed the same for both economies. This is purely for exposition, in order to focus on differences in saving rates.

In each economy the loanable funds market is brought into equilibrium through movements of the real interest rate R, which adjusts freely to equilibrate the demand and supply of bonds. Consider first what happens if there is zero mobility of capital between the two economies. This might reflect either that no financial links have developed between them – they are effectively closed economies – or that capital flows are wholly prevented by exchange-controls or other obstacles. In that case Low-saver's market clears at an interest rate of RL, where lines I and LS intersect and investment equals saving of OB, while High-saver's market clears at the lower interest rate RH, which brings investment and saving into equality at the higher value OD.

Next consider what happens if capital can flow freely between the economies, bearing in mind that bonds of similar risk and maturity composition are issued in both, and so are close substitutes. In those conditions Low-saver firms have an incentive to issue bonds at the lower interest rate in High-saver's capital market and High-saver households have an incentive to buy higher-yielding bonds in Low-saver's market. Capital will then flow from High-saver to Low-saver, causing RL to fall and RH to rise. Overall equilibrium will be established in the combined capital markets – now effectively unified as a 'global' market – when the excess of investment over saving in Low-saver exactly matches the excess of saving over investment in High-saver. (Questions of sovereign credit risk and exchange-rate risk are ignored, so the interest differential between economies is zero.) As can be seen in Fig. A the 'world' interest rate thereby established, RW, settles at the value where Low-saver's excess of investment AC equals High-saver's surplus saving CE. (This equality reflects the assumption that the two economies are of equal size in terms of GDP; if High-saver's GDP were larger than Low-saver's, AC would be larger than CE in proportion to the difference in size and the equilibrium interest rate would be lower, between RW and RH.)

The analysis so far illustrates the simple point that in an environment of high international capital mobility, capital tends to flow from high-saving to low-saving economies and the world interest rate moves to equilibrate global demands and supplies of capital. Fig. A shows that in equilibrium there is an inflow (surplus) of AC on Low-saver's external *capital* account which is equal in size but opposite in sign to the outflow (deficit) of CE on High-saver's external capital account. Since every country's total external payments must be in zero balance by definition, Low-saver's external capital-account surplus implies a current-account *deficit* of the same size, and High-saver's capital-account deficit implies a current-account surplus of equal size. Note that although international borrowing enables investment in the low-saving economy to be higher (by BC) than under capital controls, its saving is lower than in the controlled environment because of the fall in R, so the rise in its investment is exceeded by the rise in the capital stock owned abroad. Arguably the implied increase in the share of Low-saver's capital stock owned abroad could not be sustained indefinitely.

Note also that the switch to international capital mobility in this particular example does not affect global levels of investment: in Fig. A the rise in Low-saver's investment BC is exactly offset by the fall in High-saver's investment CD; similarly the decrease in Low-saver's saving AB is exactly offset by the rise in High-saver's saving DE. However, this result follows merely from the assumption of parallelism between lines LS and HS (equal marginal rates of time preference in the two economies). For example, had a lower marginal rate of time preference been assumed in High-saver, implying a lower slope for HS than for LS, RW would be closer to RH, BC would exceed CD, and both global investment and saving would be higher under a regime of capital mobility.

Now consider the contribution that fiscal policy can make to long-run sustainability in these conditions. Fig. B focuses on just the low-saving economy, omitting the high-saving economy for clearer illustration, but the results for High-saver are the exact converse of those for Low-saver. In Fig. B the respective axes and the lines I and LS (now labelled LPRS) are identical with Fig. A, representing Low-saver's demand for, and supply of, loanable funds as before. Next government saving and investment are introduced. First, Low-saver's government is assumed to pursue a 'golden rule' for fiscal policy, namely that the government always balances its current account, which means that government saving is zero, regardless of R. In that case the LS line represents both total and *private* saving, accordingly renamed LPRS. Government investment is assumed fixed at a constant proportion of GDP regardless of R, so private-sector investment is indicated by the new line PRI to the left of line I and parallel to it at the distance given by constant government investment. Thus in equilibrium under closed-economy conditions (or capital controls), Low-saver's real interest rate is again RL, with private investment OF and government investment FB. In this situation, Low-saver's private sector has net lending of FB (saving OB *less* investment OF) and this is matched by government net borrowing (an overall budget deficit) of FB.

Next consider what happens under free international capital mobility, repeating the regime change discussed above. In equilibrium the real interest rate falls from RL to RW, as in Fig. A. Low-saver's total investment rises to OC and its saving falls to OA, both as before. In this situation, if the government maintains the golden rule, government saving remains at zero and its net borrowing remains GC (= FB), but the private sector's net financial balance falls from a surplus of FB to a deficit (net borrowing) of AG. Low-saver thus becomes a net external borrower to the extent of AG + GC = AC, borrowing from High-saver at an interest rate of RW in the global capital market, as before.

Finally, consider what happens if Low-saver's government tightens its fiscal stance sufficiently not only to finance its own investment, so eliminating its net financial deficit, *but also to finance the private-sector deficit, as we recommend.* In that case government saving must rise from zero to GC + AG = AC, where AG is its net financial surplus. In Fig. B the increase in government saving is shown as a rightward shift in the LS line from LPRS to LTS (for total saving). In so doing Low-saver's government eliminates the economy's net external borrowing on capital account and thus its external current-account deficit. The assumed fiscal tightening moves the low-saving economy into external payments balance *while leaving its cost of capital unchanged.*

Note that if the government merely pursued a 'balanced budget' approach in these conditions it would not eliminate Low-saver's external current deficit, for then the rightward shift in LS would be confined to GC and the private sector would still be a net external borrower to the extent of AG.

The conclusion from this analysis is that under free international capital mobility, a tightening of fiscal policy in low-saving economies should not be expected to lead, on its own, to a reduction in the cost of capital there, other things being equal. Under our assumptions here the increase in government saving does not provide additional finance for domestic investment; it replaces relatively cheap finance from the rest of the world. A reduction in Low-saver's cost of capital would require a relaxation of monetary policy alongside fiscal tightening. Under our proposals this relaxation would require not only a cut in central-bank short-term lending rates but also open market operations to increase the share of private wealth held as money rather than long-term bonds.

9

EXCHANGE RATE POLICY

The case for exchange-rate stabilisation

Chapter 4 explained that one of the basic tenets of the 1990s synthesis was attachment to free floating for key currencies: exchange rates between the main trading currencies must be free to vary if industrialised economies are to cope with divergent productivity trends and external shocks, given the limited real wage and price flexibility that many of them still display. However, Chapter 5 argued that the large and persistent fluctuations seen in major currencies since the start of generalised floating in the early 1970s have created serious problems for industry in open trading economies. Experience over many years suggests that persistent real exchange-rate swings cause substantial resource misallocation and structural distortion in economies with large exposure to foreign trade. The consequences for industry are long lasting and hard to reverse, and over time they outweigh the advantages from floating, which in many cases merely shift the burdens of adjustment between different countries while not reducing them overall. Moreover currency floating often conceals weaknesses in monetary and fiscal policies, and these would be better addressed on the cooperative lines proposed in Chapters 7 and 8.

This chapter will argue that the time has come to revive the ideals and objectives that lay behind the original Bretton Woods project. This is of course by no means a novel or original view; similar proposals have been made by others, with more or less conviction, over the years. The novelty here is that currency stabilisation would be part of a scheme of international cooperation that would embody compatible monetary and fiscal objectives for all the major economies, and provide the machinery to implement them. The dramatic events of the past few years have created the preconditions for a comprehensive reform of this kind.

In short, governments and central banks should embark on a series of cautious, well-designed steps towards forming a global exchange-rate system, starting with informal cooperation to stabilise the key floating currencies and proceeding in due course to a multilateral pegged-rate system based jointly on the US dollar and euro as the two main global reserve currencies, under the auspices of a reformed International Monetary Fund. More speculatively, if this venture proved a success, the two currencies at the heart of the revived system might be merged to create a monetary union embracing the North American and European economies, which others might join sooner or later.

Sceptics may ask what is new in the current international environment to suggest that attempts at exchange-rate stabilisation might now succeed, given that most have failed since the collapse of Bretton Woods. Several factors encourage a positive answer. First and foremost is the evidence that, under the 1990s synthesis, the governments of most major economies have become firmly committed to price stability as a policy priority, and have largely managed to achieve it. Despite the recent upsets, the record of low and stable domestic price inflation in the developed world since the early 1990s is impressive. Only the big surges in energy and food prices in the past few years have threatened this achievement, but they have not overturned it. Those inflationary shocks originated, not within developed economies, but from supply pressures created by rapid economic growth in the big emerging-market economies of East Asia, South America and Eastern Europe. Developed-economy central banks have not allowed these shocks to pass through substantially into domestic inflation. The maintenance of low inflation for almost 20 years suggests that an essential precondition for exchange-rate stability has finally been met.

However, while inflation convergence is a necessary condition for exchange-rate stability, it is not a sufficient condition, as shown by the continuation of substantial currency volatility in the low-inflation era. This reflects that exchange rates, like other financial-asset prices, are highly sensitive to bubbles and bandwagon effects which can be both erratic and prolonged, as seen in Chapter 5. Policy must address these aberrations if currency stability is to be achieved.

A second feature of the 1990s consensus which should assist exchange-rate stability is the general acceptance by developed-economy governments that fiscal policy should be directed at economic stability over the long term. Although some governments have pursued fiscal discipline more effectively than others, the evidence suggests that most take it more seriously than before. Thus while monetary policy can fairly claim much of the credit for low inflation since the early 1990s, the greater fiscal caution generally exercised through much of this period has also helped. Nevertheless it is now clear that the relatively cautious fiscal stance (by historical standards) adopted in the Anglo-Saxon economies from the late 1990s until the crash of 2007–8 was insufficiently ambitious in countering the exceptional weakness of private saving that developed there.

If the fiscal imbalances observed between the major economies can be steadily redistributed to achieve broad external payments balance between them, all on a cyclically-adjusted basis, as we recommend, the prospects for exchange-rate stability should be much improved. The existence of large financial imbalances between the majors has been an important cause of the huge swings in the dollar, euro and pound in recent years. If pursued successfully by most or all major economies, fiscal rebalancing should lead to convergence in their long-term interest rates, at least in shock-free conditions. When added to the convergence of short-term interest rates that should result from the universal achievement of internal price stability in the major economies, this fiscally-inspired shift should help greatly to underpin exchange-rate stability.

Admittedly, powerful asymmetric shocks may continue to disturb the international environment from time to time and open up interest-rate differentials or other stresses between the major currencies. If such shocks are temporary, as many may turn out to be, the pressures thereby induced should be countered by concerted *non-sterilised* exchange-market intervention by central banks,[1] financed by official foreign borrowing if necessary. If the asymmetric shocks are permanent, as some may be, and if wage and price adjustments are insufficient to bring about the necessary long-term adjustment in relative costs and prices, appropriate exchange-rate realignments should be implemented in an orderly and cooperative way. It would be vital not to divert monetary policy from its internal counter-inflation role by calling upon it to perform external adjustment as well. Nevertheless, in time, as developed economies become increasingly diversified and adaptive to change, the need for realignments should diminish.

A third factor favouring a revival of exchange-rate management at present is the heightened concern across the world trading community that the global recession, if prolonged, could lead to beggar-thy-neighbour currency depreciations, as in the inter-war years of the last century. Several sharp depreciations have occurred in the main floating currencies during the recent crisis, including sterling and eventually the euro, confidence in which has been damaged by the sovereign debt difficulties of peripheral Euro states, as seen in Chapter 8. While depreciations like that of sterling in 2008 may cushion the effects of falling world trade on the depreciating economy (provided inflation is under control), they merely shift the adjustment burden elsewhere. In this environment, international cooperation to stabilise exchange rates should have enhanced appeal for governments in the industrial world. Moreover the election in late 2008 of a US administration seemingly intent on promoting international cooperation could herald a sea-change away from the 30-year attitude of 'benign neglect' of the dollar by successive US governments.

Two vital economic conditions for the success of currency stabilisation should nevertheless be stressed:

1. The values at which currencies are stabilised must conform to the 'fundamentals' that determine exchange rates over the long term – though these are not necessarily constant through time.
2. Stabilisation must conducted within an international policy framework that is strongly committed to stability in *all* key respects, especially price and output stability and sustainable rates of national saving.

Previous attempts at currency stabilisation have foundered sooner or later because these conditions have not been met, or have been abandoned, but this does not mean the task is doomed to failure; indeed there are reasons for thinking that it may not be as difficult as sceptics suggest. Important policy spadework has already been done under the 1990s synthesis, and the atmosphere in the wake of the current economic crisis is favourable, as observed. Furthermore, the very instability of floating exchange rates may mean that stabilising them is actually relatively easy if the appropriate macroeconomic policies are followed, as will be explained in the next section.

The sources of exchange-rate instability

It may be asked why floating currencies are so subject to instability. The answer has to be: because they are only weakly tied to the 'fundamentals'. Economists have devoted much effort to understanding exchange-rate behaviour, especially why they are so weakly related to what are widely agreed to be their fundamental determinants. Attempts at estimating equations for predicting exchange rates have been so unsuccessful that econometricians have generally concluded that the latter follow a 'random walk', i.e. that forces that determine long-run equilibrium (or sustainable) exchange rates are so weak that at any given time the best available predictor of the next period's rate is simply the rate in the current period. Thus exchange-rate forecasting in a floating-rate world is a particularly hazardous exercise and currency speculation may simultaneously be highly lucrative for some professionals and loss-making for others.

Similar conclusions have been reached by rational expectations theorists, who argue that floating exchange rates are classic 'flex' prices: they are determined in highly competitive markets where homogeneous categories of financial assets are traded by large numbers of well-informed buyers and sellers, free from barriers like exchange controls and other restrictions on international capital mobility. Under these conditions exchange rates are held to exemplify the 'efficient markets hypothesis' regarding financial asset prices. According to this hypothesis, market expectations of future prices are based on a single 'true' model reflecting fundamental factors (in the case of exchange rates, relative international costs and consumer tastes); but actual prices are affected by unpredictable changes – in either the fundamentals or other more temporary influences – which lead all agents to make forecasting errors. However, such errors (it is argued) will be distributed randomly across agents, so that on average the prices that actually emerge in the market always give the best possible forecast of future prices. That is what is meant by a 'random walk'.

However, in the real world the fundamentals that determine exchange rates are very poorly understood. There is certainly no single model that all agents accept as true, and even if there were, the underlying causal processes are slow-moving and hard to discern, and the extraneous influences tend to be powerful and unpredictable, though often short-lived. In these circumstances today's exchange rates provide very poor predictors of future rates: they may be the best available, but in normal conditions they are not much use. Only when the exchange rate departs so far from the fundamentals as to be obviously unsustainable, can the markets be confident that they can predict at least the direction of future change.

Most economists would probably agree that the main cause of the huge variability of floating currencies seen over recent decades has been the liberalisation of international capital markets. As a result of the freeing of international capital markets, much larger volumes of exchange transactions nowadays relate to capital or financial flows than to trade in goods and services. Thus exchange rates behave like financial-asset prices, not like relative goods prices. The former are driven by relative yields on assets denominated in different currencies rather than by relative production costs. Relative asset yields reflect international interest differentials and expected future exchange-rate values, extending months and perhaps years into the future. Consequently *expectations* of future interest and exchange rates play a crucial part in determining current exchange rates, and both tend to be highly uncertain, especially over the longer run.

Under the 1990s synthesis, interest-rate uncertainty has been boosted by increased reliance on monetary policy for controlling inflation and by the liberalisation of domestic financial systems, which has restored market-based interest rates as the mechanism for allocating credit across a much wider spectrum of assets than previously. Exchange-rate uncertainty is generally much greater now than it was before liberalisation because the trade fundamentals now play a smaller part in determining currency values in the short–medium term than previously. Moreover, some floating currencies are seen to be more variable than others, for historical reasons and/or because they are subject to erratic policies, and they consequently bear risk premiums which may themselves vary as national policies or institutions change through time.

Uncovered interest parity

In the floating-rate era a body of theory has been developed to explain the behaviour of floating exchange rates known as 'uncovered interest parity' (UIP).[2] This theory states that the current (spot) exchange rate between two currencies is determined by the current interest differential between them on capital-certain assets of a given maturity (say three months) and the expected future spot (uncovered) rate when the assets mature (in, say, three months' time). More specifically, the current (spot) exchange rate tends to be such that the expected yield from interest plus the capital gain or loss from holding assets in each currency is equal. Other things being given (including the *expected* spot, or uncovered, exchange rate), an increase in the interest rate on currency X will cause it to appreciate immediately but temporarily against currency Y, for only then will the expected capital loss from holding assets denominated in X compensate for the extra interest received from holding them rather than Y-denominated assets. There is some empirical support for UIP in the short term, for *negative* correlations can be found between changes in international interest differentials and subsequent exchange-rate movements over periods of up to about two years. But similar results are not found over longer periods: in general *positive* correlations are found between international interest differentials and exchange-rate movements in the medium–longer term (see Miles and Scott 2005: sec. 20.6). This may reflect that exchange-rate expectations looking more than a year or so ahead are insufficiently certain to deliver the UIP result in the longer term.

It follows that international interest-rate differentials are relatively strong influences on exchange rates in the medium and longer term, although by no means the only important influence. This holds regardless of whether interest and exchange rates are expressed in nominal or real terms, provided they are measured consistently. Thus persistent divergences in the thrust of monetary policies among the key-currency economies are likely to be one of the main explanations for the big long-period real exchange-rate fluctuations shown in Figure 5.4.

In summary, long-term exchange-rate instability is due to three main factors:

1. the trade fundamentals have only a weak influence on floating exchange rates except in the very long term;
2. exchange-rate expectations have an important influence on exchange rates in the short-medium term but are highly uncertain in the longer term; and
3. interest differentials are an important but rather unpredictable influence on exchange rates in the medium and longer term.

Nevertheless there is hope that exchange-rate stabilisation can be a manageable task if the authorities choose appropriate objectives and pursue them in a determined and consistent way. When markets are uncertain as to what are sustainable exchange-rate values, spontaneous market forces tend to be weak, and in such circumstances clear and concerted stabilisation actions by the authorities have a good chance of being effective. Such actions must of course work with the grain of the fundamentals so far as these are reflected in the markets, and the latter (i.e. relative costs and prices of tradable goods in different currencies) must themselves be reasonably stable.

There is persuasive evidence to support this view. Above all there is the acknowledged success of the Bretton Woods system in maintaining relatively stable exchange rates for major currencies for nearly 25 years after the Second World War, though this achievement was assisted by the retention of exchange controls on weaker currencies through much of the post-war era. Also favourable was the experience of the EMS for around 20 years after 1979, when small-country currencies like the Dutch guilder and the Belgian franc were kept stable against the D-mark, Europe's strongest currency, through many vicissitudes, because their authorities were committed to keeping their short-term interest rates close to those of the Bundesbank. There was also the successful though much briefer episode following the G7 action to bring about a managed depreciation of the overvalued US dollar under the Plaza Agreement (1985) and Louvre Accord (1987).[3] A more recent example was the concerted intervention led by the European Central Bank in support of the euro in autumn 2000 when, after 18 months of depreciation, it was judged to have fallen excessively against the dollar. This action was successful in arresting the euro's depreciation and putting it on a recovery path.[4]

These examples illustrate the familiar caveat that successful stabilisation depends on working with the grain of the market. Thus success in all these cases depended on the currencies in question being stabilised at or near sustainable long-run values; concerted and highly publicised central-bank intervention was undertaken to move misaligned rates towards those values; and monetary and fiscal policies were implemented to reinforce stability at those rates, at least for a time. Only when national monetary and/or fiscal stances ceased to be compatible with stable exchange rates, as in the United States towards the end of the 1960s and again after 2002; and when there were inconsistent policies among several G7 countries towards the end of the 1980s, in the wake of the Plaza and Louvre agreements (discussed in Poole 1992), did instability again break out.

Sceptics may fairly point out that several efforts at key-currency stabilisation under the conditions of high international capital mobility after the Bretton Woods era came to grief because macroeconomic policies failed to underpin exchange-rate stability, or did so only temporarily. Prominent among these failures was the expulsion of the lira and pound from the ERM in autumn 1992. Those events showed that central banks cannot resist market pressures for devaluation when it becomes clear to international investors that a currency is being held at a substantially overvalued rate. Failure in such cases has usually been due to inconsistency between participants' macroeconomic policies. Thus the speculation against the lira and pound in September 1992 arose because the Italian and UK authorities were unwilling for domestic reasons to emulate the sharp policy tightening by the Bundesbank in 1991–2, at a time when reunification was putting heavy demands on the German federal budget and creating excess demand in the reunified economy. In these circumstances the markets became convinced that realignment of the D-mark was inevitable, and when no such realignment was forthcoming (at the insistence of the French government) they were presented with a 'one-way' speculative option against the lira and sterling which no amount of official intervention (or last-minute monetary tightening) could withstand. Only if major policy conflicts are avoided can stabilisation hope to succeed.

The path to currency stability

The path to currency stability in the present century can be envisaged broadly as follows; arguably the process is already underway:

1. The starting point was a remarkable event in 1999: the launching of the euro as a global currency comparable with the dollar. The present century thus began with two large monetary unions. Around each of them are congregating groups of mainly small open economies – namely, the large number of emerging and developing economies of East and Central Asia and South America

that link their currencies more or less loosely to the dollar; and the dozen or more CEE and Mediterranean economies that aim to join the euro, or develop strong links with it. Since the start of EMU, a growing 'euro zone' has emerged in the wider Europe. For political reasons the looser type of arrangement is likely to be preferred by countries that wish to link to the dollar, for whom the alignment process has been in evidence much longer: a modern 'dollar zone' has been in existence over the past two decades.

2. The existence of two big currency areas is likely to generate a gradual but inexorable process of *polarisation*, with each area becoming an increasingly self-contained trading and investment bloc. The 'satellite' members of each bloc will be obliged to sacrifice monetary independence for the sake of stability against their reference currency, though they may retain some freedom to adjust their exchange rates if competitiveness considerations require it. The incentives and constraints generated by currency stability mean that international trade and investment will tend to become increasingly oriented within each of the two currency areas, so that each becomes more internally open but more externally closed. Eventually, unless action is taken to avoid it, polarisation may lead to increased exchange-rate instability between the two key currencies, as policies for each bloc become more inward-looking. There are some indications that this is already happening.

3. A number of large and medium-sized economies will stay outside these two rival blocs. Among them are likely to be Japan, mainland China, Russia and several of the larger CIS states (notably Ukraine), and the UK. These are all countries that have strong political and/or economic reasons for retaining monetary independence. Some (like China) may continue to stabilise their currencies more or less loosely against either the dollar or euro, depending on their particular external trade and investment affinities; but some (like the UK) may prefer to float freely, a strategy that has delivered a degree of long-term stability in *effective* terms against a trade-weighted average of the euro and dollar, though not in bilateral terms.[5] Eventually new monetary unions may polarise around the yen or RMB, if Asian regional politics permit, though at present this seems rather unlikely.

4. Despite – or perhaps because of – the prospect of increasing dollar/euro polarisation, the euro's emergence as a global currency may facilitate cooperation between them. It should be easier to agree mutual currency support when there are just two or three key currencies than when a number of European currencies had to be considered; and Euro Area representatives should find it easier to punch their weight in the G7 or successor groups. Third countries oriented towards one or other of the two major currency blocs would benefit from a stable dollar/euro rate, because it should be easier to link to one or other currency if the two are themselves linked in a stable way.

5. It is hard to foresee the exact nature of the cooperation that might then ensue, but the following sequence can be envisaged:

i. The process might start with an informal but overt agreement between the authorities in charge of the dollar, euro and yen, plus possibly sterling and the Canadian dollar as lesser associates. Initially the best approach would probably be to stabilise the key rates within broad target zones with 'soft edges'. The currencies would be kept within these zones if necessary by concerted, highly publicised, central bank intervention at or near their margins. Such action would be underpinned by uniform inflation targets (and hence compatible monetary policies) and mutually consistent fiscal targets.

ii. After several years of successful cooperation, the informal approach might give rise to a more formal intergovernmental agreement, perhaps resembling the Plaza Agreement and Louvre Accord in the mid/late 1980s. Such an agreement would set out objectives for monetary and fiscal policy on lines discussed earlier in this chapter, and create consultative machinery between the main authorities (ECOFIN and the ECB for the euro and the US Treasury and Federal Reserve for the dollar).

iii. If key-currency stability were successfully maintained for five to ten years, other currencies would be drawn into the process, and the way would be open for a formal exchange-rate system. This would probably be managed by a reformed International Monetary Fund, which would operate a pegged-but-adjustable exchange-rate system with central rates set against the dollar/euro and, initially, wide fluctuation margins. More will be said below about the institutional and technical features of this stage below.

iv. Eventually, if a high degree of dollar/euro stability were established at the centre of a formal system over a decade or more, it might be made irreversible by merging the two global currencies. The modalities of that more speculative stage will be considered in Chapter 10.

Although international interest in currency stabilisation may be gaining ground for the reasons given earlier, it would be optimistic to contemplate venturing far on the above path in the immediate future. Successful action to stabilise currencies will depend on full and credible support from monetary and fiscal policy, but overcoming the exceptionally deep and protracted recession has compelled governments to take policy risks which would be thought reckless in normal conditions. And the task of negotiating a formal system must clearly wait until the authorities have time and energy to devote to it. Yet if moves towards stabilisation are delayed far into the tenure of the Obama Administration, the opportunity may be missed.

Reforming the international monetary system

It cannot be emphasised too strongly that no serious venture in currency stabilisation could hope to succeed without clear and credible commitments to domestic economic stability by all participants, preferably via inflation and fiscal targets as proposed in Chapters 7 and 8. These targets would need to be mutually consistent and compatible, as also explained there. Initially, drawing them up would be a task for G7 finance ministers and central-bank governors, or a successor group created to accommodate the euro and the emerging Asian giants. If the initial focus were on just three major currencies – the dollar, euro and yen – the appropriate forum would probably be a 'G3' of just the United States, Euro Area and Japan; or perhaps a G4 including China, possibly with others (UK, Canada, India) as associate members. The initiative might be provided by the G20 but this would be too large and diverse a group to manage a currency stabilisation scheme effectively.

While ad hoc arrangements might suffice in the early stages, inclusion of more currencies would call for administrative support, economic advice and technical expertise, preferably from an experienced, well-resourced and widely respected international body. The International Monetary Fund would seem to be the best and indeed the only realistic candidate for this role, despite the criticisms of it by some influential economists in recent years. Reform of the IMF has been the subject of much debate at various times since the early 1970s and there is not space here to do the arguments justice. The recent debates have been keenly contested and even acrimonious at times. Criticisms arose around the turn of the century mainly over the Fund's handling of the East Asian financial crisis of 1997–9 and the transition of former centrally-planned economies after the disintegration of the USSR. Joseph Stiglitz's attack on the Fund's policies and governance after he retired as Chief Economist of the World Bank received wide attention and elicited a strong rebuttal from Kenneth Rogoff, who was in charge of the Fund's research at the time.[6] Attacks have been remounted in the past few years over the Fund's advocacy of banking deregulation even while the sub-prime mortgage crisis was breaking in the United States; and lately over its calls for fiscal retrenchment by heavily indebted economies in the Euro Area.

Some of Stiglitz's strictures seem justified but by no means all. For example, complaints that the IMF has been too secretive about its policy advice to member countries seem unfair: since the 1990s the Fund has greatly improved public access to its country reports and its consultations with members; pressure for confidentiality has usually come from the latter. And suggestions that the Fund lacks integrity as a disseminator of members' economic and financial statistics seem totally groundless. The Fund's data are widely acknowledged to be of high quality; its role in training experts and improving the collection of statistics is widely valued. On the other hand, arguments that the Fund has been impatient and insensitive at times in pressing for the removal of import and exchange controls in poorer economies with struggling domestic industries and rudimentary capital markets seem better founded, as do accusations that it has sometimes been harsh in advocating shock treatment for developing economies in the hope of getting markets to work better (removal of food subsidies, expenditure tax hikes, sell-offs of parastatal organisations, etc.). In general, the Fund's comparative advantage lies in advising economies with strong capitalist institutions, liberalised goods and financial markets, and effective macro policy instruments. It has tended to be less surefooted when it has been drawn into development and structural issues, on which its research staff tend to be less expert. If support grows for a formal exchange-rate system in due course, there would a strong case for reviving the IMF's original though long-defunct role as provider of balance of payments finance for developed economies. From time to time the Fund's leading apologists have called for a revival of that role.

Among possible reforms in anticipation of such a revival, several merit special attention in the present context. First, it would be desirable to enshrine the elements of a cooperative macroeconomic policy regime, on the lines we have suggested, in a new or amended Treaty, to which all participants would subscribe. Procedures should then be established for the setting of consistent national stability targets for inflation, output, saving, and par values against the dollar-euro, at levels to be agreed with the IMF and monitored by it. These targets, and performance against them, would then be the focus of Fund policy advice and conditions for Fund assistance in the reformed system.

A second reform would relate to Fund conditionality. The Fund's traditional function of providing temporary and conditional financial assistance to members in balance of payments difficulty should continue under a reformed system, but its conditionality has tended to be forward-looking (conditional on the applicant's future policies), whereas there is a case for making it partly retrospective (conditional on previous policies). In this way eligibility for Fund assistance would depend partly on the applicant's *past* record in relation to its policy obligations, as well as on its future intentions. This would encourage national authorities facing potential problems to follow Fund advice at an early stage, rather than wait until a crisis breaks out, as has too often happened in the past.

Third, in a reformed system the Fund should be empowered to distinguish clearly and openly between member countries 'in good policy standing', of whose macroeconomic policies it approves, and those of whose policies it disapproves. A country's standing in this respect is important not only because it determines eligibility to receive Fund assistance but also because it affects creditworthiness on the international capital markets. To have maximum impact, such badges of policy approval (or disapproval) should be published, with an explanation of the underlying reasoning. This would also encourage openness in the Fund's country reports and consultations, building on the progress already made. More explicit distinction between members' good and bad performance, and more openness generally, should help the Fund to exert more influence over countries whose policies it dislikes even when they are not subject to balance of payments pressures – especially those in chronic and substantial external payments surplus, which may be undesirable for global systemic reasons. In the past the Fund has generally been unable to exert much influence over surplus countries, although there have been times when it wished to do so.

Finally it is possible to have sympathy with the criticism by Stiglitz and others that the big developed economies have too much influence on the Fund's governance and decision-making. The United States has sole veto over Fund decision-making on account of its size, and uses that power to get its way on issues like Fund conditionality and other aspects of its lending policies.[7] Some critics believe

US dominance to have been responsible for the shift in Fund philosophy from the interventionism of the Keynesian era to the extreme free-market approach of recent decades, though other major economies also contributed to that shift. But while democratic considerations suggest that poorer and smaller economies should have more say about the terms on which Fund provides advice and financial support, the IMF cannot be an entirely democratic institution in this respect, given its heavy reliance on finance contributed by the rich economies. Admittedly it raises some finance by market borrowing, but its ability to do so depends on the creditworthiness of the rich countries that stand behind it. For this reason it is probably unrealistic to look for radical reform of the Fund's governance. But moderate changes to give developing countries more influence should be possible, for example by adjusting the formula that determines Fund quotas and voting rights to give more weight to trade and other factors and less to GDP; some progress has been made in that direction.[8] In any case, if the emerging economies continue to grow rapidly, their relative quotas will rise and the bigger ones should be in a position to challenge the United States' veto power within a decade.

Related proposals for Fund reform include a strengthening of the independence of the Directors on its Executive Board who are responsible for all its significant lending and other policy decisions. These officials are almost always government appointees and act under guidance from their sponsors. Some economists have recommended that they be accorded full, legal, policymaking independence in the manner of modern central banks, together with the accountability that goes with it (see de Gregorio *et al.* 1999). This is a bold idea whose time may come but it seems unlikely to do so soon. Developed-economy governments are unlikely to cede influence over Fund decision-making as long as they are called upon to contribute the bulk of the Fund's financial resources and shoulder its lending risks.

Choosing and pursuing exchange-rate targets

The remainder of this chapter will discuss the main technical issues that will need to be addressed if there is to be a successful return to currency stabilisation on the lines suggested. They relate to the specification of the exchange-rate targets to be adopted and the way in which they should be pursued. These are vital questions because the success of any stabilisation scheme will depend on choosing appropriate (i.e. sustainable) targets for the currencies involved. On several occasions over the years, currency stabilisation schemes have got into trouble through choice of inappropriate central rates and/or fluctuation margins.[9]

Focusing on real exchange rates

Since the object would be to maintain stable international trading conditions, rather than controlling inflation by linking to an external anchor, the focus should be on *real* rates (adjusted for relative inflation), rather than the nominal exchange rates which have tended to be the focus of targeting in the past. As argued earlier, it should be easier to achieve real-rate targets in conditions when national inflation rates have securely converged and governments are committed to price stability, than in the previous high-inflation era. Even so, unless and until countries successfully pursue uniform inflation targets, periodic adjustments of nominal rates will still be required. In addition, occasional realignments of real rates may be needed to accommodate permanent shocks or structural divergences between national economies. (For example, the transformation of the UK economy into a net oil exporter through the discovery and exploitation of North Sea oil in the 1970s probably warranted a historically high real exchange rate for sterling through the next 20 years.)

The principles underlying the determination of exchange rates over the medium and longer term have been the subject of much debate in the literature. At the risk of seeming tautological, economic theory teaches that real exchange rates depend fundamentally on relative prices (or costs) in the countries concerned, and a given exchange rate will be sustainable in the long run only if it reflects these 'fundamentals'. Yet exactly what constitutes the fundamentals is far from transparent, as argued earlier. Logic suggests that in open and competitive markets the 'law of one price' should hold, which means that it should cost the same to buy the same goods in different countries (after allowing for taxes and transport costs) when their prices are expressed in a common currency; and exchange rates should adjust over time to bring this equality about. In fact very few individual goods actually command the same price in different countries, as the famous example of the 'Big Mac' index published by the *Economist* magazine bears out (see Miles and Scott 2005: 504–9). However, there is some empirical support for the law of one price if it is extended to cover a wide range of goods and services, as under the 'Purchasing Power Parity' (PPP) approach. Under PPP a given basket of commonly traded goods and services produced in different countries should cost the same (after allowing for taxes and transport costs) when expressed in the same currency; if it does not, importers will shop around for the cheapest supplies, arbitraging between them if there is scope to do so, and exchange rates will tend to adjust until different countries' prices in a common currency come into equality.

Estimates of relative-price ratios for most developed economies, known as 'PPP exchange rates', are regularly compiled and published by the OECD, using the US dollar as the standard of comparison.[10] The evidence for the major economies suggests that actual exchange rates diverge from their PPP values for long periods and that, in general, purchasing power parity holds only over the very long run – several decades or more. Thus over the past 50 years, broad purchasing power parity has existed between the UK and the United States only for a few rather short periods, as can be seen in Figure 9.1, and the same can be said for the German/US exchange rate. Similarly, the Japanese yen has seldom been close to PPP against the dollar since 1960, though it was fairly close for a time in the late 1970s and again around 2006, according to the estimates in the chart.

Over shorter periods, which may mean up to about 25 years, real exchange rates tend to display large fluctuations, as shown earlier. Thus although the trade fundamentals do seem to reassert themselves ultimately after having been driven

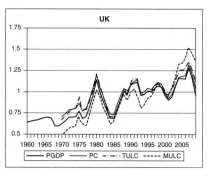

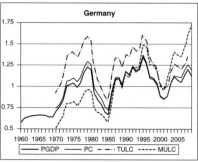

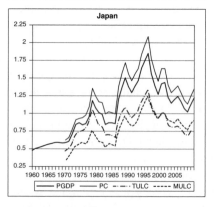

FIGURE 9.1 Real bilateral exchange rates, sterling, Deutsche mark-euro and yen against US dollar: alternative measures, 1960–2009 (source: OECD Stat online database and author's calculations).

Notes: PGDP and PC are ratios of home-economy GDP prices and consumer prices respectively to US prices, all expressed in US dollars. TULC and MULC are index numbers (base year 2000 = 1.0) of whole-economy and manufacturing unit labour costs respectively, relative to US costs, all expressed in dollars. See also the text for explanations.

apart by temporary or persistent shocks, the forces propelling them back to equality are generally weak and slow-acting (Miles and Scott 2005). It is this 'low frequency' volatility that stabilisation efforts should address.

One factor behind low-frequency real-rate volatility is the behaviour of profit margins in tradable goods industries, which tend to vary considerably over the short to medium term when exchange rates fluctuate. This type of variability arises because industrial firms tend to 'mark to market' in foreign markets, i.e. charge what the market will bear rather than applying a standard mark-up on unit production costs, as imperfectly competitive firms would be expected to do in domestic markets. Some of the variability seen in real exchange rates should therefore be avoided if stabilisation focuses on costs rather than prices. For this reason studies of international trade generally focus on relative costs – generally unit labour costs (ULCs) – in a common currency, rather than prices.[11] Yet ULC-based measures display long-run fluctuations as large, or almost as large, as those displayed by price-based measures, as may be seen in Figure 7.1. Many practitioners would therefore probably agree that price-based measures (like PPP rates) are acceptable guides to competitiveness over the very long run (20 years and more).

The choice of target values: PPP rates are best?

Because of the high uncertainty that normally surrounds a currency's long-term sustainable value, the choice of target values for real exchange rates has to be a matter for judgement. In principle there is much to be said for stabilising open-economy floating currencies at or close to their PPP values against some widely-traded reference currency, most obviously the US dollar, on the basis of either relative GDP prices or consumer prices. Indeed PPP values appear to offer a plausible guide to sustainable rates in present circumstances. This may be seen in Figure 9.1, which suggests that in 2007 both sterling and the euro (based on German GDP prices) were overvalued by over 20 per cent compared with their PPP values against the US dollar, while the yen was fairly close to its PPP value then. Since then sterling has moved close to its PPP value against the dollar owing to its sharp depreciation in 2008, but the euro, much less so; and the yen looks to have become appreciably overvalued on this basis.

However, alternative real-rate measures – for example those based on relative unit labour costs – may give somewhat different results, as may also be seen in Figure 9.1, and these differences should also be taken into account. Thus an average of price-based and cost-based measures might be preferable to either measure singly if profit margins in the tradable sector are abnormally high or low; or manufacturing measures might be preferable to whole-economy measures for a country whose trade is composed largely of manufacturing; and so forth.

Furthermore, some exchange rates may diverge so far from their PPP values for structural or other long-term reasons that the latter do not provide appropriate stabilisation targets. In such cases it might be preferable to use long-run averages or trend values of the real exchange rates in question as targets. For example Figure 9.2, using deviations of real exchange rates from their respective trends since 1970, suggests that both the euro and pound were only moderately overvalued against

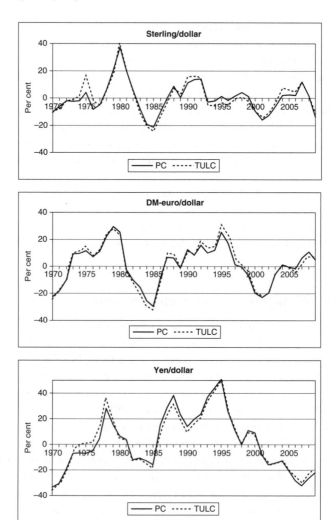

FIGURE 9.2 Deviations from long-term trends in real exchange rates, sterling, Deutsche mark-euro and yen against US dollar, alternative measures, 1970–2009 (source: OECD online database and author's calculations).

Notes: percentage deviations from log-linear trends, 1970–2008. 'PC' is the index of home-economy consumer prices relative to US prices, used in Figure 9.1; 'TULC' is the index of home-economy total unit labour costs relative to US costs, also used there.

the dollar in 2007 (by around 10 per cent or slightly less), whether on a relative consumer price (PC) basis or a unit labour cost (ULC) basis, whereas the yen was substantially undervalued (by around 30 per cent) against the dollar on both measures in that year, though it has recovered somewhat since. The yen's large real depreciation in the past decade reflects the remarkable and persistent disinflation in the Japanese economy since the early 1990s, which meant that Japanese prices and costs tended to fall substantially against US costs, despite nominal dollar deprecia-tion. While PPP *ratios* may give a better approximation of long-run sustainable values for the euro and pound, very long-run (30-year) *trends* in PC or ULC values might give a better approximation for the yen.

Perhaps surprisingly on the face of it, the high uncertainty surrounding sustain-able values for the major floating currencies may make it easier to stabilise them in some respects, as argued earlier. Where market views about underlying currency values are weakly held and widely distributed around prevailing values, market speculation will itself tend to promote stability around those current market values (in the absence of 'news' or other surprises). And the precise values targeted are unlikely to be crucial for many firms or industries. Thus, within quite wide limits (say, plus or minus 10 per cent), the values set for real exchange-rate targets are likely to be less important than a credible commitment to stabilisation at broadly sustainable rates. This seems a widely held business view: industrialists often say that they are looking for exchange-rate stability per se, rather than stability at some particular value. Nevertheless, such views should be taken with a pinch of salt, since the values at which rates are stabilised do matter, as we have argued. The point is that they matter only in broad terms.

Target ranges and realignments

If it is broad stability that matters, quite wide target ranges (fluctuation margins) can and should be set where the object is to stabilise external trading conditions over the long run. This approach is quite different from that required by international *monetary* stabilisation – the linking of exchange rates in order to promote inflation convergence. That was the main purpose of the ERM, or became so in its later years, as nominal convergence towards monetary union became the priority for most adherents to the mechanism. Thus whereas the narrow band of the EMS (the margin of fluctuation between *any pair* of member currencies) was set at 2.25 per cent in order to create a zone of monetary stability, a fluctuation range of, say, plus or minus 2.5 percentage points against the dollar should probably suffice for the type of approach we have in mind.[12] This would be considerably wider than the fluctuation margin of plus or minus 1 per cent against the dollar adopted for the original Bretton Woods system.

Relatively broad fluctuation margins against the dollar would permit the man-agers of the type of scheme recommended here to peg rates in *nominal* terms, subject to small adjustments at regular intervals (say, every 12 months) if neces-sary to accommodate modest inflation differentials against the United States. (Thus a country inflating at 1 per cent p.a. faster than the United States should allow its nominal central rate against the dollar to be reduced by 1 percentage point annually, to maintain a constant real rate.) Provided national inflation differen-tials remained small, nominal-rate adjustments should be well within the permit-ted fluctuation band and speculative market pressure for real-rate realignments on inflation grounds should be avoided. In a formal scheme, such adjustments should be made on the authority of the administrative body (i.e. the IMF) and should not need government consent on each occasion.

Real-rate realignments would also be permitted in a formal scheme, but only for structural or other long-term reasons, as explained earlier. Examples would be a substantial depletion of indigenous supplies of raw materials or energy, like UK North Sea oil reserves, or serious damage to national industry or infrastructure caused by climate change or other natural catastrophes. In a group of economies successfully pursuing compatible domestic stabilisation policies, with monetary policies dedicated to price and output stability and fiscal policies dedicated to external current payments balance, such problems would manifest themselves as increasing structural unemployment in the affected economy, rather than a chronic balance of payments deficit. Real-rate realignments would then have to be agreed between the government concerned and the scheme's managers, with the approval of the membership. In the event of disagreement, the currency in question would be suspended from the scheme. There should also be provision to suspend one or more currency targets temporarily, by common consent of the membership, in the event of serious emergencies such as a global recession on the recent scale or a major disaster or conflict of some kind.

These then would be the main institutional and technical features of the progression towards key currency stability envisaged to convert the 1990s policy synthesis into a durable regime for the present century. They would comprise a thorough redevelopment of the international monetary system, building on existing institutions, chiefly a reformed IMF; and recasting of the exchange-rate targets and methods tried, with mixed success, in the last century. Critical to future success would be the alignment of monetary and fiscal policies provided by internationally compatible inflation and saving targets for major economies. If successful, such reforms could prepare the way for a merger of the dollar and euro into a single currency around the middle of the century. The modalities of that more speculative stage will be discussed in Chapter 10, which will also review the entire reform programme.

10

REVIEW AND ASSESSMENT

The case for reform

In the early 1990s policymakers in the major economies reached a compromise between laissez-faire (neoclassical) and interventionist (Keynesian) ways of running market economies. Perhaps more by luck than good judgement they managed to escape from the oscillation that had characterised policy previously – the 'journey to Utopia and back' as Britton (2001) described it. For around 15 years the new synthesis, with its emphasis on monetary stability and inflation targets, seemed to perform remarkably well in achieving its main objective of overcoming the inflation that had afflicted major economies in preceding decades. Moreover it did so without resort to the stagflation that had gripped many of the majors in the 1980s; except in Japan, the one major economy that has continued to stagnate.

Yet the 1990s settlement harboured a number of weaknesses that worried sceptics when it appeared, and these have become more evident with time. The main ones were discussed in Chapter 5: the one-club methodology of monetary policy; asset-price instability and associated fragility in liberalised financial markets; instability between the major floating currencies; inflexible and ill-defined fiscal targets; the divorce between monetary and fiscal policy; and weak accountability, at least in EMU, the regime that came closest to embodying the new synthesis.

As the new century got under way, it seemed only a matter of time before the new settlement encountered serious threats from outside, some familiar but others unprecedented. The main ones, also discussed in Chapter 5, were: commodity-price fluctuations; ageing populations and rising dependency ratios; competition from emerging economies; and the international financial imbalances that created the 'global saving glut'.

In the past few years the 1990s synthesis has indeed been put to severe test, culminating in the crash of 2007–8 and the ensuing global recession. A number of adverse shocks and systemic weaknesses interacted to produce the crisis, as described in Chapter 6. The initial shock was the hyper-boom in economic activity led by the giant emerging economies from around 2002, which generated a big surge in commodity prices; it was accompanied by unsustainable asset-price increases in the main deregulated financial centres, emulating the earlier property booms in Japan and East Asia. House price bubbles in the United States and UK were fuelled by imprudent lending, reflecting business errors and unsound financial engineering by many banks and investment firms, assisted by a catastrophic failure by the financial regulators to address them. When the economic boom went into reverse, owing partly to aggressive monetary tightening in the major economies, the house-price bubbles burst, creating large quantities of non-performing loans in the United States and international banking systems. The failures in financial markets caught policymakers completely by surprise, and so were all the more damaging. The damage spread quickly via globalisation across developed and emerging markets. The weaknesses in 1990s regimes were compounded by errors of macroeconomic policy which allowed large financial imbalances to emerge between high- and low-saving economies and helped fuel the credit excesses in America and Europe.

Only very recently (autumn 2009) have the main economies started to recover from the ensuing credit crunch and global recession. Although it is still too early to be sure that the emergency measures taken to manage the crisis have succeeded, the worst now (spring–summer 2010) seems over. Yet the costs of overcoming the crisis have been heavy and it will take time to absorb them: high unemployment and loss of investment and output in the main trading economies; large budget deficits and accumulations of government debt in those worst hit by the crisis, namely the United States and UK; and big losses of capital, reputation and creditworthiness among financial firms large and small.

A more durable regime

Looking beyond crisis management, it seems clear that substantial improvements will be needed in the rules and conduct of financial regulation and corporate governance in the financial sector, and these are now being addressed by the relevant authorities and practitioners. Improvements will also be needed in the institutions and conduct of macroeconomic policy if the 1990s synthesis is to survive in the longer term. A programme of reforms for this purpose was offered in Chapters 7–9.

Monetary policy objectives and instruments

The main recommendation in the monetary field is that *output stability* should be incorporated alongside price stability as the main objective of monetary policy. These are congruent objectives if inflation is determined in accordance with the Phillips curve, as the evidence suggests and the 1990s synthesis accepts. According to the inflation-augmented Phillips curve, pursuit of price stability requires output to be stabilised at the level consistent with the NAIRU (the crucial rate of unemployment needed to achieve zero inflation). Far from jeopardising price stability, as critics might argue, stabilising output at this level should reinforce it: such an approach would assist in avoiding policy errors that occur because of the asymmetries still found in price behaviour in developed economies, in particular the downward stickiness of many producer prices in periods of weak activity. At present central banks tend to be slow to relax monetary policy when recession develops because they give insufficient weight to output as a policy objective.

This reform would also recognise that stability of output and employment is a desirable end in itself, readily acceptable to markets and electorates. Indeed it is explicitly recognised in the legal policy remit given to the US Federal Reserve, though less so in the remits of the ECB and the Bank of England, for both of whom output stability is only a subsidiary objective.

We also recommend that *all* central banks should adopt explicit inflation targets, and that these should be internationally compatible, meaning close to uniformity, at least among the major economies. More specifically central banks, having established credible counter-inflationary reputations, should converge on the same low-inflation target, probably in the range of 0–2 per cent. This step is warranted because inflation targets have proved to be superior to monetary targets in giving focus and precision to counter-inflation policy; they are widely understood by economic agents, and for that reason have a powerful effect in damping down and eliminating inflation expectations. The international alignment of inflation targets would be an important precondition for moving towards exchange-rate stability on the lines recommended in Chapter 9.

Responsibility for financial stability

In view of the policy errors and ambiguities that contributed to the financial crash, central-bank responsibility in the area of financial stability should be clarified and strengthened. In liberalised economies systemic financial stability should be made a formal objective for central banks, provided it is done in a way that does not cause the markets or the public to doubt the primacy of the price stability objective. Mindful as they must be of this caveat, central banks can be expected to accept this responsibility stability only if they have specific macro-prudential powers and tools. These should be distinct from monetary policy proper and usable without prejudice to price stability.

In the course of the financial crisis weaknesses have been exposed in the operation of monetary policy, characterised as the 'one-club' methodology, and these should be addressed; indeed this is already happening. The normal links in the monetary transmission mechanism have been distorted by the credit crunch, making it difficult for central banks to induce falls in commercial-bank lending rates by cutting their customary intervention rates to historically low levels. When confronted by this modern version of the liquidity trap, central banks in liberalised regimes have been obliged to resort to the form of money creation known as quantitative easing. This was an appropriate tactic in the circumstances, though not without risk. We think there are good grounds for accepting quantitative management of the money stock as a normal ancillary technique, to be used judiciously to supplement conventional money-market operations when circumstances require. In the light of the recent experience, other unconventional methods should also be adopted. For example, public debt managers should be more proactive in influencing the shape of the yield curve in support of monetary policy. In regimes where debt management is done by an independent agency, the central bank should be more closely involved in this task.

Regulatory reforms

The financial crisis has raised important questions about the interface between central banks and regulators. Calls have been made for transferring the day-to-day task of banking supervision from specialist agencies back to the central bank; indeed the new UK government in 2010 has already announced this step. Such moves would mean retreating from unified regulation via a single central agency, introduced in the UK in the 1990s and quite widely copied elsewhere (though not in the United States), and they could point towards the re-segregation of banking supervision as between commercial and investment banks on Glass-Steagall lines. On balance such moves seem inadvisable, even if corresponding action could be secured globally in all jurisdictions, which seems doubtful.

A systematic break-up of integrated banks into 'utility' and 'casino' operations would be inadvisable on microeconomic grounds because there are substantial synergies and scale economies in modern banking, some of which would be lost if multi-function banks were routinely broken up on purely prudential grounds. There are also questions whether it could be done without disrupting ordinary banking business. Even banks that are largely retail in character need to engage in some proprietary trading and investment operations in order to be able to offer a competitive service to corporate clients. In general, questions of dismembering large integrated banks should fall within the remit of *competition policy*, not prudential regulation. The preservation of inter-firm competition provides widely accepted criteria (avoidance of dominant market shares) for anti-monopoly or anti-trust action in the financial, as in the industrial, sector. It would be difficult to devise rules for limiting banks' size or segregating their activities on purely prudential grounds. As many commentators have pointed out, some banks were kept in business by official support during the financial crisis because their failure posed a systemic threat (e.g. Northern Rock in the UK), even though they were neither large in system terms nor conglomerates or investment banks.

That does not mean that the authorities in liberalised centres have to accept that few banks can be allowed to fail, and must live with the associated moral hazard. Rather it implies that size and diversification, as well as other features of a bank, should be judged on a *case-by-case* basis in the prudential field. The regulators must be intrusive in requiring banks with high-risk business to meet higher than average capital/liability ratios, as argued by the *Turner Review* and other reports.

In the event of non-compliance, or if other system concerns arise, they must have power to make banks divest themselves of high-risk operations, or protect the capital in their retail operations by firewalls or in some other way. If despite these precautions a troubled bank, large or small, requires emergency assistance from the central bank, the latter must be free to provide it, on penal terms and in confidence. Finally if a bank's solvency comes into serious question, the authorities (the central bank in collaboration with the regulators and government) should be prepared to orchestrate orderly disposals if it judges them to be necessary, involving break-ups, takeovers by other banks and even fire-sales if all else fails. With encouragement from the G20, the Financial Stability Board and the Basel Committee are working on new internationally consistent measures to address 'too big to fail' problems.[1] Ad hoc operations of this kind do not necessarily involve bailouts, though they may do so. Central banks have carried out such interventions from time to time since the early 19th century, and should expect to continue doing so.

Encumbering the central bank with substantial regulatory functions would represent a clear retreat from the 1990s synthesis, with its emphasis on the primacy of price stability and a level playing field across the whole of the financial sector. Central banks have become increasingly macroeconomic in their orientation under the new policy consensus. This seems unavoidable and it would be hard to reverse. Senior central bankers and their expert advisers should not be routinely diverted from these issues by concerns about the business decisions and practices of individual banks. Such diversions are liable to raise conflicts of interest between price stability and financial stability which a single institution should not be expected to resolve. Instead, the practical work of financial regulation should be undertaken outside central banks. The challenge is then to find effective ways of bringing the latter's macroeconomic expertise to bear on system-wide aspects of regulation like the counter-cyclical variation of banks' capital/asset ratios and other prudential standards. This should lead to closer cooperation between regulators and central bankers, from the most senior level down, with central bankers in the lead on macro aspects (and bearing the responsibility for them). At the global level, a corresponding strengthening of cooperation is needed between the regulators and the international financial institutions with macroeconomic expertise, specifically a reformed IMF, as argued in Chapter 9.

Nevertheless certain sources of systemic financial instability have become so troublesome in liberalised regimes that central banks need to address them directly, namely the house-price instability seen in the United States, UK and other mortgage-oriented markets. Central banks in these regimes should target *the long-term trend value of average house prices*, using special tools for the purpose – variable maximum loan-to-value and loan-to-income ratios for mortgage lending. Such tools should be kept separate from the monetary instruments proper but their judicious use should assist monetary policy to maintain overall price stability over the longer term. The design of the new instruments and the setting of house-price targets should be tasks for central banks, though their administration and detailed monitoring would be matters for the regulators.

While the changes summarised above should help monetary policymakers to deal better with the tests facing them in the new century, they hardly amount to radical reform in themselves. That is hardly surprising, since monetary policy has performed relatively well under the 1990s synthesis and there is no case for abandoning its objectives or procedures. However, monetary policy would be significantly affected by our reforms in other areas. The reunification of monetary and fiscal decision-making proposed in Chapter 8 would require institutional changes in both policy arms; and the revival of exchange-rate stabilisation proposed in Chapter 9 would re-impose important tasks on central banks in the area of exchange-market intervention. These themes will be resumed below.

Fiscal policy objectives

The main innovation in the fiscal field, and the most far-reaching element in our reform programme, would be the assignment of a new long-term objective to fiscal policy – a sustainable rate of national saving. This idea is not new, and is being revived by economists who see it as part of the answer to the wider problems of low-saving economies, but it would represent a basic change in the 1990s approach. Admittedly, the identification of sustainable targets for national saving may not be straightforward, but it is a question on which independent economic expertise can and should be brought to bear. The workable default rule for fiscal policy under our approach is that the government budget balance should be set to achieve broad balance in current external payments over the medium and longer term. Some developed-economy governments might prefer to aim at modest payments surpluses, to pay off external debt and finance overseas aid and investment. But they should do so only if others, mainly in the emerging and developing world, are ready to accept corresponding payments deficits overall, in order to import long-term capital and perhaps run down holdings of unstable or unremunerative foreign assets.

Such an approach would take advantage of the relevant national accounting identities, set out in Annex 1 to Chapter 8, which state that a country's external current balance must always equal the difference between its national saving (by households, firms and general government) and domestic physical investment. Governments of developed economies should aim to save at least enough to make up for any shortfall of private saving; governments of emerging and developing economies should dis-save at least enough to compensate for any excess private saving.

The idea that fiscal policy should be set to achieve balance on external payments should appeal to markets and the public generally, who should have no difficulty accepting that countries should live within their means. Moreover the task should be feasible in economies with standard national economic data and methods for simulating the results of alternative fiscal policies. Merchandise trade statistics are generally reliable and timely, and although data on trade in services and income from abroad are less so, revisions are seldom significant in relation to GDP. Data on government saving are also subject to revision, but this has not prevented governments from targeting fiscal balance; neither have forecasting errors, which are well-documented in the fiscal field. Cyclical factors are likely to be an important source of errors in forecasting both external and government financial balances, but the tendency for such errors to be offsetting should help the targeting process.[2]

Nevertheless our proposed fiscal rule could raise wider problems. One risk would be that while many hitherto low-saving economies might wish to aim at external payments surpluses for a time (to pay of external debt), few high-saving economies would be content to aim at persistent external deficits, for fear that their international credit rating would deteriorate and this might lead to downward exchange-rate pressure. If such views prevailed our approach could turn out to be deflationary overall, since from a global viewpoint external surpluses must be matched by deficits elsewhere, and a universal effort to pursue surpluses could result in global deflation (the 'pass the deficit' process referred to in Chapter 8). This risk would be greater if policymakers in high-saving economies find it difficult to stimulate their economies sufficiently to reduce their external surpluses. Japan's failure to do so in the past two decades is a significant warning in this respect.

A second, related, risk would be that the proposed fiscal rebalancing between major economies might lead, not to the elimination of external current imbalances as intended, but to counter-productive exchange-rate responses: instead of depreciating to reflect lower real interest differentials, as much theory suggests, the currencies of low-saving economies might appreciate in reflection of lower risk premiums; and the converse might happen in high-saving economies if they moved into heavy (or heavier) fiscal deficit. A third risk is that the recent recession has been so severe in low-saving economies that they would find it hard to deliver enough fiscal retrenchment to achieve budget surpluses on the required scale, and simply become mired in low activity and high deficits. This risk would be harder to avoid if high-saving economies tighten their fiscal stance as global recovery proceeds; and/or if they resist currency appreciation in those circumstances.

Minimisation of these risks would depend on a sea-change taking place in international policy cooperation. Above all, the proposed long-term fiscal objectives, as well as the monetary ones, should be adopted in a mutually consistent way by all the major developed economies; they should not be confined to just the handful of low-saving economies which have received most of the blame for the macroeconomic imbalances associated with the recent financial crisis. Second, the authorities in charge of the major floating currencies should cooperate to stabilise them at long-term sustainable rates. Neither of these developments is likely to emerge spontaneously. They would require a strong new consensus among the major economies, at G7–8 level though with endorsement by the G20, and would in due course call for coordination and surveillance by the IMF, as outlined in Chapter 9.

The fiscal policy institutions

If powerful external shocks of the kind seen since 2000 recur, tensions could well arise between the pursuit of the long-term fiscal targets envisaged above and the more flexible short-term role also sought for fiscal policy. Institutional reforms will be necessary if such tensions are to be managed successfully. First, the conduct of fiscal policy, like that of monetary policy, should be given a strong legal framework specifying explicit long-term and short-term objectives and rules, while allowing temporary overrides in emergencies. Steps in this direction were suggested in Chapter 8. The short-term fiscal objective should be exactly the same as that of monetary policy – to stabilise GDP at or near the level consistent with the NAIRU (the unemployment rate required for overall price stability). In this way international compatibility should be ensured in the short-term objectives of fiscal and monetary policy, as well as in the long-term ones.

A second important step in this context would be to reform the fiscal-policy institutions in major economies to make them less vulnerable to short-term political pressure, and more amenable to independent professional expertise, broadly as was done for monetary policymaking under the 1990s synthesis. This is likely to be difficult in the fiscal field because of the political sensitivity of tax rates and social benefits, and the complicated administrative procedures involved in changing in them. Different arrangements might be needed in different national regimes. For the UK we recommend arrangements that retain Treasury responsibility for fiscal administration, data and technical support for forecasting and policy simulation, while transferring strategic decisions to a Fiscal Policy Committee including independent experts and distanced from political pressure, as described in Chapter 8. A synoptic approach to policymaking would be provided by a high-level advisory council (the EPC), as also outlined there. Accountability of independent experts in both fiscal and monetary wings would be improved through greater exposure to public debate and parliamentary scrutiny, as also proposed there. In 2010 the new UK government has taken a cautious step to distance fiscal policy from political influence but it falls far short of these reforms.

Broadly comparable reforms should be considered in other major economies. In the United States, the CEA already provides the nucleus of an independent high-level expert body, and should be given a greater role in both fiscal and monetary policymaking; and there seem few reasons why comparable arrangements should not be introduced in other major economies. The biggest obstacles to fiscal reform lie in the Euro Area, owing to the institutional and procedural straightjacket imposed by the Maastricht Treaty. However, it is not unrealistic to hope for progress on these issues even there. The current concerns about fiscal imbalances and sovereign bailouts in the Euro Area seem to be galvanising the EMU authorities and the European Commission to move to closer central consultation on national budgetary policy, if not yet coordination in this field. Even if fiscal policy remains largely a prerogative of national governments in the EU, the reforms contemplated should not be out of reach at the national level.

Macro-prudential fiscal measures: a Tobin Tax?

In the wake of the recent crisis, attention has turned to fiscal measures that might be deployed to counter instability in global financial markets. Although such measures are generally classed as microeconomic, they could be used to further macroeconomic objectives and therefore deserve consideration here.

Chief among them is the Tobin Tax, an idea first floated by the distinguished Keynesian economist James Tobin in the 1970s as a device for discouraging speculative trading in foreign exchange markets. He proposed a uniform tax of up to one percentage point on the value of all spot purchases of financial instruments denominated in foreign currency (Tobin 1978). The tax would be internationally agreed, administered by national governments in their respective jurisdictions, and the proceeds would be paid to the IMF or World Bank for use in financing aid to poorer economies. Tobin judged the tax would cut the profitability of short-term 'round-tripping' – high-volume trades to take advantage of tiny yield differentials – but would not impinge on longer-term investment offering higher yields. Mechanical calculations suggest that a tax rate of 0.2 per cent could raise revenues of over $150 billion per annum globally. Variants of the basic idea have subsequently been put forward, including extension of the tax to cover securities trading, in the hope of discouraging short-term churning. Latterly a much broader approach has been proposed: a Financial Transactions Tax (FTT) which would amount essentially to a turnover tax on all types of financial business. In response to criticisms that the markets would be distorted by Tobin's scheme, alternatives with lower tax rates have been proposed as sources of aid financing, though they would generate much smaller revenues.

Tobin's proposal remained largely an academic curiosity until the East Asian financial crisis drew developing countries' attention to it; and interest in it finally surged after the crash of 2007–8. In December 2009 a Summit of EU leaders expressed support for an FTT based loosely on Tobin's ideas, and referred it to the IMF for study. Subsequently the G20 and the French and UK governments declared in favour of a global scheme on these lines. But despite this newfound support it remains to be seen whether an FTT-type scheme will be adopted. The US government was unenthusiastic and the IMF, initially sceptical. Their hesitation related partly to the practical difficulties of policing the tax effectively and partly to fears that a tax of the magnitude proposed would damage market liquidity and impede legitimate trading activities in hedging and derivatives. However, the chief objection was that a tax of this kind would drive financial business to uncontrolled locations. The major economies would therefore agree to it only if universal adherence were guaranteed, with regular IMF inspection of offshore centres. Even in the present receptive environment that seems questionable.

Moreover it remains unclear how far a Tobin Tax would reduce unproductive speculation and contribute to financial stability. In principle the original Tobin Tax on foreign exchange transactions might reduce short-term currency volatility, though at some cost to liquidity and efficiency in foreign exchange markets. But it would not address the problems of long-term currency instability that trouble us. Tobin himself saw it as way of mitigating the volatility he observed in floating exchange rates after the collapse of Bretton Woods; it could be no more than a marginal remedy for the massive and persistent currency swings observed under the 1990s synthesis.

Given these uncertainties, those who see the tax as a useful revenue source, perhaps to assist poorer countries or finance future bank bailouts, would seem to be on stronger ground. And there are persuasive grounds in equity and tax neutrality for introducing a broadly based turnover tax on financial services. These services have in the past been judged not to bear their fair share of value added tax, or turnover taxes in general, and the *Turner Review* seemed to agree. An FTT would redress this balance and would be an efficient way of raising revenue; if levied at a modest rate across all financial business it should not distort markets or reduce trading volumes unduly. Provided it were adopted near-universally and properly policed in offshore centres it should not drive business away from established centres. Yet an FTT might contribute little to asset-price stability or the reduction of excessive risk-taking.

The US and UK governments are nevertheless under strong political pressure to tax what are widely perceived as excessive bank profits in the muted recovery after the crisis. In late 2009 the US government announced plans to raise $90 billion from US banks over the next ten years, in the form of an insurance levy to meet the costs of government bailouts. The UK Treasury has expressed interest and might follow suit. Such plans are less ambitious in scale and intention than the Tobin Tax: the amounts of revenue raised would be much smaller and they are unlikely to curb speculation in the way that the Tobin Tax might. Yet so long as a comprehensive Tobin-style tax or FTT seems out of reach, the authorities in the major economies seem likely to prefer more modest approaches. In 2009 the UK and France introduced one-off levies on bankers' bonuses, and in 2010 the new UK government announced an annual levy rising to 0.07 per cent on the liabilities of all banks operating in the UK (reported in the *Financial Times*, 23 June 2010). The tax would raise around £2 billion in a full year, for use as general revenues rather than provision for future bailouts. It would be the first of its kind globally, though France and Germany have also pledged to introduce similar levies and the United States is moving slowly towards one. After further study the IMF is recommending a much larger 'financial activities tax' to be introduced by all G20 countries and earmarked for financing bank rescues in future crises. However, Japan and Canada have opposed such a tax and it remains to be seen whether the G20 will endorse one.

Exchange-rate policy and the international monetary system

Our advocacy of a return to concerted efforts at key-currency stabilisation is motivated by two main concerns. One is the serious damage done to industry and external trade of open economies by the large and persistent swings seen in real exchange rates. This 'low-frequency' exchange-rate instability sends misleading signals to producers and long-term investors in export-oriented industries. UK manufacturing industry was decimated (literally) by sterling's large real appreciation in the late 1970s as it became an oil-based currency. The UK economy took a long time to adjust its structure to this big change in relative costs and prices, and there are questions whether the resulting shift to financial services was wise or durable in the light of recent experience. This is far from an isolated case: currency swings have led to serious industrial misallocation in other major economies, for example the stagnation of Japanese industrial production during the 1990s following the large real appreciation of the yen against the dollar that began in 1985.

Our second concern in this context is that a global rebalancing of fiscal surpluses and deficits could be impeded by adverse exchange-rate responses, as markets reassess the creditworthiness of previously low- and high-saving economies. This concern is supported by historical experience and the properties of econometric models, which suggest that fiscal-policy actions have more leverage over output and activity when exchange rates are fixed than when they are floating. Thus, under floating exchange rates, fiscal stimuli have tended to be dissipated by the inflation caused by exchange-rate depreciation as external balances deteriorate. It was no coincidence that the collapse of the Bretton Woods system was closely followed by the demise of Keynesian economic management, as seen in Chapter 2.

Experience of previous attempts at currency stabilisation over the years has admittedly been mixed, as conceded in Chapter 9. There have been notable failures as well as successes. Success has required that action in support of weak currencies be internationally concerted and highly overt, whether through formal systems like Bretton Woods and the EMS in their heydays, or through less formal arrangements like the Plaza Agreement and Louvre Accord. Success has also required that currency-support operations work with the grain of the market, and that underlying macroeconomic policies are consistent with the currency targets. Failures have been due either to inappropriate exchange-rate targets or to conflicting macroeconomic policies, as the collapse of Bretton Woods and the traumas of 1992–3 in the ERM amply showed. Success in any future scheme will depend on the pursuit of compatible monetary and fiscal policies by participants, and on the selection of appropriate exchange-rate targets. Although identification of these targets would be a matter for expert judgement, it is arguable that PPP rates against the US dollar would provide the best starting point, and perhaps a satisfactory default option, as suggested in Chapter 9. Among the strongest merits of PPP rates are their objectivity and transparency. Few economists would dispute that they reflect the fundamental values towards which all exchange rates tend to gravitate over the very long run. Moreover, being calculated by international technicians, they cannot be subject to the national governmental pressures that so worry critics of exchange-rate management.

There are good reasons for thinking that the economic environment is now more favourable to exchange-rate stabilisation than for decades. This is partly because counter-inflation policies under the 1990s synthesis have been successful on the whole, which should remove one major cause of currency instability, and partly because, under the synthesis, governments have also accepted the need for long-term fiscal discipline, even though important mistakes have been made in fiscal policy. If these mistakes can be corrected – through the common pursuit of external payments balance – a second major source of currency instability should be removed. Finally, in the wake of the global recession and the protectionist fears it has engendered, many governments are likely to be more receptive to currency stabilisation provided it is soundly based.

Assignment of targets and instruments

A resumé of the way in which the main objectives and targets would be assigned between the three main categories of policy instruments under the foregoing proposals is offered in Table 10.1.

The chief task of monetary policy would be to maintain overall price stability. Central banks would manage short-term interest rates with a view to stabilising GDP and activity at or near the level required for consumer price stability in the

TABLE 10.1 Assignment of policy objectives and instruments

Objectives and intermediate targets	Monetary policy instruments	Fiscal policy instruments[c]	Exchange-rate instruments
Price/output stability[a] _Inflation rate 0–2% p.a._ _GDP (NAIRU level)_	Official interest rates Open market operations in government bonds[b]	1. Short-term Tax and public expenditure rates	
House-price stability _Average house-price/earnings ratio_	Variable maximum loan/value and loan/income ratios		
Sustainable national saving rate _External current balance/GDP ratio_		2. Long-term Tax and public expenditure rates	
Exchange-rate stability[d] _PPP rate v US Dollar or Euro_			Foreign exchange-market intervention

Notes: Basic policy objectives are in bold type; intermediate targets are in italics. Policy is assumed to minimise percentage deviations from intermediate targets.

[a] The two intermediate targets (inflation rate and GDP) are complementary, not competing. Policy aims to minimise deviations of GDP from the level consistent with the NAIRU (non-accelerating-inflation rate of unemployment).

[b] Quantitative easing, positive or negative.

[c] Two policy objectives are assigned to fiscal policy. In normal conditions the fiscal instruments are set to achieve a sustainable rate of national saving over the long term, the default target for which is zero balance on current external payments. However in abnormal conditions (exceptionally strong boom or deep recession) the fiscal instruments are set to assist monetary policy in stabilising GDP at or near the level consistent with the NAIRU over the short term.

[d] Exchange-rate stability is pursued by informal agreement or under a formal system, supported by consistent national monetary and fiscal targets among participants. Foreign exchange-market intervention is overt, concerted and mutually supportive (financed by pre-agreed currency swaps or standby arrangements if needed).

See the text for further explanations.

domestic economy (the NAIRU). If all central banks pursue the same (low) inflation target, short-term interest rates should converge between the main economies,
both in nominal or real terms; and they should remain converged, assuming a
shock-free environment. (Action to deal with cycles and shocks will be considered
below, see pp. 223–4.)

The chief task of fiscal policy would be to maintain sustainable national saving
rates, taking account of private saving. To this end the fiscal authorities would set
aggregate tax and public expenditure rates to achieve *balance in external payments*
over the long term. The 'default' target would be zero balance on the external
current account. More ambitiously, some countries might aim at current-account
surpluses and others deficits, provided the planned surpluses and deficits would
be approximately zero at the global level. This policy setting should ensure broad
convergence of long-term interest rates between the major economies, both in
nominal and real terms: and they should remain broadly converged in the absence
of cycles and shocks.

The chief task of exchange-rate policy would be to maintain stable real exchange
rates between the key currencies. Governments should instruct their central banks
to stabilise their currencies at or near underlying competitive levels, initially through
informal agreements on target ranges and eventually through a formal pegged-rate
system with agreed central rates and moderately wide fluctuation margins. The
default approach would target central rates at or near purchasing-power-parity values against the US dollar, though a more refined approach might focus on relative
costs rather than prices. In conditions where inflation has converged and long-term
productivity growth is broadly equal across different economies, PPP rates would
be constant. Nevertheless occasional real-rate realignments might be needed to
accommodate permanent structural shifts between economies.

The chief instrument to be used to keep exchange rates within their permitted
fluctuation ranges would be concerted and overt central-bank intervention in the
foreign exchange markets. Where necessary this would be financed by central-bank
swaps or official longer-term lending on pre-agreed terms, including IMF drawings
in the case of a fully-fledged system. Whether such financing would be conditional
on policy changes would depend on the nature and size of the disturbances in question. Whether and how central banks should sterilise the effects of their foreign
exchange intervention on domestic money supplies would be a matter for ad hoc
judgement by policymakers, with the proviso that achievement of inflation targets
should always be the dominant consideration. For example, if central-bank sales
of domestic currency to purchase foreign currency in pursuit of an exchange-rate
target threatened to create domestic inflation, the increase in the domestic money
supply should be sterilised even if it meant moving outside the exchange-rate target
range.

In the event of normal business cycles or other mild and temporary shocks, the
onus would be on monetary policy to stabilise GDP and activity at or near the
NAIRU by adjusting short-term interest rates. This action would be assisted by
the automatic fiscal stabilisers and ordinarily no fiscal action should be needed. If

the cycles or shocks were synchronised and symmetrical across the major economies, short-term interest rates should move broadly together and there should be no disruptive pressures on exchange rates. If the cycles or shocks turned out to be unsynchronised or asymmetric across the majors, moderate short-term interest differentials and external current payments imbalances would probably emerge and these might induce pressure on exchange rates. But if the effects were seen to be mild and temporary, target ranges should be wide enough to accommodate any induced exchange-rate movements.

However, in the event of abnormally powerful cycles or shocks, or ones with big asymmetric effects on or approaching the scale seen in recent years, the onus for stabilising GDP and activity would be shared between monetary and fiscal policy. Subject to the institutional checks and conditions outlined above, temporary and overt fiscal action would be taken to assist monetary policy in stabilising GDP at or near the level implied by the NAIRU. In that case large interest differentials and external current payments imbalances might emerge between the major currencies, creating strong pressures on exchange rates. The payments imbalances might be financed by spontaneous flows through the international capital markets, but if these proved insufficient and currency pressures emerged, foreign exchange intervention on the lines described above would be required to stabilise rates.

If the shocks, though powerful and asymmetric, were expected to be temporary and turned out to be so, foreign exchange-market intervention, financed if necessary by official borrowing, should suffice to overcome them. But if they proved permanent as well as asymmetric, exchange-rate realignment plus appropriate domestic policy changes would be needed, as envisaged (if seldom symmetrically applied) in the original Bretton Woods scheme. In short our proposals would not attempt to override the hard lessons of the 'inconsistent quartet', taught so forcefully by the events of the past 40 years.

A North Atlantic monetary union

If key-currency stabilisation progressed successfully to the stage of a fully-fledged exchange-rate system based jointly on the dollar and euro, attention might turn in due course to a merger between them. This would represent a logical and, in favourable conditions, a feasible extension of the proposed reform programme. Accordingly it is worth pausing to consider the pros and cons of a monetary union of the two currency areas, and the modalities involved.

Suggestions for greater integration between the economies of North America and Western Europe are not of course new, but they have generally been on the lines of a free trade area, a much looser form of association than monetary union. North Atlantic free trade proposals were first canvassed seriously in the 1960s as an alternative to the European Common Market, but they received only limited support, largely because the main European economies were intent on consolidating the ECM. Interest in them resurfaced in the 1990s as the momentum for EMU built up and opponents sought alternatives. However, they again failed to take off, as EU governments were preoccupied with EMU, and the US authorities with NAFTA (the North American Free Trade Agreement with Mexico and Canada, reached in 1994).[3] So far as the author is aware, no serious consideration has yet been given to a monetary union involving the dollar and euro. The euro has been seen mainly as a rival to the dollar, not a partner with it.

Yet the idea that policy cooperation between the main global currencies should be carried close to monetary union has a respectable intellectual lineage. Two of the leading originators of the theory of currency unions in the 1960s called in due course for determined moves in that direction. Thus in the 1980s Ronald McKinnon outlined a scheme to coordinate monetary growth between the central banks of the United States, Germany and Japan that would permit full stabilisation of their exchange rates (McKinnon 1984: sec. 5). And in the approach to EMU in the 1990s Robert Mundell recommended the re-structuring of the IMF to provide fixed exchange rates between the dollar, ecu (now euro) and yen as a way of avoiding the polarisation that he feared would emerge between them (Mundell 1993: sec. 10). These ideas are taken to their logical conclusion of monetary union below.

Pros and cons of monetary union

The main benefit from such a merger would be a permanent boost to trade and investment between North America and Europe. The rationale would be similar to that put forward by the architects of EMU: the gains from eliminating exchange-rate variation, together with the associated uncertainty and hedging costs, which must discourage some cross-border trade and long-term investment within the region. The substantial benefits expected in EMU's case were extensively analysed in the European Commission's definitive study, 'One market, one money' (European Commission 1990). That study also examined the potential savings in currency conversion costs and related benefits (such as cross-border price transparency). The latter savings were expected to be significant in time, more than compensating for the temporary costs incurred during transition, though they would be modest in relation to the gains from eliminating exchange-rate variability. Similar benefits should arise from a North Atlantic Monetary Union (NAMU). It would also benefit the numerous countries that retain their own currencies but link them in some way to the dollar or euro. A merger of the dollar and euro in due course would strengthen the then existing exchange-rate system by enlarging its nucleus and consolidating macro-policy cooperation between its key members. In the fullness of time, if the enlarged monetary union proved durable it might be joined by major economies elsewhere, provided they could demonstrate the necessary economic convergence, stability commitments and high degree of policy cooperation.

Costs and risks would certainly be involved in the formation of a NAMU. Since monetary union is much harder to undo than an exchange-rate system, the project would have to be designed with great care and carry great conviction. As explained in Chapter 5, economists have long been interested in the issues surrounding this form of regional integration and there is an extensive theoretical literature on what constitutes an 'optimal currency area'.[4] The debate was launched by the distinguished Canadian economist Robert Mundell (1961) who concluded that economies should consider entering into currency unions only if they display high cross-border mobility of labour and capital, for only through free movements of labour and capital could participants adjust effectively to external shocks without resort to exchange-rate changes. Subsequent contributors argued that small and medium-sized open economies are more likely than large closed economies to gain from joining currency unions; but others (Kenen 1969) pointed out that large, diversified economies are more likely to benefit because they can adapt better internally to external shocks, whereas single-product economies need to retain exchange-rate flexibility as an adjustment mechanism. The early literature, which focused on the costs rather than benefits from monetary union, attracted wide interest but it contained ambiguities and was far from conclusive. Its emphasis on factor mobility, price and wage flexibility, openness to trade, and diversity of production was generally persuasive, but it was unclear how the costs (if these criteria were unfulfilled) would measure up against the benefits in a real-world analysis.

Later, when interest grew in EMU, the debate acquired more empirical content. Quantitative investigations were made of comparative labour mobility, regional unemployment, wage and price flexibility, and susceptibility to 'asymmetric shocks' (external events which affect different economies differently) among potential candidates. Although the results were still quite hard to interpret, they encouraged the view among independent economists that the candidate states should be separated into a 'core' of between six and eight relatively compatible, adaptable economies (essentially Germany and its neighbours), which were well capable of forming a monetary union, and a 'periphery' of others much less capable.

This impression was reinforced when, in the immediate approach to EMU, policymakers' attention shifted to questions of nominal convergence between candidates, i.e. convergence on low rates of inflation and nominal interest rates, stable exchange rates within the ERM, plus moderate fiscal deficits and falling government debt/GDP ratios. These concerns led to increased emphasis on compatible monetary and fiscal policies among participants, a point that had been made by some contributors to the theoretical debate. The view gained ground that, even after German reunification, Germany and its neighbours were closely converged in these respects, whereas others, principally Italy and Belgium, clearly failed to meet the fiscal criteria, and France barely did so. Yet in the event EMU went ahead with almost all member states that wished to join (Greece was the only one initially excluded). When the chips were down, European political imperatives prevailed over the economic arguments.

After a decade of experience with EMU it is still too early to be sure that the venture is a success, but until the global crisis the record was broadly encouraging. Contrary to some initial expectations, the single monetary policy has functioned fairly effectively for the area as a whole: after a slow beginning, output and activity in the Euro Area picked up over the first five years and the trend in unemployment was then slightly downward, at least until the events of 2007–8. Price stability has been well maintained, and the euro has become a major global currency with an increasing role as a haven for international financial investment and reserve-holding.

As expected, EMU membership has created economic stresses as well as benefits for weaker-performing states: some have found it difficult to adapt to its fiscal disciplines and to the deterioration in external competitiveness due to the euro's real effective appreciation which started in 2002 and lasted through much of the decade. These problems have been greatly augmented by the recent global recession, as seen in Chapter 8. The sovereign debt difficulties confronting several peripheral states have created major headaches for the Euro authorities and for the stronger-performing economies, who have called for strong corrective fiscal action as a condition for providing a rescue fund of €750 billion for the heavily indebted economies (*Guardian*, 11 May 2010).

Yet in other respects the Euro Area appears to have performed relatively well in comparison with its Anglo-Saxon rivals. There is evidence that intra-Area trade has been stimulated, and inward FDI from outside the Area seems to have been encouraged at the expense of other destinations (see Taylor 2008).The downside of these shifts is felt mainly by the Euro Area's main competitors. As the author has argued elsewhere (Taylor 2002), EMU is likely to involve diversion of trade and investment from partners outside the region, notably the UK but also the dollar area, and in time this could lead to polarisation between the euro and dollar unless action is taken to avert it. If so the North American economies, together with the UK and others that have so far avoided EMU, would have a particular interest in efforts to stabilise and eventually merge the two global currencies.

Inevitably questions would arise as to whether the main players – the United States and the big Euro economies, and possible new adherents (principally the UK and the Nordic countries that are presently EMU bystanders, and Canada) – could confidently expect to gain from creating a monetary union of two such large and politically independent regions. As was the case in the pre-EMU debate, the 'optimal currency area' arguments in relation to NAMU are rather inconclusive. There is clearly high mobility of financial and business capital between North America and the European Union, but labour mobility between them is much more limited. Yet labour might become more mobile in time if political pressure developed to promote NAMU. Collectively neither the United States nor the Euro Area are very open to external trade by global standards, but many individual member states are extremely open to business with third countries, and there seems plenty of scope for these activities to grow between the two continental areas if currency instability and conversion costs were removed. Empirical studies generally find wage and price flexibility to be significantly higher in the United States than the EU, but market rigidities in Europe are being whittled away under the pressure of EMU and extension of the Single European Market into sheltered sectors of services and finance. Above all, both existing monetary unions are highly diversified economic regions, able to absorb external shocks relatively well. Some big disturbances (like oil price fluctuations or the sub-prime mortgage crisis) may affect individual states very unevenly, but they are likely to be more even across the United States and the Euro Area when considered as whole regions.

Sceptics might question whether North American and European political and social objectives will ever cohere sufficiently to motivate a successful monetary union. Only time will tell. Similar doubts prevailed in Europe after the Second World War. It took over 40 years for Continental Europe to move from the Common Market of six, formed in 1957, to EMU, even though a few visionary politicians shared that early ambition. Yet much of the political-economy spadework for NAMU would have been done if our proposals for cooperation between the major economies are successfully implemented over the next 10–20 years. If a formal exchange-rate system were well established with the dollar and the euro as its joint reference currencies, a permanent merger would seem a less radical step than appears now.

Clearly NAMU could be a realistic possibility only if the underlying causes of the sovereign debt problems presently troubling the Euro Area can be successfully overcome. If these problems lead to major defections from EMU, whether by a group of small states unwilling to accept fiscally-induced austerity, or Germany if it is unwilling to accommodate the weaker performers in the ways proposed, any prospect of a merger between the euro and dollar would be off the agenda. The possibility would be worth considering only if EMU survives and prospers. That will require, among other things, the Area's national governments to adopt and successfully pursue the objectives and modes of fiscal policy cooperation advocated here. The same applies to all the major economies that embark on the road to exchange-rate stability recommended here.

Modalities of forming NAMU

On the (perhaps bold) assumption that monetary union between the dollar and euro might occur by around mid-century, it is worth considering what practical steps would be involved. A crucial requirement for any successful monetary union is of course permanency: the locking of exchange rates must seem irreversible to the markets and public. In previous projects of monetary union, permanency has generally (though not always) required the adoption of a single currency, and EMU was no exception. Accordingly an eventual NAMU would probably mean replacing the dollar and euro with a new currency.[5] The new currency would need to be given material form as notes and coin, but a prior and important question would be its value. Convenience for users and savings in conversion costs would suggest that the new currency should be denominated one-for-one with either the dollar or euro (to permit existing notes and coin to be used for a time in at least one of the two regions, and to reduce the amount of redenomination of existing prices and financial assets and liabilities). However, political expediency might demand an intermediate value for the new currency – say, close to the simple average value of the dollar and euro, subject to rounding.

Even assuming that the dollar–euro rate will be substantially realigned over the next decade (as seems likely) and eventually settle near the purchasing-power-parity rate, as recommended in Chapter 9, some redenomination of both currencies would still be needed if the new currency would be required to have a value somewhere between them. However, that redenomination would probably be modest in size, which would ease the transition.[6] If inflation turns out slightly lower on average in the United States than in the Euro Area over the next two decades – not an improbable prospect if the dollar appreciates further against the euro – the euro/dollar PPP rate could equal 1.0 at some point within that period, at which point the new currency could be introduced as a one-for-one replacement for both currencies. This would have the huge advantage that existing notes and coin could continue to be used in both regions after NAMU, and prices and asset values would not need redenomination in either region. However, it would be optimistic to rely on such a convenient solution to the conversion problem.

A second crucial requirement for a successful monetary union is that the single currency should be issued and managed by an independent and credible central monetary institution, firmly committed to the project's objectives. The ECB clearly provides a compelling model, but sceptics might question whether two such powerful and independent central banks as the ECB and the Federal Reserve could contemplate a merger, let alone replacement by a new, untried, institution. (Similar doubts were expressed about the Bundesbank before EMU; they were overcome because the ECB's constitution was based on a mainly German blueprint.) However, arguably neither replacement nor a full institutional merger of the two central banks should be needed for NAMU, bearing in mind that only two institutions would be involved, they represent regions of broadly equal economic size, and both are already well-shielded from political interference. The analogy with moves to EMU is not close in these respects.

Instead it should be possible for the Fed and the ECB to align their operational targets and procedures sufficiently to produce a single monetary policy across their two regimes. Their governing bodies could meet regularly (perhaps alternately in Washington and Frankfurt) to agree common intermediate targets and oversee their achievement.[7] They could have equal voting rights on all policy decisions, subject to a casting vote by joint chairmen – or the chair could alternate between the Fed Chairman and the ECB President. A new joint governing body could appoint a management committee to undertake the day-to-day operation of the single monetary policy, replacing the FOMC and the ECB Executive Board. With modern electronic communications it should not matter much where the committee met, though political expediency might require some alternation between Washington and Frankfurt. Its task would be to set the key policy instruments – the official deposit, discount and intervention rates – and ensure they were the same in both regions, and that the operating procedures were compatible and fair to counterparties across both. Commercial banks in both regions would continue to hold operational reserves at their parent central banks, as at present, the remuneration rates on which would be identical. Both central banks would guarantee to accept deposits and provide liquidity denominated in the new currency on identical terms.

Many other technical and organisational issues would need to be resolved in the course of forming NAMU. The adoption of the new currency would have to be perfectly synchronised across both regions, in a manner recalling the 'Big Bang' adopted for EMU. The alignment of central bank intervention rates and harmonisation of wholesale market operations would probably precede similar steps in the retail banking field, and the actual introduction of new notes and coin could be left to the final stage, as in EMU's case. Operation of the new currency would probably call for an integrated and efficient payments clearing system to handle wholesale transactions across the entire monetary union, modelled perhaps on the TARGET system set up for the euro.

The new regime would need to be given a strong international legal framework, which would need to cover not only the monetary elements but also other key policy areas (fiscal and exchange-rate policy). As these latter policies are likely to remain ultimately the prerogatives of national governments, and many governments might eventually join NAMU, the associated fiscal and exchange-rate objectives might be most easily dealt with in an intergovernmental agreement (recalling EMU's Stability and Growth Pact). But in order to give NAMU the necessary credibility there would be strong grounds for setting out the monetary objectives and institutions in a new treaty, which would also cover the fiscal and exchange-rate elements This would mean amending the parts of the EU treaty dealing with EMU and associated policies, but that would also probably be the case if NAMU were implemented purely by intergovernmental agreement.[8]

Given the current stresses affecting the euro, creation of a NAMU is hardly something that EU governments could contemplate in the foreseeable future. But the prize of permanent stability between the euro and the dollar might appeal strongly to some in due course, particularly the French government, which has long favoured transatlantic exchange-rate stability; and for smaller countries it might offer a welcome counterweight to increasing German hegemony over the Euro Area. As the Area's membership expands, the appeal of NAMU, fully open to transatlantic trade and investment and less dominated by Franco-German interests, might well gain ground in time. And the rising competitive power of other trading regions in Asia and South America might persuade non-aligned governments of NAMU's merits.

Finally NAMU could appeal to countries that have so far opted to remain outside EMU, principally the UK and several Nordic countries. A good reason for UK hesitation to join EMU lies in the fact that about half UK external current receipts arise outside the Euro Area (if investment income is included), and that proportion may grow as the weight of non-euro economies in world trade rises (Taylor 2002). If exchange-rate stability and trade openness are important benefits, the UK would gain more from joining NAMU than EMU; and similar arguments might weigh with other EMU waverers.

Towards a new economic order

The recent global economic crisis has confirmed that the 1990s policy synthesis suffered from at least two serious flaws, the second potentially fatal: a system of light-touch financial regulation that proved unfit for purpose; and an ill-defined and unsatisfactory conception of the long-term role of fiscal policy. Both of them should be addressed if 1990s regimes are to survive and prosper in the new century. Other important weaknesses in the 1990s model also need remedying, notably the one club-methodology of monetary policy, pusillanimity about the short-term role of fiscal policy, and the susceptibility of floating currencies to long-period instability.

The author has trodden lightly in the field of financial regulation because it lies mostly outside the macroeconomic sphere. He nevertheless agrees with those more versed in this field who conclude that a substantially tougher approach is needed. The challenge will be to strengthen the rules and procedures where laxity has permitted imprudent risk-taking by banks and other credit institutions, while leaving them free to innovate and compete sensibly in a rapidly changing technical and commercial environment. Raising the capital and liquidity requirements for risky banking business and setting higher standards of creditworthiness for borrowers is surely the key to improvement in this sphere, together with the beefing up of industry-financed insurance provisions to protect retail depositors. Legal provisions to limit banks' size and separate traditional banking activities from more speculative business seem more questionable; these problems would be better addressed through case-by-case intervention by regulators and central banks, and where necessary their powers to do so should be strengthened. They should certainly be able to call on the financial resources of governments in emergencies but the latter's law-making powers should be kept in reserve.

A special avenue of reform in the regulatory field nevertheless falls within our ambit, namely the strengthening of macro-prudential inputs into financial regulation. At the national level this would entail finding effective ways of bringing macroeconomic expertise to bear on the supervision of banks and other credit institutions, through closer contacts and cooperation between central banks and supervisors. The introduction of special market-based instruments to stabilise house prices in the Anglo-Saxon economies would give point and thrust to these endeavours. The counterpart at the international level would be augmentation of co-operation and surveillance between the national regulators to give greater weight to macroeconomic inputs. The requirement there is not so much for harmonisation of rules as for closer consultation between the regulatory bodies and the global institutions, to bring macroeconomic expertise to bear on the supervision of international banks. Global bodies like the new Financial Stability Board should have more input into the design of prudential rules and standards and more responsibility for monitoring the system-wide results. Surveillance of the system-wide aspects should be principally a task for a reformed IMF. These steps would not be radical but in strengthening international cooperation they would be very much in tune with our central recommendations.

Macroeconomic policy

In the field of macroeconomic policy, the main plank of the reform programme would be the adoption of a positive long-term role for fiscal policy: the pursuit of sustainable levels of national saving. This would involve setting a target for national saving and using the fiscal instruments to deliver it, while allowing for private saving. The default target would be to achieve zero balance of current external payments over the long term. Although this reform in itself would hardly amount to a new economic order, it would represent a basic change in the accepted role of fiscal policy and would have some far-reaching international and institutional implications.

If these proposals are to have more than local impact and avoid negative feed-backs they would require the adoption of compatible national saving objectives and associated fiscal targets in most, and preferably all, major economies. Compatibility in this context means that each economy's budget balance should be set to deliver broad equality between national saving and aggregate domestic physical investment in cyclically-adjusted terms. If such targets are met by most or all the majors, they should be in or near collective external current payments balance at satisfactory levels of activity. Compatibility also means that uniform inflation targets should be pursued by most or all major economies. Preferably national rates of consumer price inflation should converge to low single figures over a transitional period, though temporary divergences might be allowed to accommodate asymmetric external shocks. Inflation convergence would remove one important source of exchange-rate instability and facilitate progress towards the real-rate stability sought under our programme.

Exchange-rate stability would be desirable not only in itself but also to support the other proposals because, without it, the global fiscal rebalancing could be frustrated by perverse exchange-rate responses. The major economies would need to take concerted steps to avoid this happening. Currency stabilisation might be difficult if conducted in a vacuum but it should be manageable if undertaken as part of a comprehensive exercise in macro policy cooperation on the lines indicated. Without such cooperation, the survival of the 1990s policy model will remain in serious doubt.

Pursuit of these proposals would manifestly require international policy co-operation of a kind and on a scale not seen for many years. Such cooperation would be difficult because it would mean abandonment of important elements of the 1990s consensus, notably the commitments to broad fiscal balance and key-currency floating. In the present environment it might be especially difficult to secure agreement by the governments of high-saving economies to abandon the balanced budget objectives that many have pursued with more or less success over the past 10–15 years. There are bound to be objections to retreating from the hard-won fiscal discipline of this period. The task in this context would be less difficult if the factors which have contributed to persistent excess private saving in high-saving economies gradually recede. There is hope that this may happen in due course. The huge private-sector financial surpluses experienced in fast-growing emerging economies like China may be a temporary phenomenon, reflecting low real wages, high job insecurity, inadequate social provision and undeveloped local financial systems. These problems seem likely to be ameliorated in the catch-up process that will almost certainly take place over coming years. Similarly, there is hope that the persistent shortfall in household saving observed in low-saving economies may be gradually corrected in due course, as better financial regulation discourages excessive risk-taking by lenders and borrowers, and awareness of the saving gap leads to pension reform and other incentives to personal saving. If so, the global fiscal rebalancing proposed above should be less onerous than currently appears.

Without appropriate flexibility, the ambitious long-term role envisaged for fiscal policy would leave little scope for the active use of the fiscal instruments for short-term stabilisation purposes. Yet the recent credit crunch and global recession amply illustrate the occasional need for discretionary fiscal action to stabilise output. Flexibility is defensible in this context because fiscal stimuli may be needed to support monetary policy at times; in deep recessions (if less so in booms), monetary policy on its own may have difficulty in sustaining activity. But serious tensions could arise if fiscal policy has the dual role of assisting short-term stabilisation while also being assigned to long-term saving objectives. Such tensions are likely to be hard to resolve if fiscal policy is left exclusively to national finance ministries which are highly subject to short-term political pressures. The solution lies in distancing the conduct of fiscal policy from the political arena and increasing the influence of independent advisers, much as was done for monetary policy under the 1990s synthesis. These are unlikely to be easy steps: institutional innovations like those recommended for the UK are undeniably novel and would be controversial in many national regimes. But they will be essential if fiscal policy is to acquire the objectivity and credibility that monetary policy now enjoys.

Manifestly the suggestions in these pages do not imply abandonment of the 1990s synthesis. To do so would mean a return to the interventionism tried and found wanting in the last century. That is not the intention here. But the revival of substantive macroeconomic cooperation between developed economies would represent a radical change in the 1990s model. Ever since the collapse of Bretton Woods, cooperation has been out of favour among the leading players, except during the Plaza-Louvre phase in the 1980s: the G7 has had little impact on macroeconomic policies since that episode, and the IMF has had little to do in this field since the early 1970s (until the recent crash). Even though doubts are reappearing about recovery from the global recession, and conflicting macroeconomic priorities seem to be re-emerging internationally, governmental interest in the G7 or a small-group successor remains at a low ebb. This is partly because the G20 is seen as more relevant in a globalising world, but 20 players with diverse interests seem too many to carry currency stabilisation forward. In a macroeconomic regime which has largely turned its back on cooperative ideals, the formation of EMU has stood out as a huge and remarkable exception, but its scope is regional not global, and for the time being the EMU authorities have their own systemic problems to overcome.

Yet the post-crisis environment offers an exceptional opportunity for bold new moves in the direction of multilateral cooperation and integration. At this unusual juncture it does not seem totally unrealistic to hope that a new economic order, based on the 1990s synthesis but oriented towards internationally consistent objectives and policies, might be attainable by the middle of the present century. The reforms suggested in these pages might not constitute such a revolution but they would go a long way towards it.

NOTES

2 The demise of economic management

1 The CCC scheme was set out in a consultative document (Bank of England 1971a: 189) and explained in a subsequent lecture by the Chief Cashier (Bank of England 1971b: 477).
2 For a description of the SSD scheme see Bank of England (1974: 37).
3 A full account of the inception, rules and operations, and eventual collapse, of the Bretton Woods system can be found in Tew (1982; Part Three).
4 One of the earliest commentators to draw attention to the tendency for fiscal stimuli to occur before general elections was the *Financial Times* columnist Samual Brittan after his spell in the UK Treasury (Brittan 1971).

3 The monetarist experiment and its legacy

1 Hayek's political defence of free-market institutions and philosophy ideas was famously expounded in the *Road to Serfdom* (Hayek 1944), for which he was later awarded the Nobel Prize. His economic ideas had been developed earlier in Hayek (1931). Brunner's strict theoretical monetarism can be sampled in Brunner and Meltzer (1971: 784–805).
2 In practice, monetary control was supposed to work through varying the opportunity cost of holding cash balances rather than interest-bearing assets, but this mechanism was prone to be frustrated if a large segment of the controlled aggregate itself contained deposits bearing market-related interest rates, as was the case with £M3 and other broad aggregates.
3 Described in the Bank's *Quarterly Bulletin* (Bank of England 1987: 212–19). M4 remains the aggregate preferred by the Bank of England when monitoring monetary conditions. Both versions of M3, along with M1, ceased to be published in July 1989, as a consequence of the sharp break in the series when the Abbey National Building Society became a commercial bank.
4 An account of New Zealand's early experience under its inflation target can be found in Fischer (1995).
5 The Bundesbank's difficulties in controlling central bank money as the D-mark increasingly became the anchor currency of the ERM caused it to switch the monetary target to

M3 in 1987. For an assessment of the role of monetary targeting in controlling inflation in Germany, see Von Hagen (1995).

6 Note for example the sharp tightening of German fiscal policy in 1975–9, and again in 1985–9, as shown in Chart B of Box 1.1 earlier.

7 In fact the decision not to adopt monetary base control was made by the government, not by the Bank, as Christopher Dow pointed out in an academic study later (Dow and Saville 1990: x, fn. 7).

8 The new dictum originated as an observation by the Bank's chief monetary adviser of the time, Charles Goodhart, who pointed out that ordinary market-based relationships like those governing the supply and demand for money tend to break down when weight is put on them for control purposes.

9 See also Dow and Saville's response to Laidler (Dow and Saville 1990: 'Preface to the paperback edition').

10 The doctrine of Ricardian equivalence argues that a fiscal stimulus will have only temporary effects on aggregate demand because consumers anticipate that tax rates will have to be raised in the longer run in order the service the extra government debt created by the fiscal action, and will raise their saving accordingly. The argument depends on consumers being rational and far-sighted enough to forecast the increase in the burden of debt service accurately, and ignores the possibility that higher aggregate demand will stimulate investment and thus create additional productive capacity to service the higher interest burden in due course.

11 The crowding out argument holds that a fiscal stimulus will have only temporary effects on aggregate demand because long-term interest rates will have to rise in order to finance the additional government borrowing due to the fiscal action, with the result that private investment will be discouraged – crowded out – by the increase in the cost of finance. The argument overlooks the possibilities that (1) private investment may be depressed anyway if aggregate demand remains weak in the absence of the fiscal stimulus; and (2) monetary policy may be relaxed sufficiently to accommodate the stimulus, thereby avoiding an interest rate increase.

4 The 1990s synthesis

1 The term 'neo-liberal consensus' has been used by Joseph Stiglitz among others to refer to the set of free-market policies adopted by the International Monetary Fund to cope with the East Asian financial crisis of 1997–9 (Stiglitz 2002: ch. 3, 74). This package of policies had originally been identified and named the 'Washington Consensus' by John Williamson ten years earlier, but later this term was used to refer to free-market policies more generally (Williamson 1999). Thus although the Washington policies were originally designed for emerging-market economies, there is clearly an overlap with the approach described here.

2 Officially the ECB's preferred monetary aggregate (M3) is supposed to have equal status with its conditional inflation projections as the 'twin pillars' of its monetary strategy (see European Central Bank 2001: ch. 3). However in practice the inflation target seems to be given more weight in setting the ECB's policy interest rates.

3 A notable late developer among this set of ideas was inflation targeting itself, first introduced in 1989 in New Zealand, as a last resort after a series of unsuccessful efforts to overcome inflation.

4 An accessible assessment of the Maastricht Treaty and its implications can be found in Kenen (1995); see also the author's review of the pros and cons of EMU (Taylor 1995: chs. 4 and 5). For a longer perspective on the genesis of EMU, see Dyson (1994).

5 'Big Bang Day' in the City, 27 October 1986, was actually the day on which fixed commission charges were removed on the London Stock Exchange, as part of a series of changes to open up market-making to free competition between non-specialist securities

traders. These changes included the ending of the traditional demarcations between specialist jobbers and brokers, and replaced open-outcry by screen-based trading.

6 For a short non-mathematical introduction, see Sargent (1987). See also John Flemming's introductory textbook on inflation (Flemming 1976: chs. VI and VII) which remains one of the most accessible syntheses of monetarist and alternative theories of inflation.

7 For example although John Flemming, who succeeded Christopher Dow as Chief Economist of the Bank of England in 1984, stressed the role of inflation expectations in wage determination, he doubted that the 'efficient market hypothesis' applied to the labour market. He believed that labour markets were best characterised by adaptive expectations rather than by the stronger forms of rational (forward-looking) expectations. See Flemming (1976: 58–60).

8 A leading exponent of the cost-push view was Wilfred Beckerman, who argued that inflation subsided after the mid-1970s because commodity prices fell sharply, not because unemployment was allowed to rise in the major economies (Beckerman and Jenkinson 1986).

9 An explanation of the mechanics of the Phillips curve is appended to this chapter. An introduction to the expectations-augmented curve and implications can be found in Sloman (2000: ch. 21).

10 Whether inflation actually becomes negative at rates of unemployment above the NAIRU, and accelerating negative inflation develops at those rates, must depend on whether wages and prices are flexible downwards. In strongly unionised economies, falls in nominal wage rates have traditionally been rare except when unemployment has risen to very high rates, as in the 1930s. But wage rates have tended to become more flexible downward in economies where labour-market rigidities have been dismantled, as in the UK under the Thatcher government, or where employees are accustomed to more paternalistic relations with their employees, as in Japan, where wage inflation has been persistently negative in response to the high rates of unemployment of the past decade.

11 The existence of a stable inverse link between unemployment and GDP in the short term is known as Okun's law, after the economist who first drew attention to it.

12 The term 'inconsistent quartet' was applied to four mutually incompatible policy objectives – free trade, capital mobility, monetary independence and fixed exchange rates – in the Padoa-Schioppa Report (Padoa-Scioppa et al. 1987). This report was influential in providing a coherent rationale for monetary union in Europe, as explained in Padoa-Schioppa (1994: especially ch. 6).

13 The description of the NCM model here relies heavily on the account given by the Cambridge economist Philip Arestis (Arestis 2007). His version of the model draws on several sources, principally Meyer (2001: 1–15), McCallum (2001: 145–60) and Woodford (2003); and he acknowledges its New Keynesian origins in papers by Goodfriend and King (1997) and Clarida et al. (1999: 1661–707). Although Arestis gives a scrupulously neutral account of the standard NCM model, he points to a number of weaknesses and mounts strong criticisms from a Keynesian perspective in subsequent papers (for example Arestis 2009).

14 The latter observations echo the views expressed 30 years earlier by John Flemming, noted above.

15 Even Arestis seems to support this questionable conclusion (2009: 3–4).

5 Problems under the 1990s synthesis

1 The historical behaviour of US stock prices is well analysed by Shiller (2000: ch. 1).

2 For example an influential study by Rogoff and others found a significant impact of exchange-rate instability on long-term productivity growth, but only for countries which are relatively undeveloped financially; no effects were discovered for financially advanced economies (Aghion et al. 2006). However the main measure of volatility used

was relatively short-term – volatility and productivity growth over successive non-over-lapping five-year periods: probably too short a timespan to capture the long-term effects of misalignment.

3 A study of the income and price elasticities of exports and imports in the G7 economies using data from 1970 (or earlier) to the 1990s found that, for five of the seven, the price elasticities were generally stable and strong enough to imply that a sustained real exchange rate depreciation would improve the trade balance (see Hooper *et al.* 2000). The price elasticities satisfied the 'Marshall-Lerner' conditions, meaning that the sum of long-run export and import price elasticities (in absolute terms) for each country summed to more than unity. The exceptions were Germany and France, where the results were affected by coefficient instability in the 1990s, but this was attributed to the effects of German reunification. Some subsequent studies have confirmed these broad findings.

4 An empirical exercise using simulations of a large multi-country econometric model – the IMF's MUTLIMOD – warned that the implied fiscal tightening would result in deflation unless accompanied by a general relaxation of monetary policy, and expansionary policies in low-deficit economies (Hughes Hallett and McAdam 1996).

5 On the author's reading, Keynes never actually used the term 'liquidity trap' in the *General Theory*, though the problem was of course discussed at various places there (Keynes 1936: chs. 13 and 15).

6 For example Sir Bryan Hopkin and Sir Douglas Wass, respectively former chief economic adviser and permanent secretary to the UK Treasury, wrote a newspaper article entitled 'The Flaws in Central Bank Freedom': 'But monetary policy is only one of many instruments of policy which have a bearing on inflation. Government borrowing, taxation, competition policy and public sector pay all have some part to play in the fight against inflation. If beating inflation is so important and the politicians cannot be trusted to give it the priority it deserves, logically we should take out of their hands not only monetary policy but a range of other policies as well' (*Financial Times*, 22 January 1993).

7 A fuller exposition of the arguments in this section, including an assessment of the arrangements for ECB accountability, comparisons with other regimes, and proposals for strengthening policy accountability and cooperation in EMU, can be found in C.T. Taylor (2000).

8 There is not space here to do justice to the growing economic literature on climate change. Interested readers are referred to recent studies such as the Stern review (Stern 2007).

9 For a short introduction to the problems of pay-as-you-go pension commitments in Europe, see Taverne (2000). A discussion of the relative merits of PAYG and funding approaches to pension provision, and a useful bibliography, can be found in Davis (2002).

10 A wide-ranging discussion of these issues in a UK context can be found in the first report of the Pensions Commission, set up in 2002 under Lord Turner's chairmanship to recommend reforms in the UK pension system (Pensions Commission 2004). See also the concluding section of Chapter 8.

11 The original dual-economy models were built in the 1950s and 1960s to explain growth in poorer economies with distinct urban and agricultural sectors (see Fields 2007 for a short review and bibliography). The principles have since been extended to the problems experienced in developed economies as a result of low-cost competition from the developing world. See for example the evidence put forward by Adrian Wood, who discovered a strong association between the fall of manufacturing's share in total employment in developed economies and developing-country import penetration from 1970 to 1990 (Wood 1995).

12 The rate of physical investment in China is known to be exceptionally high (around 45 per cent of GDP on some estimates) but the saving rate is put even higher at some 50 per cent (González-Páramo 2006).

13 Without sterilisation the intervention would have inflated the domestic money stock on a one-for-one basis; but sterilisation of the intervention would have raised government bond prices and reduced interest rates; either outcome would have been inflationary, other things being equal.

6 The global financial crisis

1 For a timeline of events from spring 2007 to mid-2009 see Bank of England (2009a: Annex).

2 After several amendments to the bailout provisions, Congress eventually passed the Emergency Economic Stabilization Act on 3 October 2008. This Act gave US Treasury Secretary Henry Paulson the authority he had been seeking to launch the government's 'Troubled Assets Relief Program' (TARP) with capacity to acquire up to $700 billion of mortgage-backed securities from US banks.

3 A diagnosis on these lines, typical of many in the broadsheet press at the time, appeared in a 12-page special review 'The 2008 Crash' in the *Observer* newspaper, 5 October 2008; especially the article by Will Hutton (Hutton 2008: 8–9).

4 Principles-based regulation – until now the preferred approach in the UK and other Anglo-Saxon regimes – sets the broad prudential principles by which financial institutions should be managed and assesses performance against them. In contrast a rules-based approach – generally favoured in Continental European regimes – sets precise quantitative requirements (like minimum capital/asset ratios) and inspects the institution's accounts to verify that they are met. In general the latter approach is more mechanical, whereas principles-based regulation involves more judgement. In practice most regimes are mixtures of both approaches.

7 Monetary policy

1 An alternative, though compatible, explanation for this pattern is that consumers' inflation expectations have become subject to considerable inertia under inflation targeting, a feature to which Blanchflower (2008) has drawn attention. Thus if inflation expectations of low single figures become strongly established in consumers' minds through successful monetary policy, unemployment may rise well above the NAIRU before inflation turns down.

2 Between spring 2008 and autumn 2009, CPI inflation in the UK actually rose from a 12-month rate of around 2.5 per cent to some 3.5 per cent, even though unemployment rose from around 5 per cent to 8 per cent in the same period. (Admittedly, commodity prices will have contributed to higher UK inflation then.) In contrast CPI inflation turned briefly negative in the United States after the very sharp rise in unemployment in 2007–8, but even there inflation had returned to an annual rate of nearly 3 per cent in autumn 2009, while the unemployment rate then approached 10 per cent, perhaps double any plausible estimate of the United States' NAIRU.

3 Strictly, a non-accommodating policy stance requires lending rates to be unchanged in real terms, but provided inflation expectations do not become established as a result of the shock, unchanged nominal rates should suffice to give the same result.

4 Lorenzo Bini-Smaghi, an ECB Director and former senior economist at the Banca D'Italia, argues that 'the central bank should not target asset prices but should take asset prices into account in forecasting inflation and in assessing whether the economy is embarking on unsustainable debt accumulation' (Bini-Smaghi 2008: 5). Lucas Papademos makes similar points, and while accepting that the General Council of the ECB (27 governors of the national central banks plus the ECB President and Vice-President) will be voting members of the European Systemic Risk Board as recommended by the Larosière Group and agreed by the European Council, he insists that 'the ESRB will not be responsible for implementation of macro-prudential policies'. That responsibility

should remain with the national supervisors and other national authorities (Papademos 2009: 5).
5 Existing rules have generally required capital adequacy requirements for banks and other financial institutions to be *raised* during recessions, to provide against higher default risks, whereas counter-cyclical adjustments would lower capital requirements in recessions, in order to encourage lending.
6 So far as the author is aware, nothing in the EMU rules would prevent member central banks of the ESCB from introducing such targets and instruments.

8 Fiscal policy

1 Gross national income (GNI) is equal to gross national output GDP plus net income from abroad. See the Annex to this chapter for fuller definitions.
2 In this context more than most, the precise duration of the 'medium term' will depend on the length of business cycles experienced by developed economies, since fiscal balances in most economies are highly sensitive to the state of the cycle.
3 Generally termed the government's 'net borrowing requirement' in UK fiscal parlance.
4 Investment in the domestic economy here means physical investment in buildings, machinery and equipment and in stocks (inventories), but under standard national accounting conventions all investment abroad is counted as *financial* investment (acquisition of financial assets), even if it involves acquiring a controlling stake in foreign businesses (known as 'foreign direct investment').
5 All governments would of course be free to undertake domestic physical investment financed either by their own saving, or by borrowing to the extent that there is a surplus of saving over investment in the private sector. (Investment decisions in the public sector would continue to be subject to sound economic criteria where possible and appropriate.)
6 The big deterioration of the UK budget position after the crash of 2007–8 led to the suspension of the Golden Rule in November that year. By mid-2009 the official date for returning to budget balance had been put back beyond 2016.
7 A rigorous exposition of this theory can be found in Levačić and Rebmann (1982, 272 et seq.).
8 The comparable proportions are over 45 per cent for the United States and nearly 30 per cent for the UK (BIS 2010).
9 A report on the MPC's policies and their impact on the UK economy in its first ten years of operation can be found in the Bank's evidence to the House of Commons Treasury Select Committee (Bank of England 2007). For a recent account of the committee's composition and work, see Bank of England (2009).
10 The EPC would commission regular forecasts from the official or independent forecasting bodies using its own information or assumptions about exogenous variables and residual adjustments which are usually crucial to forecast results.
11 Alan Greenspan served as a member of the CEA for a spell in the 1970s, well before his appointment as Federal Reserve Chairman, but in his speech recollecting that experience he makes no mention of working on monetary issues there and does not include them in the three main themes that recurred during his tenure (Greenspan 2005). In his personal reflections as Chairman of the CEA in 1982–4 Martin Feldstein emphasises the frequency of his contacts with government departmental and agency heads at the White House and mentions that they were joined 'on some rare occasions' by Fed Chairman Volker. He adds (with possibly a tinge of regret) that 'these breakfast meetings were just about the only time during my time at the CEA when the Fed Chairman participated in a discussion inside the administration' (Feldstein 1992).
12 In response to the massive deterioration in the UK budgetary position during 2009, the Commission was obliged to postpone the deadline for correction of the UK's excessive deficit from 2009/2010 to 2013/2014.

9 Exchange rate policy

1 Non-sterilised intervention is foreign exchange market intervention by central banks which is not accompanied by offsetting intervention in domestic money markets, and is therefore allowed to impact fully on the domestic money stock, other things being equal. It is distinguished from sterilised intervention, under which, for example, an increase in the money stock due to central-bank sales of domestic currency to purchase foreign currency is mopped up by domestic money-market operations.

2 An introduction to UIP can be found in Miles and Scott (2005: ch. 20); see also Blanchard (2003: 387–90).

3 Academic research at the time concluded that the currency interventions under these agreements were successful in stabilising the dollar because they were well concerted and well publicised and worked with the grain of the markets (see for example Catte *et al.* 1992).

4 A fuller account of this episode can be found in Taylor (2004).

5 The UK is a somewhat special case in this respect, in that sterling has dual affinities with both the euro and the dollar, and might therefore be advised to stabilise against a *weighted average of the two*, rather than solely against the euro (by joining EMU). Clearly any scheme to stabilise sterling would be facilitated if the dollar/euro rate were itself stable. A fuller exposition of these issues is available in Taylor (2002).

6 See Stiglitz (2002: ch. 9). Joseph Stiglitz was Chief Economist at the World Bank until 2000 and, before that, Chairman of the Council of Economic Advisers during the Clinton Administration. His policy strictures were roundly rejected in an open letter by Kenneth Rogoff, issued when the latter was Director of Research at the IMF. Rogoff admitted that the Fund had made some mistakes, particularly in situations where economies go bankrupt, but dismissed Stiglitz's ideas for improving the Fund's macro-policy advice as 'at best highly controversial, at worst, snake oil' (Rogoff 2002).

7 For decisions on Fund policy and other strategic matters an 85 per cent majority vote is required. Only the United States with its voting share of around 17 per cent has an effective blocking vote.

8 Every member of the IMF has a quota which determines its financial contribution and voting power in the Fund. The quotas are based on a formula with weights for GDP, openness, economic variability and reserves, and are reviewed every five years. In April 2008 a major quota reform was agreed which increased the representation of fast-growing economies and gave low-income economies more say in decision-making. The US quota was reduced to just below 17 per cent. For an up-to-date account of the Fund's quota system, see International Monetary Fund (2009).

9 For example a number of economists believe (and argued at the time) that sterling was put into the ERM at too high a rate in 1990; and it was partly for that reason that the pound was forced out of the mechanism in October 1992.

10 The principles are as follows. Suppose the same basket of goods costs $1,500 when bought in the United States and £1,000 when bought in the UK. The UK's PPP exchange rate against the dollar is then 0.67 (1000/1500). If the market exchange rate is actually 0.5 (£1 = $2), so the relevant basket bought in the UK costs $2,000, sterling is overvalued by 33.3 per cent (100 × (2000/1500 − 1)). The UK will then tend to have a trade deficit with the United States until sterling has depreciated in that proportion against the dollar (from 0.5 to 0.67). According to the PPP approach, trade between two countries will be in equilibrium only when their market exchange rate equals the PPP rate, other things being equal. Thus in equilibrium the UK's real exchange rate – its nominal rate of 0.67 divided by its PPP rate (also 0.67) – will be 1.0. Moreover in equilibrium, if inflation rates are equal in the UK and United States, the UK's nominal exchange rate and its PPP rate will both be constant through time, as also will be its real rate; but if the UK is inflating at a different rate from the United States, its PPP rate will change (i.e. rise if the UK inflates faster), and its nominal rate must then change (rise) in step with the PPP rate if equilibrium is to be maintained. Thus a condition for

long-run equilibrium under PPP conditions is that changes in market exchange rates exactly compensate for differences in national inflation rates.

11 Practitioners differ as to which relative-cost measure is better for explaining trade flows. Some hold that relative ULCs in manufacturing (the MULCs referred to in Box 5.1) are the better measure, because manufactures still comprise the bulk of goods exports. Others hold that 'whole-economy' or total costs (TULCs) are preferable, because services are increasingly important in developed-economy trade.

12 This would permit the *total amplitude* of fluctuations between currencies other than the dollar to be ten percentage points, whereas the corresponding amplitude in the EMS narrow band was just 4.5 percentage points.

10 Review and assessment

1 Banks and other financial firms will be required to anticipate such emergencies by drawing up 'Recovery and Resource Plans' under guidance from the regulators. These plans will resemble 'living wills' which provide advance information and analysis for the authorities about survival or disposal in the event of a stress situation (see UK Treasury 2009b: 15–16).

2 For example, if an economy's GDP turns out higher than forecast because of cyclical factors (a corporate investment boom or temporary fall in the household saving ratio), its external trade deficit is likely to be temporarily higher than forecast, but so is its government saving (surplus of tax receipts over current-account spending).

3 At a White House meeting in April 1995, Prime Minister John Major suggested a North Atlantic free trade agreement between the United States and the EU to President Bill Clinton. The issue had been under discussion with European governments for at least six months, had some support in US industry and labour unions, and was well received by the US Administration (Report by the Knight Ridder/Tribune News Service, 5 April 1995).

4 A review of the optimal currency area literature can be found in Taylor (1995: ch. 4).

5 An obvious (if rather unimaginative) name for the new currency would be the Eurodollar, though that term's earlier connotations – in the 1970s it referred to dollar balances held in Europe and elsewhere, to escape US exchange control – might not be thought propitious.

6 In 2008 the purchasing power parity rate between the euro and the dollar was €0.85/$1.0 and the market rate averaged €0.68/$1.00. On this basis the dollar was undervalued by some 25 per cent or 100[(0.85/0.68) − 1.0]. If future inflation rates in the United States and Euro Area are equal over time and the dollar/euro rate approaches the present PPP rate in due course, the market rate would rise by 25 per cent to reach €0.85/$1.00. A gap of about 15 percentage points or 100[(€0.85/$1.00) − 1.0] would then remain between the unit values of the two currencies. This could be bridged by a single currency using conversion factors of plus 7.5 per cent for the dollar and minus 7.5 per cent for the euro.

7 One question to be resolved would be the locus of authority for setting the inflation target under NAMU. In EMU this authority lies with the ECB, whereas the choice of a future US inflation target might lie with the US government. Governmental authority for the target would be preferable but that would require amendment of the ESCB Statute and the EU Treaty.

8 But EU Treaty amendment would not be required to include the euro in an informal stabilisation scheme, or even put it into a formal exchange-rate system. Provision for those steps was made in the Maastricht Treaty, which reserved policy for the euro for EU ministers, subject to a number of hurdles involving the ECB and the European Commission (see Taylor 2004: Part I).

REFERENCES

Aghion, P., P. Baghetti, R. Ranciere and K. Rogoff (2006) 'Exchange rate volatility and productivity growth: the role of financial development', National Bureau of Economic Research Working Paper 12117, May.

Arestis, P. (2007) 'What is the new consensus in macroeconomics?' in P. Arestis (ed.) *Is There a New Consensus in Macroeconomics?* Houndmills and New York: Palgrave Macmillan.

Arestis, P. (2009) 'New consensus macroeconomics: a critical appraisal', Working Paper No. 564, The Levy Economics Institute of Bard College, May.

Arestis, P. and A. Ross (2007) 'Introduction' in P. Arestis (ed.) *Is There a New Consensus in Macroeconomics?* Houndmills and New York: Palgrave Macmillan.

Bank of England (1971a) 'Competition and credit control', *Quarterly Bulletin*, May.

Bank of England (1971b) 'Competition and credit control: extract from a lecture by the Chief Cashier of the Bank of England', *Quarterly Bulletin*, June.

Bank of England (1974) 'Credit control: a supplementary scheme', *Quarterly Bulletin*, March.

Bank of England (1987) 'Measures of broad money', *Quarterly Bulletin*, May.

Bank of England (2007) 'Submission regarding the economic context', memorandum of evidence submitted to the House of Commons Treasury Select Committee, *Inquiry into the Monetary Policy Committee of the Bank of England: Ten Years On*,19 February. Online. Available at: www.bankofengland.co.uk/publications/other/treasurycommittee (accessed 20 December 2009).

Bank of England (2009a) *Financial Stability Report*, June.

Bank of England (2009b) 'Monetary Policy Committee (MPC)'. Online. Available at: www.bankofengland.co.uk/monetarypolicy/overview (accessed 20 December 2009).

Bank for International Settlements (BIS) (2010) *80th Annual Report 2009/10*, 28 June.

Bank of Japan (2009a) 'Functions and Operations of the Bank of Japan', edited by Institute for Monetary and Economic Studies. Online. Available at: www.boj.or.jp (accessed 12 November 2009).

Bank of Japan (2009b) 'Policy and Operations'. Online. Available at: www.boj.or.jp/en/theme/index.htm (accessed 25 December 2009).

Barr, C. (2009) 'The truth about credit swaps', *CNN/Fortune Magazine*. Online. Available at: http://money.cnn (accessed 16 March 2009).

Barrell R. and M. Weale (2009) 'Fiscal policy, fairness between generations and national saving', National Institute of Economic and Social Research Discussion Paper No. 338, September.

Beckerman, W. and T. Jenkinson (1986) 'What stopped the inflation? Unemployment or commodity prices?' *Economic Journal*, March.

Bernanke, B. (2002) 'Deflation: making Sure "it" doesn't happen here', Remarks before the National Economists Club, Washington, DC, 21 November. Online. Available at: www.federalreserve.gov/BOARDDOCS/SPEECHES/2002 (accessed 19 March 2008).

Bernanke, B. (2005) 'The global saving glut and the U.S. current account deficit', speech at the Sandridge Lecture, Virginia Association of Economists, Richmond, Virginia, 10 March, updated at the Homer Jones Lecture, St Louis, Missouri, 14 April. Online. Available at: www.federalreserve.gov/boarddocs/speeches/2005 (accessed 19 March 2008).

Beveridge, W.H. (1944) *Full Employment in a Free Society*, London: Allen and Unwin.

Bini-Smaghi, L. (2008) 'Financial stability and monetary policy: challenges in the current turmoil', speech at the CEPS joint event with Harvard Law School on the EU-US Financial System, New York, 4 April. Online. Available at: www.ecb.int/press/key/date/2008 (accessed 10 September 2009).

Blanchard, O. (2003) *Macroeconomics*, 3rd edn, Pearson International Edition, New Jersey: Prentice Hall.

Blanchflower, D. (2008) 'Inflation, expectations and monetary policy', speech at the Royal Society, George Street, Edinburgh, 29 April. Online. Available at: www.bankofengland.co.uk/speeches (accessed 14 May 2009).

Bordo, M. and B. Eichengreen (1993) *A Retrospective on the Bretton Woods System*, Chicago: University of Chicago Press.

Brittan, S. (1971) *Steering the Economy*, revised edn, London: Penguin Books.

Britton, A. (1991) *Macroeconomic Policy in Britain 1974–87*, National Institute of Economic and Social Research, Economic and Social Studies XXXVI, Cambridge: Cambridge University Press.

Britton, A. (2001), *Monetary Regimes of the Twentieth Century*, Cambridge: Cambridge University Press.

Brunner, K. and A.H. Meltzer (1971) 'The uses of money in the theory of an exchange economy', *American Economic Review*, December.

Buiter, W. and A. Sibert (2007) 'The central bank as the market maker of last resort: from lender of last resort to market maker of last resort', 13 August. Online. Available at: www.VoxEU.org (accessed 13 March 2008).

Buiter, W., G. Corsetti and N. Roubini (1993) 'Excessive deficits: sense and nonsense in the Treaty of Maastricht', *Economic Policy*, April.

Callen, T. and J. D. Ostry (2003) *Japan's Lost Decade: Policies for Economic Revival*, Washington, DC: International Monetary Fund.

Catte, P., G. Galli and S. Rebecchini (1992) 'Concerted interventions and the dollar: an analysis of daily data', paper prepared for the Ossola Memorial Conference, Banca D'Italia, Perugia, 9–10 July.

Clarida, R., J. Gali and M. Gertler (1999) 'The science of monetary policy: a new Keynesian perspective', *Journal of Economic Literature*, 37(4).

Corden, W. Max (2007) 'Exchange rate policies and the global imbalances: thinking about China and the IMF', Paper for the James Meade Centenary Conference, Bank of England July 2007, revised August.

Council of the European Communities/Commission of the European Communities (1992) *Treaty on European Union*, Luxembourg: Office for Official Publications of the European Commission.

Davis, E.P. (2002) 'PAYG versus funding'. Online. Available at: www.geocities.com/e-philip-davis (accessed 24 June 2007).

De Gregorio, J., B. Eichengreen, T. Ito and C. Wyplosz (1999) *An Independent and Accountable IMF*, Geneva Reports on the World Economy 1, International Center for Monetary and Banking Studies, London: Centre for Economic Policy Research.

Dow, J.C.R (1964) *The Management of the British Economy*, Cambridge: Cambridge University Press.

Dow, J.C.R. and I.D. Saville (1990) *A Critique of Monetary Policy: Theory and British Experience*, Oxford: Clarendon Press.

Dyson, K. (1994) *Elusive Union: The Process of Economic and Monetary Union in Europe*, London and New York: Longman.

Eichengreen, B. (1990) *Is Europe an Optimal Currency Area?* London: Centre for Economic Policy Research, Discussion Paper 478, November.

Ellerman, A.D. and B.K. Buchner (2007) 'The European Union emissions trading scheme: origins, allocation and early results', *Review of Environmental Economics and Policy*, 1.

European Central Bank (2001) *The Monetary Policy of the ECB*, Frankfurt: European Central Bank.

European Commission (1990) 'One market, one money', *European Economy* 44.

European Commission (1993) 'Stable money – sound finances', *European Economy* 53.

European Commission (2009) 'Public finances in EMU', *European Economy*, 5 June

Feldstein, M. (1992) 'The council of economic advisers and economic advising in the United States', *Economic Journal*, September.

Feldstein, M. (2008) 'The dollar is falling at the right time', *Financial Times* comment and analysis. Online. Available at: www.ft.com/cms/s (accessed 27 March 2008).

Fields, Gary S. (2007) 'Dual economy', Working Paper 17 in the ILR Collection, Industrial and Labour Relations School, Cornell University. Online. Available at: www.digitalcommons.ilr.cornell.edu/workingpapers (accessed 3 October 2009).

Financial Stability Forum (2008) *Report on Enhancing Market and Institutional Resilience*, Washington, DC, 7 April.

Fischer, A. (1995) 'New Zealand's experience with inflation targets' in L. Leiderman and L.E.O. Svensson (eds) *Inflation Targets*, London: Centre for Economic Policy Research.

Fisher, I. (1911) *The Purchasing Power of Money*, Basingstoke: Macmillan.

Flemming, J.S. (1976) *Inflation*, Oxford: Oxford University Press.

Foot, M.D.K.W., C.A.E. Goodhart and A.C. Hotson (1979) 'Monetary base control', *Bank of England Quarterly Bulletin*, June.

Friedman, M. (1968) 'The Role of Monetary Policy', *American Economic Review*, March.

Friedman, M. and A. Schwarz (1963) *A Monetary History of the United States 1870–1960*, Princeton: Princeton University Press.

Geddes, P. (1987) *Inside the Bank of England*, London: Boxtree Limited.

Gonzáles-Páramo, J.M. (2006) 'Central banks and imbalances: introduction to the round table', International Conference on Central Banks in the 21st Century, organised by the Banco de España, Madrid, 9 June.

Goodfriend, M. and R.G. King (1997) 'The new neoclassical synthesis and the role of monetary policy' in B.S. Bernanke and J.J. Rotemberg (eds) *NBER Macroeconomics Annual: 1997*, Cambridge, MA: MIT Press.

Goodhart, C.A.E. (1989) 'The conduct of monetary policy', *Economic Journal*, June.

Goodhart, C.A.E. (1993) 'The political economy of monetary union', reprinted in P.B.

Kenen (ed.) *Understanding Interdependence: The Macroeconomics of the Open Economy*, Princeton: Princeton University Press, 1995.

Goodhart, C.A.E. (2007) 'The future of central banking' in P. Arestis (ed.) *Is There a New Consensus in Macroeconomics?* Houndmills and New York: Palgrave Macmillan, 61–81.

Goodhart, C.A.E. (2010) 'Is a less pro-cyclical financial system an achievable goal?', *National Institute Economic Review*, 211.

Goodhart, C.A.E. and S. Smith (1993) 'Stabilization' in European Commission, 'The economics of community public finance', *European Economy: Reports and Studies 5*.

Greenspan, A. (2005) 'Receipt of the Truman Medal for Economic Policy', remarks before the Truman Medal Award and Economics Conference, Kansas City, Missouri, 26 October. Online. Available at: www.whitehouse.gov/cea/about (accessed 1 December 2008).

Hayek, F.A. (1931) *Prices and Production*, Chicago: Unversity of Chicago Press.

Hayek, F.A. (1944) *The Road to Serfdom*, London and New York: Routledge.

Healey, D. (1990) *The Time of My Life*, London: Penguin Books.

Hicks, J.R. (1937) 'Mr Keynes and the classics: a suggested interpretation', *Econometrica*, 5, 147–59.

Hooper, P., K. Johnson and J. Marquez (2000) *Trade Elasticities for the G-7 Countries*, Princeton Studies in International Economics, No. 87, August.

Hughes Hallett, A. and P. McAdam (1996) 'Fiscal deficit reductions in line with the Maastricht criteria for monetary union: an empirical analysis', Global Economic Institutions Working Paper Series No. 8, Economic & Social Research Council, March.

Hutton, W. (2008) 'This terrifying moment is our one chance for a new world', *Observer*, 5 October.

Institute for Fiscal Studies (2007) *Press Release: the IFS Green Budget,* January.

International Financial Services London (2009) 'Sovereign wealth funds', IFSL Report, 2 March. Online. Available at: www.ifsl.org.uk (accessed 7 March 2009).

International Monetary Fund (IMF) (1996) *Annual Report 1996.*

International Monetary Fund (IMF) (2009) 'IMF quotas', IMF Factsheet. Online. Available at: www.imf.org (accessed 10 September 2009).

Italianer, A. and M. Vanheukelen (1993) 'Proposals for community stabilization mechanisms: some historical applications' in European Commission, 'The economics of community public finance', *European Economy: Reports and Studies 5*.

Kay, J. (2008) 'More regulation will not prevent next crisis', *Financial Times*, 26 March. Online. Available at: www.johnkay.com/print/541 (accessed 30 March 2008).

Kenen, P.B. (1969) 'The theory of optimal currency areas: an eclectic view', *Monetary Problems of the International Economy*, Chicago: University of Chicago Press.

Kenen, P.B. (1995) *Economic and Monetary Union: Moving beyond Maastricht*, Cambridge: Cambridge University Press.

Keynes, J.M. (1936) *The General Theory of Employment, Interest and Money*, London and Basingstoke: Macmillan.

King, M. (2009) Speech at the Lord Mayor's Banquet for Bankers and Merchants of the City of London at Mansion House, 17 June. Online. Available at: www.bankofengland.co.uk (accessed 3 September 2009).

Krugman, P. (1998) 'It's baaack: Japan's slump and the return of the liquidity trap', *Brookings Papers on Economic Activity* 2, Washington: Brookings Institution.

Krugman, P. (2003) 'Who lost the US budget?', *New York Times*, 21 March. Online. Available at: www.nytimes.com/2003/03/21/opinion (accessed 19 December 2009).

Labour Party (1976) *Annual Conference Report*, October.

Laidler, D. (1989) 'Dow and Saville's critique of monetary policy: a review essay', *Journal of Economic Literature,* September.

Larosière Group on Financial Supervision (2009) *Report on Enhancing Market and Institutional Resilience,* 25 February. Online. Available at: www.ec.europa/internal market/finances/docs (accessed 17 March 2009).

Levačić, R and A. Rebmann (1982) *Macroeconomics: an Introduction to Keynesian-neoclassical Controversies,* 2nd edn, London and Basingstoke: Macmillan.

Llewellyn, J. (2009) 'Lessons from the financial crisis'. Online. Available at: www.llewellyn-consulting.com (accessed 5 March 2009).

Lucas, R.E. (1976) 'Econometric policy evaluation – a critique' in K. Brunner and A.H. Meltzer (eds.) *The Phillips Curve and Labor Markets,* Amsterdam: North Holland.

Lucas, R.E. (1987) *Models of Business Cycles,* Oxford: Basil Blackwell.

McCallum, B. T. (2001) 'Monetary policy analysis in models without money', *Federal Reserve Bank of St Louis Review,* 83(4).

MacDougall Report (1977) *Report of the Study Group on the Role of Public Finance in European Integration,* Brussels: the European Commission.

McKinnon, R.I. (1984) 'An international standard for monetary stabilization', *Policy Analyses in International Economics,* Institute for International Economics, Washington, DC, March.

Maddison, A. (1995) *Monitoring the World Economy, 1820–1992,* Paris: OECD.

Matthews, R.C.O. (1968) 'Why has Britain had full employment since the war?', *Economic Journal,* September.

Meade, J. E. and M. Weale (1995) 'Monetary union and the assignment problem', *Scandinavian Journal of Economics,* 97(2).

Meek, P. (1982) *U.S. Monetary Policy and Financial Markets,* New York: Federal Reserve Bank of New York.

Meyer, L.H. (2001) 'Does money matter?', *Federal Reserve Bank of St. Louis Review,* 83(5).

Miles, D. and A. Scott (2005) *Macroeconomics: Understanding the Wealth of Nations,* 2nd edn, Chichester: John Wiley and Sons.

Minsky, H.P. (1992) 'The financial instability hypothesis', Working Paper No. 74, Jerome Levy Economics Institute, Bard College. Online. Available at: www.levy.org/pubs/wp74.pdf (accessed 17 December 2009).

Mundell, R.A. (1961) 'A theory of optimal currency areas', *American Economic Review,* September.

Mundell, R.A. (1993) 'EMU and the international monetary system: a transatlantic perspective', expanded version of a paper presented at the Austrian National Bank, 25 May, *Oesterrichische Nationalbank Arbeitspapier,* Nr. 13, July.

Muth, J.F. (1961) 'Rational expectations in the theory of price movements' reprinted in *The New Classical Macroeconomics,* Vol. 1, Aldershot: Elgar, 1992.

National Institute of Economic and Social Research (NIESR) (2003) 'Commentary', *National Institute Economic Review,* 183, January.

National Institute of Economic and Social Research (NIESR) (2005) 'The Labour government's economic record and economic prospects', *National Institute Economic Review,* 192, April.

Nickell, S. (2006) 'The budget of 1981 was over the top', speech to the Institute of Economic Affairs Panel Discussion, London, 13 March 2006. Online. Available at: www.bankofengland.co.uk/publications/speeches/2006/speech269.pdf (accessed 23 October 2009).

Organisation for Economic Cooperation and Development (OECD) (1985) *Exchange Rate*

Management and the Conduct of Monetary Policy, OECD Monetary Studies Series, Paris: OECD.

Osborne, G. (2010) Speech at the Lord Mayor's Dinner for Bankers and Merchants of the City of London at Mansion House, 16 June. Online. Available at: www.hm-treasury. gov.uk/press (accessed 21 June 2010).

Padoa-Schioppa, T. (1994) *The Road to Monetary Union in Europe: the Emperor, the Kings and the Genies*, Oxford: Clarendon Press.

Padoa-Schioppa, T., M. Emerson, M. King, J.-C. Milleron, J. Paelinck, L. Papademos, A. Pastor and F. Scharpf (1987) *Efficiency, Stability and Equity: A Strategy for the Evolution of the Economic System of the European Community*, the Padoa-Schioppa Report, Oxford: Oxford University Press.

Papademos, L. (2009) 'Financial stability and macro-prudential supervision: objectives, instruments and the role of the ECB', speech at the conference 'The ECB and its Watchers XI', Frankfurt, 4 September. Online. Available at: www.ecb/press/key/date/2009 (accessed 8 January 2010).

Pensions Commission (2004) *Pensions: Challenges and Choices: First Report of the Pensions Commission*, London: the Stationery Office, 12 October.

Pensions Commission (2005) *A New Pension Settlement for the Twenty-first Century: Second Report of the Pensions Commission*, London: the Stationery Office, 30 November.

Phelps, E.S. (1967) 'Phillips curves, expectations of inflation and optimal employment over time', *Economica*, August.

Phillips, A.W. (1958) 'The relation between unemployment and the rate of change of money wage rates in the UK 1861–1957', *Economica*, November.

Pigou, A.C. (1943) 'The classical stationary state', *Economic Journal*, December.

Poole, W. (1992) 'Exchange-rate management and monetary-policy misalignment: a study of Germany, Japan, United Kingdom and United States after Plaza', *Carnegie-Rochester Conference Series on Public Policy*, 36.

Pomerantz, O. and M. Weale (2005) 'Are we saving enough? The macroeconomics of the savings gap', *National Institute Economic Review*, 191.

Radcliffe Committee (1959) 'Report of the Committee on the workings of the monetary system', London: HMS0, Cmnd. 827.

Reddaway, W.B. in collaboration with J.O.N. Perkins, S.J. Potter and C.T. Taylor (1967) *Effects of UK Direct Investment Overseas: an Interim Report*, Cambridge: Cambridge University Press.

Rogoff, K. (2002) 'An open letter to Joseph Stiglitz', International Monetary Fund, Washington, DC, June. Online. Available at: www.imf.org/external/np/vc/2002 (accessed 4 June 2010).

Rogoff, K. (2005) 'Let it ride', *Foreign Policy* 47.

Sachs, J. and X. Sala-i-Martin (1989) 'Fiscal federalism and optimum currency areas: evidence for Europe from the United States', reprinted in M. Canzoneri, V. Grilli and P.R. Masson (eds) *Establishing a Central Bank: Issues and Lessons from the US*, Cambridge: Cambridge University Press, 1992.

Sargent, T. (1987) 'Rational expectations' in J. Eatwell, M. Milgate and P. Newman (eds) *The New Palgrave: a Dictionary of Economics*, 2nd edn, Vol. 4, Basingstoke and New York: Palgrave Mac,illan.

Shiller, R.J. (2000) *Irrational Exuberance*, Princeton and Oxford: Princeton University Press.

Skidelsky, R. (1998) 'The growth of a world economy' in M. Howard and W. Louis (eds) *The Oxford History of the Twentieth Century*, Oxford: Oxford University Press.

Sloman, J. (2000) *Economics*, 4th edn, Harlow: Pearson Education.

Spiegel, M.M. (2006) 'Did quantitative easing by the Bank of Japan "work"?', Federal Reserve Bank of San Francisco Economic Letter, 2006–28, 20 October.

Stern, N. (2007) *The Stern Review: the Economics of Climate Change*, Cambridge: Cambridge University Press.

Sterne, G. (1999) 'The use of explicit targets for monetary policy: practical experience of 91 countries', *Bank of England Quarterly Bulletin*, 39(3).

Stiglitz, J. (2002) *Globalization and its Discontents*, London: Penguin Books.

Svensson, L.E.O. (2007) 'Inflation targeting' in L. Blum and S. Durlauf (eds) *The New Palgrave Dictionary of Economics*, 2nd edn, 2008, Basingstoke and New York: Palgrave Macmillan.

Tarullo, D.K. (2009) 'Financial regulation: past and future', Speech at the Money Marketeers of New York University, New York, 9 November. Online. Available at: www. federalreserve.gov/newsevents/speech (accessed 22 December 2009).

Taverne, Dick (2000) *Can Europe Pay for its Pensions?* Federal Trust Report, London: Kogan Page for the Federal Trust.

Taylor, C.T. (1995) *EMU 2000? Prospects for European Monetary Union*, Chatham House Paper, London: Royal Institute of International Affairs.

Taylor, C.T. (2000) 'The role and status of the European Central Bank: some proposals for accountability and cooperation' in C. Crouch (ed.) *After the euro: Shaping the Institutions for Governance in the Wake of European Monetary Union*, Oxford: Oxford University Press.

Taylor, C.T. (2002) 'Sterling volatility and European Monetary Union', National Institute of Economic and Social Research Discussion Paper No. 197, May.

Taylor, C.T. (2004) 'An exchange-rate regime for the euro', *Journal of European Public Policy*, Special Issue, 11(5).

Taylor, C.T. (2008) 'Foreign direct investment and the euro: the first five years', *Cambridge Journal of Economics*, January.

Taylor, John B. (1993) 'Discretion versus policy rules in practice', *Carnegie-Rochester Conference Series on Public Policy*, 39.

Tew, B. (1982) *The Evolution of the International Monetary System*, 2nd edn, London: Hutchinson.

Tobin, J. (1978) 'A proposal for international monetary reform', *Eastern Economic Journal*, July/October.

UK Central Statistical Office (1990) *Financial Statistics: Explanatory Handbook, 1990 Edition*, London: HMSO, June.

UK Financial Services Authority (2009) *The Turner Review: A Regulatory Response to the Global Banking Crisis*, 18 March. Online. Available at: www.fsa.gov.uk/pdf (accessed 30 March 2009).

UK Treasury (1998) *The Code for Financial Stability*, November. Online. Available at: www. hm-treasury.gov.uk/d/fiscal_stability.pdf (accessed 20 December 2009).

UK Treasury (2009a) 'Reforming financial markets', statement by the Chancellor of the Exchequer to the House of Commons, 8 July. Online. Available at: www.hm-treasury. gov.uk/newsroom & speeches (accessed 8 August 2009).

UK Treasury (2009b) 'Risk, reward and responsibility: the financial sector and society', Discussion Document, 10 December. Online. Available at: www.hm-treasury.gov.uk/ pdf (accessed 20 December 2009).

US Federal Reserve (2005) *The Federal Reserve System: Purposes and Functions*, 9th edn. Washington, DC: Board of Governors of the Federal Reserve System, June.

US Securities and Exchange Commission (2008) *Testimony Concerning Turmoil in U.S. Credit Markets: Recent Actions Regarding Government Sponsored Entities, Investment Banks and Other*

Financial Institutions, by Christopher Cox, Chairman, before the Senate Committee on Banking, Housing and Urban Affairs, 23 September.

US Treasury (2009) 'Financial stability plan', Fact Sheet. Online. Available at: www.financialstability.gov (accessed 21 December 2009).

Von Hagen, J. (1995) 'Inflation and monetary targeting in Germany' in L. Leiderman and L.E.O. Svensson (eds) *Inflation Targets*, London: Centre for Economic Policy Research.

Wadhwani, S. (2008) 'Should monetary policy respond to asset price bubbles? Revisiting the debate', *National Institute Economic Review*, 206.

Williamson, J. (1999) 'What should the Bank think about the Washington consensus?' paper prepared as background to the World Bank *Development Report 2000*, Washington, DC: Peterson Institute for International Economics, July.

Wolf, M. (2008) 'Why financial regulation is both difficult and essential', *Financial Times*, 15 April.

Wood, A. (1995) 'How trade hurt unskilled workers', *Journal of Economic Perspectives*, 9(3).

Woodford, M. (2003) *Interest and Prices: Foundations of a Theory of Monetary Policy*, Princeton: Princeton University Press.

Woodford, M. (2006) *How Important is Money in the Conduct of Monetary Policy?* paper for the Fourth ECB Central Banking Conference, 'The Role of Money: Money and Monetary Policy in the Twenty-First Century', 9–10 November.

Woodford, M. (2009) 'Convergence in macroeconomics: elements of the new synthesis', *American Journal of Economics-Macroeconomics*, 1(1).

Wren-Lewis, S. (2007) 'Are there dangers in the microfoundations consensus?' in P. Arestis (ed.) *Is There a New Consensus in Macroeconomics?* Houndmills and New York: Palgrave Macmillan.

INDEX